A Culture of Rapid Improvement

Creating and Sustaining an Engaged Workforce

A Culture of Rapid Improvement

Creating and Sustaining an Engaged Workforce

Raymond C. Floyd

CRC Press
Taylor & Francis Group
Boca Raton   London   New York

CRC Press is an imprint of the
Taylor & Francis Group, an **informa** business

A PRODUCTIVITY PRESS BOOK

Productivity Press
Taylor & Francis Group
270 Madison Avenue
New York, NY 10016

© 2008 by Taylor & Francis Group, LLC
Productivity Press is an imprint of Taylor & Francis Group, an Informa business

No claim to original U.S. Government works
Printed in the United States of America on acid-free paper
10 9 8 7 6 5 4 3 2 1

International Standard Book Number-13: 978-1-56327-378-0 (Hardcover)

Library of Congress Cataloging-in-Publication Data

Floyd, Raymond C.
  A culture of rapid improvement : creating and sustaining an engaged workforce / Raymond C. Floyd.
    p. cm.
  Includes bibliographical references and index.
  ISBN 978-1-56327-378-0 (alk. paper)
    1. Organizational change. 2. Organizational effectiveness. 3. Organizational behavior. I. Title.

HD58.8.F57 2008
658.4'063--dc22

2007048386

Visit the Taylor & Francis Web site at
http://www.taylorandfrancis.com

and the Productivity Press Web site at
http://www.productivitypress.com

I wrote this for Marsha.

Everything I do is done for Marsha.

Contents

Foreword by
H. Eugene McBrayer

A Culture of Rapid Improvement

In 1986, I had the very good fortune of being promoted to the position of President of Exxon Chemical Company. For more than 30 years, I had been "laboring in the vineyards" of the Exxon organization learning and preparing myself for the day that I might be lucky enough to land this job—I considered this the very best job in the Exxon organization. The position I inherited was that of being the top manager of a large and capable industrial organization. Over the next six years I learned how to change and to become the leader of what I believe was the most capable team of high-performing individuals in the chemical industry.

In 1986, Exxon Chemical was a large, successful, and profitable business, manufacturing and marketing a wide array of petrochemical products throughout the world. We had excellent technology, economies of scale, and a very capable international workforce. Our management structure was a many-layered matrix that brought strong checks and balances to our business decision-making. We knew how to make careful, analytical business decisions and avoid making big mistakes. We were *good* at what we did. But, I believed that we were not yet the *best* that we could be. I felt that our goal should be to become *the best international chemical company.*

The principal reason that I believed we were falling short of being the best was that we operated with too much of a top-down command and control approach to our business life. As a result, we were not realizing all of the creativity and potential of our very capable workforce around the world—there was just too much "holding back and waiting for proper instructions from above." In order to unleash that potential, it seemed to me that we had to change our culture.

Culture change is not an easy thing, particularly for a large, successful organization. Overcoming years of inertia is tough. Many organizations proclaim their desire to change and make things better, but far too often those proclamations become a "do as I say, not as I do" exercise. So, wary old-timers in the organization correctly brand such proclamations as "management's flavor of the month."

To start with, I felt our matrix structure was stifling individual initiative and creativity. Therefore, one of the first things we did was eliminate the matrix structure and replace it with a much flatter organization. With this step, we eliminated fully one-third of our total executive positions. This forced us to place greater reliance on people in the organization who were closer to our operations and customers.

I was fortunate to have a very wise organization development advisor who convinced me that we needed to focus our attention on the values that were driving our culture. If we were to empower more people to take individual action, we needed to make sure that all were acting from a common set of values and beliefs. Consequently, we started spending a lot of effort debating our common values and what they should be if we were to become *the best*. Over a more than two-year period, we held offsite two-week workshops for approximately 500 of our middle and upper managers, giving these individuals a chance to debate our values and learn new leadership skills. I personally participated for a day in each of these workshops, giving each participant an opportunity to test me on my conviction concerning our values and the need for culture change.

I also spent significant time traveling around the world meeting with small and large groups of employees in their work locations, expressing my convictions about the importance of our values and seeking their input. From these multifaceted interactions, we wrote down the 12 core values that we wanted to be the bedrock of our work-related activities. The widespread dialogue with and among so many of our worldwide employees created broad buy-in for the values. Also, it gave a large number of our people throughout the organization a chance to know and evaluate me better. In addition, it reinforced my conviction about how truly capable our people really were.

We also became convinced that *total quality management* (TQM) could provide extremely valuable tools for focusing and aligning the groundswell of new energy growing out of our people becoming more empowered to take personal action. W. Edwards Deming and many Japanese companies have shown the way for quality management and continuous improvement. Several U.S.-based companies have adopted these techniques to improve the way they work. We benchmarked several of these organizations and concluded TQM should become a way of life for us too.

We began broad quality training across the organization. Also, there were several of our key managers already using quality management tools for improving performance in their parts of our company. One of these managers was Ray Floyd. Ray had originally worked for General Motors (GM), where he was introduced to the importance of quality management in durable goods manufacturing and became a disciple for W. Edward Deming's teachings.

After GM, Ray moved to Gilbarco, an equipment manufacturing company that was owned by Exxon. Ray was instrumental in introducing TQM and a culture of continuous improvement there. Gilbarco's Greensboro, North Carolina, plant was later designated as one of "America's Ten Best" plants by *Industry Week* magazine. Although Gilbarco was no longer owned by Exxon by that time, Gilbarco management graciously acknowledged that Ray had created the strategies and practices that led to this achievement and invited him to Greensboro to share the award ceremony with them.

In 1987, Ray Floyd joined Exxon Chemical, bringing his knowledge and experience with TQM and continuous improvement to bear on our operations and our quest to become the best. He quickly embraced our values and culture change process and showed us how to use quality management tools to align and focus the efforts of people at all levels in the company. In 1991, while he was the leader of our U.S. butyl polymers business, he and his organization won the Shingo Prize, which many consider the Nobel Prize of manufacturing. This award is named in honor of the late Dr. Shigeo Shingo, a pioneer in Toyota Production Systems, and is normally associated with excellence in durable goods manufacturing. Ray and his team demonstrated how quality principles like "just-in-time" and "single-minute-exchange-of-dies" are equally applicable to continuous chemical manufacturing processes. As a result, our butyl polymer manufacturing throughput was greatly increased and product inventory reduced significantly.

Later, Ray became the site manager for our large manufacturing complex in Baytown, Texas. There he demonstrated how the powerful merging of our values with quality management techniques could build high-performing teams. A core value that I felt strongly about was valuing our diversity. In the early 1980s, our efforts in "diversity" were more exercises in filling quotas than using our diversity as a key to gaining improved productivity.

Ray and his team fundamentally changed that at Baytown. They established an extensive awareness-training program, using a volunteer group called Diversity Pioneers to "seek out and understand the differences in people around them" and to view behavior "through cultural lenses." By challenging the prevailing white male culture to begin valuing differences in people, overall employee performance improved and an atmosphere was created where each person could contribute to his or her fullest ability. It was amazing to observe the impact of this culture change as it spread across the site, as well as throughout our company.

At Baytown, Ray and his key leaders turned the entire 2,000-person work-force into an improvement-idea-generating machine. Everywhere you went in the plant you found a quality station, which was a local focal point for improvement activities. These somewhat informal "stations" all served the same basic purposes: to convey overarching business goals to individual work teams in ways meaningful at each level and to provide a mechanism for stimulating ideas and measuring progress for each local team. A major innovation with this process was the translation of overall goals into terms that were meaningful at the grass-roots level. This alignment created an additive and multiplying effect of all the employee ideas and avoided one person's idea canceling out the impact of another's.

Over the seven-year period that Ray Floyd was site manager at Baytown, this processing complex changed from a troubled plant to a world-class example of manufacturing excellence. Manufacturing efficiency improved at a rate of 16% each year and employee participation grew to a level of 40 improvements per person per year—all resulting in outstanding bottom line profitability. In October 1993, the Exxon Baytown Chemical Plant was designated as one of "America's Ten Best" plants by *Industry Week* magazine. Of great importance for a capital inten-sive manufacturer, Baytown was also designated as Best in Large Industry by *Maintenance Technology* magazine. These awards were well deserved.

After I retired as president of Exxon Chemical Company, I lost touch with the organization and often wondered how our culture change was surviving without the "care and feeding" that I had enjoyed giving it. Although I have no firsthand information, I have been told that the culture change is still alive and well. The words that describe it have changed—for instance, "empowerment" has now become "engagement," but many of the middle managers that had been converted to the new way of working kept on doing it and spread the vision to others. When Exxon and Mobil merged and the chemical organizations of both companies were combined, I heard that our "engagement" approach to operations management was documented as "best practices" and spread to the Mobil plants as well. It is heartwarming to learn that the lessons we learned more than 15 years ago are still being used to positively impact the work lives of so many people.

When Ray Floyd told me of his book and asked me to write the Foreword for it, I was honored, delighted, and excited. I know of no one better than Ray to record and teach the lessons we learned starting in the 1980s. He knows well the theory of empowering people. However, he has the added advantage of having put the theory into practice and having personally led organizations to new higher levels of performance and personal satisfaction. I know that what he teaches in this book really works. I am convinced that if more industrial organizations adopt this "culture of rapid improvement," they will leave their competition in their dust.

H. Eugene McBrayer, President, Exxon Chemical Company (Retired), was also Chairman of the Chemical Manufacturers Association (now the American Chemistry Council), a founder and Director of Clean Sites, Inc., and a Trustee of the Malcolm Baldridge National Quality Award Program. While an officer of the CMA, he and several other chemical company CEOs launched the Responsible Care initiative, which over the past 20 years, has become one of the most important and successful industry-wide safety, health, and environmental performance improvement initiatives in American industry. In 1992, Gene was awarded the Industry Medal by the Society of Chemical Industry in recognition of his substantial contributions to the chemical industry.

Following retirement from Exxon, Gene served as a Director of Hercules, Inc., American Air Liquide, and Air Liquide International. He also served on the Advisory Committee of the Pacific Northwest National Laboratory.

Now retired from all corporate activities, Gene and his wife, Fay, live in Seattle, Washington, where he continues to pursue his passion for flying airplanes. He also contributes his leadership and energy to the Museum of Flight, which is located in Seattle and recognized internationally as one of the world's premier air and space museums.

Preface

I am frequently asked how long it takes to create a culture of rapid improvement. The answer that I give is generally the same: *it takes two years*. Let me explain the details of that expectation.

Improvement

The first benchmark on this journey is that you should be able to make progress of noticeable benefit to your business performance during the first six months. The rate of progress as you enter the second six-month period should be faster than the pace at which you entered the first six-month period. There truly is no part of this book that requires a lot of preparatory work from you in advance of beginning to experience real progress. Two important attributes that world-class businesses share are (1) they improve rapidly, and (2) they sustain rapid improvement once it has been achieved. Your actual performance should improve in each six-month period, and you should be operating with near–world-class performance at the end of two years.

Culture

The second benchmark of your improvement effort is that you should have all of the elements of the new culture in place throughout your organization by the end of two years. You will not yet enjoy a strong and mature new culture at the end of two years, but you will be clearly positioned to do so and you will already have many attributes of a new culture, including strong, autonomous improvement teams throughout your enterprise. After that, your culture will become more stable and more productive with time. It will become more like you and your people want it to be. But the critical issue related to the speed of implementation is that all the fundamental elements of your new culture should be in place within two years, and you will have substantially improved performance along the way.

Schedule

In the last four chapters (Chapters 14–17), I provide a pro forma schedule of activities to achieve culture change within two years. The schedule of implementation is the same for all businesses because organizations generally have a capability to improve that is consistent with their size. Over the years, I have led improvement at several businesses, ranging in size from $80 million to several billion dollars. At the $80 million business, the improvement was strategically created and tactically supervised by me personally. At the global multibillion dollar business, we had a staff of people in Baytown, Texas, supporting people in Houston, Brussels, and Singapore, who further supported many other people leading change in individual businesses and plants throughout the world. So whether your business needs one person or many full-time people, you more than likely already have a capability that is proportional to your need. You will probably need to redirect some of your capabilities, but if you use your organization as described in this book, you can, and should, have your culture of rapid improvement within two years.

Leadership

This book is intended for people who will lead change in their organization and for those who will help or advise the leaders. This material may also be of interest to anyone who is joining the conversation or who wants to influence the outcome. I understand that leaders generally have three critical responsibilities during periods of great change:

■ They must operate the business successfully as it exists today.
■ They must strategically improve the business for the future.
■ They must develop the organization.

Be assured that I understand and appreciate the difficulty of operating a business every day, but this book addresses only the second and third of these responsibilities; daily operation is a topic for another time. Also, in the nature of leadership, it is perfectly acceptable for other people to assist the leaders by doing many of the things described here for which leaders have ultimate responsibility. When a leader must do something personally, I state that clearly.

Because the focus of this book is industrial change, and more specifically change that produces improvement at the front line of manufacturing, I have adopted the practice of referring to leadership as "engineers and managers." I fully appreciate that businesses have other important leaders who will participate in leading the culture change and business improvement. Feel free to consider "engineers" as representing technical specialists in all fields of practice.

Adaptation

Leaders and their advisors must adapt this material to their own situations. When I was with General Motors during the 1970s, we began to hear about lean manufacturing (then called "just-in-time" manufacturing) and also about employee engagement (then called "quality circles"). Although we knew that Toyota was making wonderful progress with exactly those capabilities, during that early time very few of GM's leaders were able to adapt those concepts to our work. Obviously, we did make those technologies work with real success at a later time.

When I introduced those same technologies into the petroleum and chemical industries beginning in 1987, it was quite clear that most senior managers believed that the technologies did not apply in liquid continuous process manufacturing. Again, we ultimately did make it work. In fact, we made that technology work so well in the petrochemical industry that we were the 1991 recipients of the Shingo Prize.

In each case, both the problem and the solution were matters of industrial culture. Industrial culture in this case implies satisfying both the needs of the people and the needs of the business by applying the technologies of improvement in ways that are uniquely appropriate to each situation. Many early Western adopters of lean manufacturing and other improvement methods failed because they attempted to reproduce the exact practices that had been observed in Japan. Success in the auto industry came later, when we learned the theory that made Japanese practices successful and we applied that theory to construct practices that would work within our own culture. Changing industries from autos to chemicals worked in much the same way. Rather than adopting the practices of the auto industry, we used the theory of improvement and created practices appropriate to the needs of the chemical industry.

The key issue is that what you will read here will be theories of culture that are derived from my education and from my experiences. The examples and anecdotes are based on events that happened to me within the several companies and industries that I have served during the past 40 years. As I have moved throughout the world, across industries, and across functions within an industry, I have used the theories and practices that I brought with me from my prior experience to create new practices appropriate to each new situation. You will need to do the same.

Rituals

Over the years, I have had many, many people from many countries and many industries come to visit my operations to learn from what we have done. By the end of the visit, I generally knew from the questions that they asked which ones would succeed and which would fail. The successful managers asked: "Why did you do that?" Those who would fail asked: "Will you tell me exactly what you did?"

As the leaders of your business, you will need to learn the theory of culture change that I present and apply that theory to understand the practical elements of the examples from my experience. Then you can reconstruct the rituals and practices that I have used to create new rituals that match the needs of your own business and your own people. That is a job that requires a thorough understanding of your business and your people as well as a good understanding of the cultural improvement process. It also requires a leader with a creative mind.

Many People Make Culture Change Happen

Finally, I need to be clear about the "voice" of this book. With the advice, consent, and participation of many people who know far more than I do about the process of writing a book, I have adopted the convention of writing with two principle actors: "I" as the author and "you" as the reader. Although I understand the need for that practice, I feel that it is important to say that, quite literally, none of the activities or experiences described here were mine alone. Therefore, as you read this book, please know that whenever you see the word "I," what it really means is, "with the advice, consent, and participation of many people."

Acknowledgments

Like all significant tasks in which I have engaged, the completion of this book owes much to others who have freely given inspiration, advice, and outright help. Some individuals have influenced my career in ways that enabled me to have something to write about. Others have helped principally with this project. Most of my friends and colleagues are between those extremes: they are very important to me but won't be mentioned here.

Beginning at the beginning, I owe my early appreciation of the people side of business to Lewis Campbell. During our years together at GM, Lewis was the first person that I saw demonstrate the leadership that inspires great teams. Next in time are Gene McBrayer and John Webb. Together, Gene and John set a strategy to create great change at Exxon Chemical by establishing a very early focus on quality with a capital "Q"—as John said: "Quality in all we do." They made it happen so successfully that most of Exxon Corporation tagged along for the ride. I was very lucky to be part of their team.

I owe special debts to Don Powell, John Webb, and John Laibe. They each helped me to progress in my career in ways that made it possible to enjoy the experiences described in the book. Don convinced Exxon to hire me in the early 1980s, when the oil industry was in deep recession and the corporation already had more executives than needed. As Exxon Enterprises was closing, John Webb, who had already moved on, reached back and took me with him into the Chemical Company. John Laibe recognized that I could not progress with credentials only as a manufacturer, so he found an important business unit for me to lead and taught me the commercial side of industry.

Maura May, Michael Sinocchi, Ruth Mills, and Jose Leon all contributed to the production of this book. Maura and Michael talked me into writing it. Ruth edited the manuscript and formatted it for publication. My friend and colleague Jose agreed to the onerous task of reading the manuscript in "prepublication" form to ensure that it did not contain any material that is inconsistent with my ongoing commitments to Exxon. Quite literally, without their participation this book would not exist.

Finally, I want to acknowledge the many contributions of my wife, Marsha. She has been a true inspiration to me for many years. She has taught me real empathy through the simple process of continuous demonstration. Most important, at least for these purposes, she actually knew how to write a book.

About the Author

Raymond C. Floyd began his career as a production foreman with Inland Division of General Motors, a manufacturer of more than 30 families of automotive components. Following 10 years of increasingly responsible roles in manufacturing and engineering with General Motors, Ray joined Exxon as an affiliate vice president in Exxon Enterprises, an aggregate of more than 40 small and medium-size companies, each operating in a different industry segment. As a result, although Ray is best known for his work with Exxon Chemical, he has spent nearly half his career working broadly in discrete manufacturing.

Ray is generally recognized as among the first people in the world to practice lean manufacturing within the liquid industries. The ability to adapt the technology and examples from prior experience to new business and social cultures was critical to his success. Using exactly the theory and practices described in this book, Ray led Exxon Chemical's giant Baytown, Texas, site to international recognition for operational excellence. Later, as Global Manager of Manufacturing Services, Ray spread these practices to every plant in Exxon Chemical and used these practices to facilitate integration of operations when Exxon and Mobil joined in the world's largest merger.

Ray is the only person leading organizations in both discrete and liquid manufacturing to receive the "America's Best" designation from *Industry Week* magazine. Organizations that Ray has led have also received the Shingo Prize for Manufacturing Excellence and the "Best in Large Industry" designation from *Maintenance Technology* magazine. Ray received the Andersen Consulting Award for Excellence in Managing the Human Side of Change. Ray was appointed by President Reagan to participate in the Japan Business Study Program as a guest of Japan's Ministry of International Trade.

Raymond C. Floyd has degrees in chemical engineering (BS, Case Western Reserve University), law (JD, Capital University), and business administration (EMBA, University of Houston). He has also completed senior executive programs at the Institute for International Studies in Fuji City, Japan, and the Institute for Management Development in Lausanne, Switzerland. He is licensed as a registered professional engineer, attorney-at-law, and patent attorney. His wife, Marsha, is also an attorney-at-law. Ray and Marsha have two daughters who are both physicians.

Chapter 1

Industrial Culture: The Human Side of Change

> **Key Idea:** This book is about improving your business. More specifically, this book is about improving your business rapidly through the joint efforts of all the people who work in your company. Teamwork—and your company's unique concept of teamwork—is central to this discussion.

To be as successful as you can be, you need each person who works in the business to add his or her own best personal contribution to the efforts of the collective business team. They will do this by playing their personal roles well—and by playing their personal roles in close and structured collaboration with all your other team members. As described in detail in Chapter 12, the best companies are receiving autonomous improvements at a rate in excess of 40 improvements per person per year. That is nearly 3,000 times the average rate of autonomous improvement currently experienced in North American businesses. Once you understand that, you know the difference between average business performance and world-class performance.

Most of us have experienced or at least have a good understanding of the fundamentals of teamwork. We can create and lead teamwork in small teams consisting of 5 to 30 individuals. But how do you lead really large groups to create really big teams: teams of 500, 1,000, or even more individuals? The answer is *culture*. Culture is the driving force behind the big team version of teamwork.

The principle differences between a small team and an enterprise-wide industrial culture are differences of *scale* and *formality*. Members of small teams share values and beliefs that drive appropriate behavior based on their intimate personal knowledge of the goals of the team and their personal interaction with teammates. People within an industrial culture also share values and beliefs that drive appropriate behavior. However, as the size of the group grows, that growth requires that the communication of values, beliefs, and appropriate behavior must become more formal in order to preserve its integrity as it moves throughout the population. In a large group, knowledge of appropriate values, beliefs, and behavior is no longer sustainable based solely on intimate personal relations with other group members. In a very large culture, knowledge of values, beliefs, and behavior can only be sustained on the basis of shared formalities, deeply ingrained ritual, and visible social support or exclusion.

> **Key Idea:** Independent of the size of your business, you can create an industrial culture so that every person in your organization shares the values and beliefs of your business. You can create a culture in which everyone in your organization acts together in a way that is appropriate to those shared values. This book will give you both the theory and practice to design such a culture in a way that is especially appropriate to your business and your people.

Although sharing a common culture will promote behavior that is generally appropriate to the expectations of the group, the behavioral direction provided by cultural imperatives alone is somewhat amorphous and indirect. In order to achieve the specific outcomes and the rigorous schedules required for successful industrial performance, we still need to add the precise and closely directed actions of small, well-led teams at the front line and elsewhere throughout the business. As we discuss the subject of leading rapid improvement, we will address both the creation of a new culture for your business that draws all your people together, as well as a new culturally appropriate way to lead the activities of the small teams that conduct the detailed implementation of your strategies.

Improve the Performance of Your Business by Creating a New Industrial Culture

The most critical issue for this discussion of industrial culture is always improvement. Although there is necessarily a great deal of social content in any discussion of culture, this is not a social experiment of any type. The only reason to create a new industrial culture is to improve the performance of your business.

Unfortunately, as business leaders, we know that there is no "control knob" that we can seize upon to dial up improved performance through our own direct action. There is not even a physical or technological tool that we can deliver to our people with the certainty that, if they follow our instructions for the use of the tool, they will create improvement. Causing creative improvement through other people requires a much more complex and engaged relationship than the current industrial practice of supervising people to perform against a fixed standard.

It is difficult, but relatively straightforward, to directly manage the performance of a small team to meet a fixed standard. For example, General Motors trusted me to lead a group of about 30 people to meet their production standards beginning on my first work day as a newly graduated engineer. But *improvement* is different. When we manage large-scale improvement, we need the personal creativity and initiative of many other people. Therefore we always manage large-scale improvement indirectly. We manage improvement by creating within people the capability to cause improvement and by creating around people a culture that provides appropriate direction for those improvement efforts and a culture that provides social support for people as they practice improvement.

This is not to suggest in any way that leaders cannot personally conceive and direct some improvements. The big ideas that leaders and engineers (or other professional specialists) have are an important component of industrial improvement. The critical understanding is that implementing the good ideas that leaders and engineers have has long been an integral part of achieving normal business performance. As a result, implementing the improvements led by managers and engineers is necessary, but that alone will only produce performance that is within the current range of normal expectations.

Bad leaders produce performance at the low end of the normal range, and good leaders produce performance at the high end of the normal range. But even the best leaders and engineers acting alone do not often produce a pace of improvement that is world class. World-class performance requires implementing the good ideas from the leaders and engineers as well as implementing the good ideas from everyone else. Leaders and engineers acting alone can never produce enough improvement.

Knowing this, some organizations have reduced the number of leaders and engineers and adopted a very flat organizational structure. The bulk of the improvement in that situation is derived from the people on the front line of the business. Although saving the cost of leaders and engineers results in a nice one-time benefit, these very flat organizations also rarely produce performance that is outside the range of normal expectations. The experiences of many very flat organizations have clearly demonstrated that front-line people acting alone also cannot produce enough improvement. World-class businesses need both the contribution that can only come from leaders and engineers as well as the contribution that can only come from engaged people on the front line.

That is the secret of world-class improvement. Normal industrial improvement in Western Europe and North America averages about 3% each year, with a range from negative improvement (in other words, things got worse) to about 6% annual improvement. World-class improvement is generally believed to occur at a more rapid sustained pace of 10% or more each year. Note that the measure of world-class performance is progress against the strategic objectives of the business. Even in the most outstanding businesses, it is impractical to rapidly change everything. In fact, strategic focus for harmonizing the many different improvements is a significant part of achieving world-class results.

Sustaining rapid improvement, once it has been achieved, is another critical issue in determining that a business has become a world-class business. There are many business situations—such as the introduction of a new or reinvented product or recovering from a prior period of very bad performance—that allow a company to temporarily exceed the normal range of improvement and even penetrate the world-class range for a short while. When a business sustains a world-class pace of improvement year after year, then you know it has the right culture.

The Importance of a Culture of Rapid Improvement

The deciding factor in creating and sustaining a world-class pace of business improvement appears to be the culture of the people within the company. More specifically, the deciding factor is that the company provides a cultural environment that unites management, engineers, and others throughout the business into a single, very large, high-performing team.

What exactly does culture mean in an industrial context? In general, all cultures exist in a state of constant evolution. Cultures grow from, mature, and reinforce the values and beliefs that are shared among the people of the culture. People who share the values and beliefs of a culture also define among themselves the behavior that is appropriate to and consistent with those values and beliefs. Therefore culture—as a combination of values, beliefs, and behavior—determines how people will conduct themselves as individuals, as groups, and as individual members of a group. *Industrial cultures* are the same in this respect as *social cultures*.

Behavior that is consistent with the values and beliefs of a culture is encouraged and rewarded with social support. When culturally appropriate behavior attracts social support from others, it becomes self-reinforcing. On the other hand, behavior that is inconsistent with the values and beliefs of the culture attracts unfavorable social attention, often described as peer pressure. Practitioners of the undesirable behavior may even be shunned or excluded from the group until they abandon the unacceptable practices. For industrial purposes, this social relationship is very important. In a strong industrial culture, people will behave in a generally appropriate manner without specific direction or even without the presence of a leader or manager.

Together, values, beliefs, and behavior define a culture, either industrial or social. For very large groups, both industrial and social, a significant component of behavior that unites the group is *shared rituals*. Rituals are prescribed actions that are repetitively practiced by members of a culture as part of their cultural identity. In industry, establishing rituals can ensure that critical tasks are performed in the expected way, with the expected outcome, as part of each person's social contract with peers.

The business culture that drives the behavior of people at work today is often quite weak. The most common industrial cultures have not been created to provide a strong work culture in support of business success. Most existing industrial cultures are not much more than an informal adaptation of a social culture. As a result, a normal industrial culture today does not have shared values and beliefs that are related to the business. Adapting a social culture to the workplace provides very little guidance for business behavior, and uniting very large teams to improve the business is practically impossible in an essentially social culture.

In fact, today's work culture is often an impediment to progress. Many work cultures seek to reduce the social tension that arises as different personal cultures merge in the workplace. As a result, work cultures often value personal anonymity within the group. Work cultures that have matured in an environment of union conflict, restructuring, or outsourcing also have a strong value for self-preservation or preservation of the group. When an individual cooperates with management to improve productivity, that cooperation often raises a great many social concerns. The concerns range from personal jealousy toward an individual who attracts distinction among peers to the concern of group preservation that a successful improvement in the work may result in a reduction in the workforce.

If your work culture discourages cooperation with management, then there will be very real difficulties for even the best-planned improvement initiatives. Forced participation in improvement-related activities may occur under close supervision, but supervision will never produce enough improvement in that manner to succeed, and the improvement created in that way will rarely be sustainable.

> **Key Idea:** Ultimately the truth of culture at work is this: the people of your company will join with you to improve the business only to the extent that your people value cooperation with management as culturally appropriate behavior. Recognizing that cooperating with management to improve the business is not a value component of any social culture, practicing improvement at a world-class pace always requires converting the existing informally adapted social culture into an on-purpose business culture.

In nearly every situation where a powerful tool of improvement has failed to yield good performance, the underlying problem is that the people in the business have failed to accept the use of that tool as appropriate behavior within the culture of their company. Similarly, in situations where seemingly inappropriate improvement methods have yielded great success, it was likely due to the existence of a work culture that produced eager participation. Most or all of the people produced literally the best possible result from the tools they were given.

How Your Culture Affects the Potential for Improvement

As a group of people who have agreed (at least in established practice) how they will behave when they are working together, the people of your business, including management, have already created a culture for the workplace they share. Your goal is to convert the *existing* culture into a culture of *rapid improvement*. The distinguishing change is to engage nearly all the people to help you improve.

I have used the phrase "nearly all the people" because I understand that even in the best companies (and best societies) there are individuals who thrive by exhibiting countercultural behavior. Dealing with these troublesome individuals will be discussed more in Chapters 6 and 10, so for now, do not worry excessively about them. You will do fine if you get most of the folks to join you. As your culture of improvement becomes stronger, the social pressure on the noncompliant individuals will be on your side.

Sustained world-class performance rarely results from continuous reinvention of the products of a business, and sustained world-class performance is never the result of recovering from previously bad performance. Sustained world-class performance does not result exclusively from either big events led by management or from small events led by unsupervised workers. A world-class pace of improvement results primarily from the combined, and focused, effort of nearly all individuals: each making his or her personal best contribution. Engineers and managers make their unique contributions, and everyone else does as well. Most important, the contributions are all strategically aligned, and it is culturally acceptable for both groups to cooperate.

The combination of strategic focus and ubiquitous action appears to be critical to rapid, large-scale improvement. People who operate the business and make small improvements provide a stable base for the big events of engineers and managers. Building on the stable base, engineers and managers produce more and better big events. The big events, in turn, provide an evergreen field of action for future small-event improvement, with no danger of experiencing an environment of diminishing returns. A clear strategic direction provides focus to unite all the improvements into an additive and compatible whole.

It is truly possible to realize a genuine synergistic outcome when it becomes culturally appropriate for everyone to practice strategic improvement together. In that environment, the best companies push far beyond normal performance to achieve the sustained world-class results that we all desire.

How Culture Is Influenced by Strategy

Most leaders who succeed share two characteristics: they are following a good strategy, and they have the active support of their full team. As always, the initiating factor in improving a business for future success is strategy. If the leaders do not carefully identify the future needs of the business and respond with focused timely action to satisfy those needs, then nothing else will matter very much. Selecting the wrong method for improvement is often a mistake that can be accommodated by a willing team. Selecting the wrong strategic goals for the business is often a serious mistake that cannot be overcome. As a result, we will probably spend more time discussing strategy than you expected to find in a book on culture.

Immediately following strategy in importance is an industrial culture that encourages and enables people to support the strategy. Strategy addresses the business need to do the right thing. Culture addresses the human need to engage people to help make the strategy happen. At the intersection of these two elements of business success, the *strategic direction* of the business assumes the status of a *shared value* for the industrial culture.

The most successful industrial companies—that is, those with a culture of rapid improvement—are achieving sustained progress toward their strategic goals at a pace of 10% or more each year. However, nonstrategic elements of even the best businesses are progressing at not much more than an average pace of improvement. The real success of the best businesses lies not in an enormous volume of random improvement, but rather in the amazing rate of progress that they achieve toward implementing their strategic goals.

In such an environment, every individual—including engineers, managers, and front-line operators—works at a *sustainable level of diligence*. There is no need for a few heroic but unsustainable efforts. Each person makes his or her own best contribution to the strategic goals by taking *tactical action* that is possible within their normal scope of activity. There is no confusion of objectives or actions, and there are no people left off the team.

A Simple Model of Culture

It is convenient to think of culture—either business or social—as comprised of four elements: values, beliefs, behavior, and rituals. The logic chain of this model is explained in the following sections.

Element 1: Values

People hold certain personal or social values that are very important to them. Often these values have matured naturally through a lifetime of experience, with little formal development. As a result, those values shape people's beliefs, but they are rarely expressed or apparent. For industrial purposes, we need to create *business values* that people can share at work as naturally as they currently share *personal* or *social values* away from work.

A critical understanding is that, for people to adopt our industrial values, we need *corporate* values that are compatible with the social values that people already hold. People want to do a good job, and people want to be proud of their workplace. Many people will happily adopt corporate values at work that are well considered and well presented. But they will not adopt corporate values that are inconsistent with their existing personal values. People with different personal social cultures who are diminished or excluded by the society of the workplace will not adopt your business values in any way.

Element 2: Beliefs

Based on their values, people form beliefs about themselves, about other people, and about the world around them. Those beliefs direct a person's actions and also form the basis for a person's attempt to interpret the actions of others. Unlike values, beliefs are quite open and are often discussed.

It is possible that people who share the same values will hold different beliefs. Through discussion or persuasion, it is possible for an individual to remain committed to a personal value while changing his or her belief about transforming that value into action. As you introduce a culture based on business values, most of the conversation to reconcile corporate values with personal or social values will center on the beliefs that lead to action.

As the people of your business begin to experience the intense personal interaction of small-improvement teams, much of the conversation to resolve the interpersonal differences that interfere with team success will center on reconciling personal beliefs as they are used to interpret the values and actions of others.

Element 3: Behavior

Behavior, of course, is the most open component of culture. Behavior has three culturally critical characteristics in the workplace.

First, when people behave in a manner that is consistent with what they value and believe, their actions are comfortable and sustainable. As we create the new values and beliefs of our corporate culture, we want people to behave naturally at work in a way that advances the business.

Second, interpersonal behavior is the single most important factor when you create small teams that will carry out the detailed work of the business at the front line. As you create a culture of rapid improvement, based on the actions of small autonomous teams, you will want the interpersonal behavior of your people to draw the teams together and help to make them successful.

Third, culturally appropriate behavior attracts social support, and culturally inappropriate behavior can attract peer pressure to conform to the standards of the team. As team leaders receive increasing social support in managing behavior within a team, the team leaders can focus more time and attention on supporting the improvement and operational efforts of the team.

Element 4: Rituals

Rituals are a special form of behavior that serves two culturally specific needs. First, people agree to mutually practice the rituals of the culture as a way to demonstrate that they are all part of the same culture. Rituals are comforting, collegial, and unifying. Second, rituals ensure that certain critical tasks of the culture are always done in the prescribed manner. By establishing business-critical work as a ritual of the industrial culture, people can enjoy greater autonomy, while management retains the certainty that performance of the critical elements of the business is secure.

Management can delegate *action* to autonomous teams, but you can never delegate *responsibility* for the results. Even in the most autonomous culture, management must have certainty in business-critical areas, and the use of pre-scribed rituals of conduct and practice ensures that those critical expectations are met.

How to Use This Simple Model of Culture

The value of this simple model is that it provides a handle to grasp the amorphous concept of culture in a way that most people can actually use. The purpose for possessing a usable theoretical model of culture is to enable you to apply the theory to your specific situation as you design a unique corporate culture that is mindfully appropriate to your people and to your business. We can all learn from examples of the specific practices that others are using, but you must temper the details of those examples through the theory of culture to create unique practices for your own specific needs.

A usable model of cultural theory also provides a basis for communication on cultural issues, especially behavioral issues, among many people of different personal cultures. Cultural discussions, including discussions on differences in personal behavior, will be very valuable as you form and operate a strong cadre of autonomous teams.

In my experience, this simple three-part model (three-part because rituals are a subset of behavior) is both effective and productive. A more theoretically exact model of culture might be too complex, intellectually inaccessible, and therefore unusable for many people. A more detailed model might be a better model, but nevertheless a model with lower value.

The typical expression of a cultural model that is even simpler than this one often stops at discussions of behavior without referring to the underlying roots of behavior. Behavior-only models of personal and social culture typically result in a stereotypical assessment of individuals, and that is often more offensive than useful. Simpler cultural models often cause even more interpersonal problems than they resolve.

Through the communication and understanding facilitated by this model of culture, you can begin the process of creating an "on-purpose" corporate culture that is specifically designed for your people and your business needs. You can begin managing the interface between your corporate culture and the several personal cultures of the people in your business. Finally, you can give your people a way to form and sustain fully functional teams of people from different social cultures. Intelligent and inoffensive cultural discussion often allows teams to work together, despite behavior by team members that is com-fortable and natural to some people, but is initially either offensive or completely inexplicable to others.

Designing a Corporate Culture

This model of culture is presented to you at the beginning of the book to enable you to consider the rest of the material and your own situation in light of the model. The value of the model is principally in its use as a theoretical basis for you to design an industrial culture that is especially appropriate for your people and for your business. For leaders, the model provides some additional structure for your thinking. As you consider adoption and practice of the theory and examples presented here, use the model to help you transform the material into the culture that you want.

As you create your business strategies, do so in a way that your people will accept them as a shared value that is consistent with their personal and social values. As you create the social elements of your corporate culture, do that in a way that will draw the specific individuals who work with you together into a successful team and enable all your people to behave comfortably at work and to work comfortably together. As you create and use the rituals of a business culture, such as quality stations, do that in a way that will reinforce the commonality of purpose and action that you want to be shared broadly across the organization.

Elements of a Culture of Rapid Improvement: An Overview of How This Book Is Organized

Among the many tasks of a leader who intends to achieve world-class performance, including of course the task of operating the business on a daily basis, is the creation of an on-purpose culture of rapid improvement within the business. As I understand it, creating that new culture requires four things from leaders, so I have devoted one section of this book to each of these four:

1. Leaders must establish the *strategic direction* for the business that will enable each person to contribute to success through tactical actions that are within their normal scope of activity. Establishing a useful strategy for the business includes making the strategy memorable and visible in the workplace. Think of the strategy as establishing the shared values of your business culture. This is the subject of Section I.
2. Leaders must provide the *framework for improvement*, including the objective and subjective support that people need in order to engage with the business and with others. Within this framework, people will have new capabilities for improving their work. Think of the framework and these new capabilities as providing the shared beliefs and rituals of the new culture. This is the subject of Section II.

3. Leaders must create a new *on-purpose culture* for the business. Informal business adaptations of social cultures tend to exclude or diminish people who have a different personal or social culture outside of the workplace. The new culture for your business must specifically include everyone. This is the subject of Section III.

4. Leaders must *manage* and *sustain* the new culture. Even cultures such as Christianity that have existed for millennia receive regular attention from leaders to ensure that the values are upheld and the details of daily application of the culture evolve correctly, and to ensure that the people of the culture remain unified. You will need to provide the same support for your culture, especially in the early days. This is the subject of Section IV.

In the first four sections of the book, I describe the theory and practice of creating and sustaining a culture of rapid improvement by fulfilling each of those leadership responsibilities. The subject of Section V is a detailed description of activities during the first two years that will lead you to your goal.

Also, throughout the book I offer "Key Ideas" that appear in boxes (as in this chapter as well). I have also included a useful chapter summary at the end of each chapter to remind you of the key points you need to implement in your own organization. Finally, numerous case study "Examples" are described throughout the book, based on my experience working with many organizations in different industries and nations during my nearly 40-year career.

Summary of Chapter 1

- ■ Culture is *teamwork* on a large scale.
- ■ Small teams share *values*, *beliefs*, and *behavior* based on intimate personal knowledge of the team goals and the other team members.
- ■ In large populations, people share values, beliefs, and behavior based on *formalities* and *rituals*.
- ■ It is possible to create an industrial culture with shared values, beliefs, and behavior that is *uniquely appropriate* to your people and business.
- ■ Behavior guided by the values and beliefs of an industrial culture is not sufficiently granular for industrial operations. It is necessary to create *new rituals* and *new leadership* for directing the detailed work of small teams.
- ■ Improvement practiced by everyone acting together as a *strategically focused high-performing team* is required for world-class improvement.
- ■ Common *industrial* cultures today are informal adaptations of *social* cultures.

- Practicing improvement at a world-class pace requires converting the informal social culture at work into an *on-purpose* business culture.
- An understandable, synergistic boost to the pace of improvement results from a *strategically focused culture* that unites and enables everyone.
- Both social and industrial cultures can be considered to consist of *four elements*:
  1. Personal or business *values*.
  2. *Beliefs* that transform values into action.
  3. *Behavior* that is consistent with the values and beliefs of the culture.
  4. *Rituals* that reinforce the unity of people in the culture and also ensure that culturally critical tasks are performed as expected.
- The leadership elements of culture change are
  1. *Strategic direction* for the business that people can help implement.
  2. Objective and subjective *support* for the teams and people who will help implement the strategies.
  3. Developing an *on-purpose* culture of inclusion for all the people who will help implement the strategies.
  4. *Sustaining* the culture as it matures and evolves.

ESTABLISH THE VALUES AND BELIEFS OF YOUR NEW CULTURE

A particularly useful place to begin the discussion of industrial culture is by discussing the *strategic goals* of the business, the *tactical goals* that support the strategic goals, and the *tactical actions* that people will take to achieve those goals. Ultimately these business goals will serve as the shared values of your culture.

We begin the discussion of *culture* with a review of *strategy* because, as industrial leaders, we want a new culture for business purposes, not for social purposes. More specifically, we want to create a culture that enables the vast majority of our people to receive social support as they autonomously engage with us to improve the business. In the process of enabling autonomous action to improve the business, we need to be clear that we specify exactly what needs to improve and precisely how people can help. The strategy of the business is critical to that communication. Improvement that does not advance the strategic goals of the business has little value, and inappropriate actions will detract from, rather than contribute to, the overall effort.

Without clear strategic direction, it is relatively easy for an honest, hardworking person to decide wrongly that what is good for his or her group must also be good for the organization.

Example: In a research and development (R&D) organization where I once consulted, there was a laboratory function critical to the process. Essentially, after the scientists who worked at the research bench shaking beakers had created a new molecule, a sample of the new chemical was delivered to the lab (called the PCL) as the first step in developing the new molecule into a commercially useful product.

The PCL functioned principally as a service to the scientists. Because of this relationship, the PCL was notoriously inefficient, as many service organizations are. Some days there would be little to do, and other days there would be far too much to do. So a new lab supervisor decided to improve the efficiency of the PCL by smoothing the work flow.

The way he chose to do this was to establish a backlog of work ahead of the lab. On busy days, the lab would work at a normal pace and leave some work to accumulate for the next slow day. On slow days, they also worked at a normal pace by consuming work from the backlog. Efficiency in the PCL did in fact improve greatly.

The problem, of course, is that the lab did not exist to be an efficient lab. Instead, the lab existed to make the scientists more effective in developing new materials. As the lab improved its efficiency, two other things happened: the scientists waited longer for results, and the product development cycle slowed. The new efficiency in the lab diminished the capability of the R&D organization to carry out its mission.

In the three chapters in this section, we will discuss establishing the basis for engaged people to take autonomous improvement action by creating a clear understanding of what improvement the business needs and how people throughout the enterprise can help achieve that improvement:

- Chapter 2 tells how you can *establish strategic goals* for the business that are useful as the foundation for the shared values and beliefs of your culture.
- Chapter 3 shows how you can *translate the strategic goals of the business into local tactical goals and actions* that enable each person or team to make their own best contribution as an integral part of the larger business.
- Chapter 4 shows how to make the tactical goals and actions visibly apparent at each work location. This visibility enables autonomous improvement in a way that also enables unobtrusive management and technical oversight to ensure alignment among teams and to provide certainty to business-critical work.

Chapter 2 describes a strategic planning process that will produce a "gap analysis" strategy. That strategic format will be used consistently in the discussions throughout this book. Although there is more material on strategic development here than you might expect in a book on culture, the essence of this discussion is creating your strategy for the business in a way that can serve your need for broad communication of the objectives for improvement, and further, for using strategic communications as a basis for concerted action by many people. If you consider the *strategy* as the basis for the *values* and *beliefs* and *actions* of an industrial culture, then it makes more sense. For that reason, even if you are confident that you have a successful strategic planning process, it will be valuable to read Chapter 2 as a basis for the material that follows.

Chapter 2

Strategy: The Values and Beliefs of an Industrial Culture

Key Idea: Strategic goals are the organizing start to an ongoing communication that will provide both direction and focus to the actions of the entire organization for an extended period. In the terms of our simple model of culture, the strategies are the basis for business-related values and beliefs that will be shared by the members of the culture.

Improvements are not all created equal. As we saw in the introduction to this section, in extreme cases, it is even possible for local "improvements" to impede the mission of the overall organization. A more common effect in large organizations is for many people to each have a different idea of what might constitute a valuable improvement, with the result that a lot of time and money is consumed making local or personal improvements, but the performance of the business never improves. Real performance improvement requires that many people make many changes, all of which are additive and compatible in pursuit of the strategic goals of the business. The only way to achieve this outcome is for the leader to be quite specific in communicating what change is needed and how people can help. This chapter starts this process by describing an approach for establishing strategic goals that are specifically structured for organization-wide communication.

Establishing Strategic Goals for Your Organization

Setting the strategic goals for a business is much easier than most people make it seem. The reason that strategic goal setting is easier than expected is that strategic goals do not need to be precise. Strategic goals are intended only to provide a common direction toward a future state of the business that will unify and focus many tactical goals and subsequent tactical actions, that will occur during a period of perhaps five years or even more. A perfectly acceptable, and directionally correct, strategic goal can be as simple and as imprecise as a statement such as, "We need to participate in the Asian market."

Although strategic goals do not need to be precise, they do need to be *correct*. It may be that the vital need for correctness is the reason that strategic development has earned a reputation for being difficult. Directional accuracy of strategies is certainly important. Deciding to participate in the emerging market of Asia may preclude participation in the other emerging markets of Africa, Eastern Europe, or South America. If you decide to focus your emerging market efforts in the Asian market, then the success of your business requires that the Asian strategy be the right direction for the future of the enterprise.

The great benefit of strategic goals is that they quickly focus the field of action for the slower, more rigorous, and more precise work of establishing and progressing tactical goals and tactical actions. By eliminating Africa, Eastern Europe, and South America, the seemingly imprecise goal of entering the Asian market reduced your field of action for developing markets by three-fourths.

On the other hand, unlike strategic goals, tactical goals and actions do need to be precise. If a company with the strategy to participate in the Asian market decided to do so by building a new plant in China, that is a very precise decision. Such a decision might very well require years of detailed analysis before the project is launched and yet more years of design and construction to bring the new plant to fruition.

Although the use of strategies that are only directionally correct may seem uncomfortably imprecise for most managers, it is actually quite a satisfactory practice. I like to think of strategy as "defining the future journey of the business." For example, one of the most successful actual journeys of adventure and exploration in American history was the Lewis and Clark Corps of Discovery. When Meriwether Lewis and William Clark began their travels, they did not know the end point of their journey with any precision. They only knew that they were going to move along the rivers and lakes of North America toward the northwest until they found a water passage to reach the Pacific Ocean. That strategic direction alone was enough for great success. At the end of the trip, they reached the Pacific Ocean at what is now Seaside, Oregon.

By defining the strategic objective only as "northwest to the Pacific," they enabled an immediate commencement of travel and years of successful interim goals and tactical actions along the way, each of which advanced the ultimate goal of mapping a Northwest Passage across North America to the Pacific. Their simple goal enabled success because it also *limited and focused* the field of action. No one among them got confused and traveled toward Boston or New Orleans. Obviously there was more required for success than simply knowing where they were going. But that was a great start, and that clarity of intent enabled them to focus on everything else.

Similarly, your organization can begin work promptly and make a lot of tactical progress on the journey toward your strategic business goals long before you need a precise understanding of the end point. By defining a strategic direction, you also define all other directions as nonstrategic. That provides both focus and commonality of action.

In practice, most businesses never reach a strategic end point such as the Pacific Ocean and declare victory. Business is ongoing. As tactical progress occurs against the original strategies, the strategic horizon continually extends farther into the future, defining or refining the direction for the following years. For this reason, Chapter 3 discusses a process for periodically refreshing strategic goals to recognize progress as well as changes in the environment.

Establishing Your Organization's Tactical Goals

Tactical goals are a necessary companion to strategic goals. Tactical goals represent specific interim subsets of a strategic goal. For example, if the strategic goal for a five-year horizon is "to move toward the northwest from Houston," then a tactical goal could be, "We will be in Amarillo within six months."

These tactical subsets of the strategic goal are not merely directionally correct. Tactical goals define specific future achievements. There is room within a tactical goal for several optional actions. For example, you could get to Amarillo within six months by walking, running, or biking along any of several routes. As you commence practical progress toward your tactical goals, you will continually define and implement the most appropriate tactical actions. This is one reason that we will spend a lot of time in Chapter 4 and beyond on establishing visibility for tactical goals and actions at the team level. The life span of tactical goals is much shorter than the life of strategic goals, and the life of tactical actions is shorter still. As a result, tactical goals and actions will likely be updated several times throughout the years within the strategic horizon.

Tactical goals and actions with immediate performance expectations ensure that the organization begins strategic implementation promptly and makes good progress in the right direction. It is fine for the strategic direction to be somewhat imprecise, but practical progress must be both prompt and certain. Together, the strategic direction, tactical goals, and tactical actions provide all the information that people will need to begin making real progress.

For the first six months and the first year, it is irrelevant whether at the end of a five-year journey you will ultimately end your northwest travel in Seattle, Portland, or Vancouver. For the initial six-month period, you need only be certain that you are moving in the right direction and making good progress. I am not suggesting that establishing a strategy is truly simple, only that selecting a direction for travel should be much easier and faster than making the trip.

Setting Strategic Goals Is the Responsibility of the Senior Leader

Strategic goals for the business as a whole are the responsibility of the most senior leader of the organization. The goals are normally developed with the participation of the few people who report directly to the most senior leader. There are two implications of this requirement that the most senior leader must own the goals.

First, the senior leader is principally responsible for the future of the business, and the strategy will define that future. It is perfectly acceptable for a leader to use the resources of the organization in the normal way those resources are used, but at the end of the day, the direction the strategic goals give to the organization and the written words that state that direction must unequivocally belong to the leader.

Moreover, business is difficult. Every day there are conflicting priorities that arise. As we used to say: "When you are up to your neck in alligators, it is difficult to remember that your objective is to drain the swamp." Only the most senior leader can protect the strategic goals from the daily distractions of running a business over a multiyear period, and no senior leader will chose to do that unless he or she owns the goals as a personal obligation. Finally, only the most senior leader can require that all other people in the organization devote appropriate time and effort to make the goals a reality.

The second implication of the requirement that the most senior leader of the organization must own the goals is that not all senior leaders are at the very top of the enterprise of which they are a part. It is also fully acceptable for a middle manager with responsibility for an operating unit within a larger business to undertake goal setting and managed improvement within that unit. If you are at the top of your own organization, including an organization within a larger enterprise, and if you set goals appropriately compatible with the success of the larger entity (remember the lesson of the laboratory leader in the Section I overview?), then the goal-focused improvement process will work as a foundation for you to manage your part of the enterprise, whatever that part may be.

> **Example:** On three different occasions when I led two different organizations to performance that was recognized as among "America's Ten Best" by *Industry Week* magazine and led a third organization to receive the Shingo Prize, I was not at the top of the entire corporation. But on those occasions, and several others, I was the most senior leader for a discrete piece of the enterprise. Within the responsibility that I was given, I did everything that is described here.

A Process for Establishing Strategic Goals

There is no value in rehashing the full process of setting strategic goals; that is well covered in many other books. If you walk the business aisle of any good bookstore, you should be within arm's reach of several fine books on corporate strategy. The lesson of this book, however, is the use of strategy as the basis for the *shared values* of a corporate *culture* and as a *communication* device for organizing the efforts of many people. Therefore I will take just a quick look at the bones of the strategic planning process to provide a common basis for proceeding with the discussion of strategic communications.

For most ongoing businesses, the strategic planning process is primarily intended to ensure that management mindfully looks to the future to identify the "environmental" factors to which the company must respond in order to compete successfully. The process continues with an equally careful assessment of current internal capabilities that are aligned against the future external demands. The future external demands and the current internal capabilities define the *strategic gaps* that the business will need to close in order to be successful in the future. These gaps may be large if you need to enter the Asian market and today have no Asian capability. Or they may be much more modest. The only critical element is that the gaps be carefully defined from good data describing both internal capabilities and external demands.

Look Outside Your Organization

Typically gap assessment covers at least the major stakeholders in the future of the business: customers, owners, employees, and communities. The next four subsections of this chapter offer a brief description of the assessment appropriate to each of these stakeholders in order to indicate the possible considerations that you may encounter.

Evaluate Your Customers and Competitors

The future needs of your customers certainly must be a major part of your strategic direction. If you lose your customers, nothing else matters. The customer assessment should also include adequate consideration of capabilities that are being demonstrated or developed by your competitors. Competitor capabilities will strongly influence future customer expectations. You also should consider the future needs of potential customers. Assessing the actions needed to meet the future demands of "aspirant customers" often provides a very compelling direction for the evolution of your business.

> **Example:** For a three-year period, I was the senior manager of a synthetic rubber business that operated in North and South America as well as throughout Europe. This is the same business that received the 1991 Shingo Prize. During each of those three years, Goodyear Tire designated us as their "best" global supplier. Yet, every time that I met with Goodyear management during that period, they had a long list of new and different things that they wanted for the future. I truly believe that customers want more from the business partners they respect than from those they do not. Receiving a customer's list of future expectations is a great indication that they intend to share that future with you.

Consider the Owners of Your Business

The second external group to be considered is the people who own the business. For these purposes, the owners represent the external expectations of business performance within the investment community, and those are generally financial. Investors may want growth, cash flow, return on investment, or a variety of other specific business results. Aspirations for financial growth may drive you to new products, new customers, or new markets.

Unfortunately the time horizon for investors is often not strategic. Understanding how you will accommodate or placate your investors is an important part of ensuring that you can sustain your strategy.

> **Key Idea:** In combination, the assessment of customers, competitors, and owners will help determine the future direction for your business.

Do Not Forget to Consider Your Employees

Management also needs to consider the stakeholders known as employees. Employees are not precisely an environmental factor: employees are an integral part of the company. But employees also have many strategic characteristics of a third party. Strategically, as you adopt a new culture, there will be many changes in the ways employees participate in the future of the business. The business factor represented by employees also includes labor unions, if any, who represent your people.

Autonomous employee participation in your industry, and in the best companies that you are seeking to emulate, is a critical consideration of cultural change. In the future, your people will need to participate autonomously at least to the same extent as the best competitor in your industry. You may also want to meet the standard of employee participation set by the best companies in *any* industry. If you intend to develop a workplace where each person makes 40 or more improvements each year, then the current capabilities and future expectations for your employees is a very real strategic factor.

The principle caveat in considering your employees as a strategic factor for change is that people want to believe that they will somehow work better or harder if the conditions in which they work are improved. In most cases, in the industrial situation that exists in North America and Western Europe, though, that is not often true.

Studies conducted between 1927 and 1932 at the Western Electric Hawthorne Works in Chicago demonstrated that people did, in fact, work harder in response to changes in their working conditions. Those same studies also demonstrated that the effect was only sustainable if the working conditions changed constantly and changed in insignificant ways, such as changes in the color of the walls or the intensity of the lighting. Most reports of that study overlook the ultimate conclusion that people were responding to the interest and attention they were receiving rather than to the actual physical changes in their environment.

Sustainable improvement in personal performance results from changes in the *work* or changes to the *work process*, but does not often result from changes in the *work environment*. Chasing betterments to the work environment is often a fatal mistake when initiating employee engagement. I have seen this effect become so pervasive that it has resulted in abandonment of the engagement effort because it became expensive and unproductive.

> **Example:** During the last of my 10 years at General Motors, management conducted a "quality of work life" survey broadly across the corporation. At the time, I worked in a 70-year-old building in Dayton, Ohio, that had originally been built as part of the Wright

Brothers' Airplane Company. As engineering superintendent with responsibility for hundreds of millions of dollars of annual production, I recall winter day meetings in my office where we needed to wear our coats to keep warm. But at the end of the day, we got our work done in a fully satisfactory manner. The building was old, cold, and ugly, but it was adequate for the work we did.

In fact, the "quality of work life" survey results for the impact of facilities on the performance of people in my terrible old factory building were exactly the same as the results from a virtually new executive office building at the General Motors Technology Center in Detroit. Completely independent of the actual state of the facilities we occupied, both groups felt (or at least communicated) that better facilities would improve our performance. It is likely that improving the facilities would not have changed sustainable performance in either situation.

Assess the Needs of Your Organization's Community

The stakeholder known as "community" includes all of the legal, regulatory, and financial reporting requirements placed on your business by others, as well as the relationship of your business with the neighbors who live along your fence line or in proximity to your operations.

> **Example:** Probably a lot depends on the nature of your business and the community in which you operate. When I worked for General Motors in Vandalia, Ohio, the part-time mayor of Vandalia was also a General Motors employee. In Baytown, Texas, the situation was much the same. The part-time mayor of Baytown was also an Exxon employee. In both cases, we had huge industrial complexes in small towns, and a lot was expected of us.
>
> However, when I worked at Exxon Corporate Headquarters in Manhattan, before the company moved to Texas, I was surprised by how few people in Manhattan knew where the Exxon Building was located. In Manhattan, we were just another office building in a big town full of office buildings.

Similar to the needs of your customers, the community considerations that will be important to you in the future are those that are specific to your business. The key issue is to identify the ways in which the community might impact your license to operate and to take a careful look outside to see what is coming.

Key Idea: For all these stakeholder issues, the intent of looking mindfully at the external environment in which you operate is to develop a clear understanding of what success will require from you and your business in five or more years.

Next, Look Inside Your Organization

Now that you have looked carefully outside to understand what will be required of you in the future, look with equal care inside your organization to assess your existing capabilities against those requirements. For each strategic need that you have identified for the future of your business, assess your current capabilities. If your customers want more variety or more consistency, you should assess what your current capability is to perform to those expectations and what your history has been with improving those capabilities. This internal review occasionally unearths some interesting results.

> **Example:** In 1991, the chemical industry was deeply engaged in the adoption of statistical quality processes. Customers were beginning to request products with a well-defined statistical process capability, and the use of statistical methods was clearly the direction for the future. Surprisingly, at that time, it was still common practice in the industry for some products (such as low-value commodities) to be sold by name only with no exact chemical specification agreed upon between the customers and suppliers.
>
> Without an agreed specification, it is impossible to assess statistical product quality and process capability. During our external assessment, we found that our customers were moving toward a requirement for which we had no internal capability or other operating basis. That gap between our customer's future requirements and our current internal capabilities identified a real strategic issue that was a classic example of a change that could be either a future threat or an exciting opportunity.

The important part of comparing internal capabilities against external needs is that you must be careful to take an honest look at both the good and bad aspects of your existing ability to meet the future business needs that you have identified. This is really where you will need to pass the "bulletin-board test" with the folks who operate your business. Remember that you are establishing strategies as one part of a communications process that will enable all the people in your business to help you succeed. Ask yourself how people will react when you write down your opinion of current capabilities and hang it on the wall for everyone to read. (You will have to do this. There will be more on this in Chapter 4.)

While you are looking at your capabilities, it is fine to recognize that you have recently introduced new capabilities or that you are about to do so. The fact that your existing capabilities are changing is an important part of the assessment.

At the same time, be careful not to convince yourself that the introduction of new capabilities is, in itself, a strategic goal: as Albert Einstein said, "Perfection of means and confusion of goals seems to characterize our age." Lean manufacturing, six sigma, autonomous improvement, and other technologies of that sort are only capabilities or means to the end of improving your business. None of these capabilities should become business goals in themselves.

> **Key Idea:** In my personal experience, and in conversation with many others, it is clear that when leaders become confused and allow the deployment of the means for improvement to become the strategic objective of improvement, then the effort is more likely to fail than to succeed. When the means becomes the objective, the two most likely failure modes are excessive, costly, and unusable training coupled with "improvements" that are great demonstrations of the tool but contribute little to the business.

Analyze the Gap between Your Current Capabilities and Your Future Requirements

With a good understanding of what will be required for future success, as well as an equally good assessment of your existing and developing internal capabilities to meet those demands, you can define the precise strategic gaps that need to be closed. There will be a lot of management judgment applied in this process. You will undoubtedly discover far more gaps than you will elect to include in the strategic focus for your future. You may also want to group some gaps together as a generic category of improvement. For example, I once combined several needs for improvement in manufacturing operations such as quality, quantity, flexibility, and return on investment into the single goal of "improve capability and capacity with investment less than depreciation."

Your strategic need at this point is to use your gap analysis, combined with management judgment, to describe a few directionally correct paths for your organization to follow into the future. You need to exercise great care in

selecting the business elements that will become your strategi
dilution or loss of focus, each business element that you select
necessary for future success. To ensure success, all the strategic
do select, when taken together, must be *sufficient* to meet the external demands.
By deciding which gaps you will close, and how you will do that, you will begin
the process of communicating to your people how they can help you succeed.
Remember that at this point you have to be directionally correct, but it is not
necessary to be precise. That precision will come later as you progress to tactical
goals and tactical actions.

Write Your Goals

It is now time to write your strategic goals, as they will be used in the communication process. In general, I prefer to have just a few goals, each of real importance. In round numbers, I think that in most situations, five or six strategic
goals are adequate; three is often not enough, and eight is too many.

The important lesson of this chapter is the communication, not the goals.
The reason for the preceding brief review of goal setting by gap analysis is that
our discussion of goals as a communication device will follow the format that
this process for goal setting produces:

1. Future need.
2. Current capability.
3. Actions to close the gap.

Always keep communication in the forefront of your mind as you write
your goals. The intent is not to produce a wonderful document. The intent is to
initiate communication of the direction for the business. For communication
purposes, a good goal has five specific components, listed below. These elements
make your written strategic goals a living document that you will use as the basis
of ongoing conversation about the strategies and conduct of your business and
of your improvement efforts. Each of these will be discussed separately in detail
in the next subsections:

1. Strategic goals have a simple, memorable statement of the gap you are
   closing.
2. Strategic goals have a directionally correct statement of the future needs of
   the business.
3. Strategic goals have a credible statement of the current capability of the
   business to meet future needs.
4. Strategic goals have a few objective measures that define progress.
5. Strategic goals have interim tactical performance targets to be achieved.

1. Strategic Goals Have a Simple, Memorable Statement of the Gap You Are Closing

The intent of the goal statement is to serve as a mnemonic that will enable people to carry the goal and all its components around in their heads each day.

> **Example:** A mnemonic is a memory-enhancing technique that enables people to remember something unobvious, complex, or confusing by remembering first something that is simple and memorable. More than 50 years ago, I was taught that the colors of the rainbow occur in the sequence: red, orange, yellow, green, blue, indigo, violet. That sequence is unobvious and might be hard to remember except for the mnemonic "Roy G. Biv" that I was given at the time. With Roy to help me, I have always been able to easily and quickly remember this information.

The simple phrase that makes goals memorable is what enables goal-focused improvement to become a part of how each person makes operating choices throughout each day. By remembering the simple and attractive phrase that describes the goal, people will be able to remember and use the more complex details of the goal itself. For the purpose of using strategies as a value of the industrial culture, you want a goal statement that people can conveniently use to exchange mutually reassuring communications that strengthen the teams. As you will see in the sample goals presented later in this chapter, a goal statement might be as simple as "Improve the capability and capacity of the plant." In pursuit of that goal, people in different parts of the plant may be doing very different things, but by exchanging the phrase "capability and capacity," they will know that they are working on the same team, toward the same end, even if they appear to be doing different things. This is the place where you say your own version of "We are seeking the Northwest Passage to the Pacific." You will want one memorable statement for each goal that communicates the gap that you have discovered between future needs and current capabilities.

2. Strategic Goals Have a Directionally Correct Statement of Future Needs

In one or two paragraphs of a few short sentences each, describe for each goal the vision of the new future state when the goal has been met and the reasons that you have found for moving toward this new future state. Be careful not to describe the *intended actions* to achieve that future state. The intent is not to imply a limit on permissible actions by describing a few possible actions, but rather to describe the rationale and result of all possible actions that will close the business gap that you have identified. It should be clear to people that the gap you are closing leads to this future state.

3. Strategic Goals Have a Credible Description of Current Capabilities

Again, in one or two paragraphs of a few short sentences, describe the current capabilities that you assess your organization to have related to your future needs. Be certain that you keep this credible to the folks who will read it: a fair statement will be of more value to you in the long term than any possible inspiration obtained from inaccurately describing a pending disaster. It is perfectly acceptable to recognize while describing the current state that capabilities are changing and to report the recent trends of that change. Together, it should be apparent that the statement of future needs and the statement of current capabilities defines and clarifies the performance gap described in the goal statement.

4. Strategic Goals Have a Few Objective Measures That Define Progress

There will be a lot more detail on measurement in Chapter 12, but for now, for communication purposes, keep the number of measures in the goal statement small, and make the measures as objective and understandable as possible. For some people, the paragraphs describing the future state and current capabilities will establish the strategic path. For others, the measures will be the best descriptor of what you intend to achieve. Independent of what people understand the goal to be as a result of the written materials, for almost every member of your team, the measures will be the best indicator of what they will actually do in response to the goals.

Key Idea: Think about the measures as a communication device in exactly the same way the words are structured to communicate. Be certain that the measures you adopt accurately and objectively measure the strategic path forward.

I have seen far too many measurement systems that were superficially or indirectly related to the goal. That practice is both distracting to the communication as well as an invitation to folks to do the wrong thing in pursuit of the measure rather than in pursuit of the goal.

---

5. Strategic Goals Have Interim Tactical Performance Targets to Be Achieved

We will discuss in Chapter 3 that the goals need to be refreshed periodically in order to sustain improvement over a long period of time. As you begin practicing a disciplined approach to strategic goals, you should identify the date of your next formal update. For at least the period until the first scheduled refreshment, which will likely occur in two years, you should have a specific performance target designed to achieve ratable progress against each goal for each six-month period.

As mentioned, strategic goals may be directionally correct, but imprecise. This does not imply in any way that it is acceptable for progress to be slow or uncertain. Good performance targets for each six-month period help ensure that you get started promptly and continue diligently.

Present Your Goals to Your Organization

All five components of each goal as described above must be able to fit on one side of a normal sheet of paper when the goals are written for presentation to the organization. This is the time to be concise in your writing. As hinted at earlier, ultimately you will hang these few sheets of paper on the wall throughout the facility so that everyone can see exactly what you are all going to be doing together. Goals have a limited value in engaging people unless everyone can see them and talk about them.

Figure 2.1, Figure 2.2, and Figure 2.3 illustrate the form and substance of strategic goals. For the record, because they have been written from my own experience, these documents appear to be goals that I might have used in my prior life, but they are not. These are only examples.

The value of the sample goal documents is that they represent several types of goals that you might need, along with some pro forma indication of the considerations for each type of goal. Here are a few observations on the sample goals.

First, look at the goal statement that heads each sheet. The intent here is to create a mnemonic to provide people with a handle that they can use to remember the entire goal based on some simple and easily remembered phrase. They can then use that handle to carry the entire goal around in their heads. Normally for these three goals, people would learn to remember:

- "License to operate," which represents the community goal of Figure 2.1.
- "Involve all people," which represents the employee goal of Figure 2.2.
- "Improve capability and capacity," which represents the customer/owner goal of Figure 2.3.

Strategic Goal:
Maintain our license to operate

Vision of the future
Our business needs to demonstrate that our operations are absolutely legal, safe, honest and ethical. We need to be recognized as good neighbors. By year end 2010, we will meet or exceed all then-current legal and regulatory requirements for safety, health, financial and audit controls and personnel standards. We will have in place a process to anticipate future requirements, and this will be a primary input to our operations and business planning. We will improve personal relations with our neighbors and the local civic entities to become a trusted and valued member ofthe community.

Today's reality
We are required to comply with various standards mandated by law, govemmental regulations, industry associations, financial accounting standards or corporate policies. Our method for achieving compliance is often reactive, and we do not achieve compliance as well or as effectively as we would with adequate anticipation ofnew requirements.

Community involvement is excellent and community support is adequate. Workplace safety is far better than industry average, but not as good as we want. The effectiveness of our efforts in wellness initiatives is not measured and not well known. We are in compliance with all applicable laws and regulations. Our current compliance with accounting standards and corporate policy is not satisfactory but is improving.

Measurements
Monthly
- Total recordable incident rate (TRIR) for all people including both employees and contractors.
- Count of community complaints.
- Count of regulatory actions
Quarterly
- Total Air, Water and Land environmental emissions and trends.
Annually
- Safety and wellness program assessments using standard assessment format.
- Financial and internal controls audits using standard audit format
- Count of Govemmental actions or complaints and measured regulatory action
- Legislative advocacy program development in cooperation with industry association.

Performance Targets
- TRIR equivalent to or better than average of top five US industrial companies by 2010 with ratable progress toward that achieved during each six months.
- Community complaints reduced by 90% by 2010 with ratable progress each six months.
- Total environmental emissions in tons reduced 50% by 2010 with ratable progress each six months.

Figure 2.1 Sample goal for meeting the future needs of communities.

Strategic Goal:
Involve all people in the improvement process.

Vision of the future
The best companies in industry improve through the combined efforts of all the people. We need that capability as well. By year end 2010, all people in our business will be full participants in the success of our organization. The capability of each individual and team to contribute will be recognized. The diversity of people and their different contributions will be valued. Each person will contribute improvement to change our business in pursuit ofour strategic goals at a pace equivalent to the best businesses in North America. Management will demonstrate that no employee will lose his or her employment due to improvements. Greater participation and autonomy will improve the perception of our company as an employer.

Today's reality
The goal deployment process is well known here and used in several places already. The elements of engagement are known and practiced, but generally at an early stage of development. The activities to understand and value our diverse population have a strong basis, but much more is needed. The people of our business are good honest hard working people who generally want more opportunity to ensure the future of the enterprise. Existing participation through autonomous change is unmeasured, but believed to be about average for North American industry. Relationships are good and far better than average, but not as good as we need for meeting our goals.

Measurements
Monthly
- Count of improvements per person at each team's work location and aggregate counts throughout each organizational unit.

Quarterly
- Autonomous improvement against strategic goals and routine performance indicators assessed by subtracting capital project effects from bulk measures of the business.

Annually
- Formal and informal employee complaints including complaints made directly to management or indirectly through a union or a regulator.

Performance Targets
- Counted improvements per person each year should reach 8 by year end with ratable progress each six months thereafter to a level of 50 improvements per person per year by year end 2010.
- The aggregate value of autonomous improvements as derived from the bulk measures of performance will reach $2,500 per person by year end with ratable progress each six months thereafter to a level of at least $20,000 per person per year by year end 2010.

Figure 2.2   Sample goal describing employee value, inclusion, and participation.

Strategic Goal:
Improve the capability and capacity of our plant with new investment less than depreciation.

Vision of the future
Customers constantly demand new or different specialty products and greater consistency in commodity products. The market for our products is constantly growing. Our business is both capital-intensive and cyclical.

The ability to improve operating performance without capital will allow us to satisfy our customers and increase our market position throughout the cycle as well as make us more attractive for future investment due to our improved return on capital employed.

Today's reality
Our historic progress improving capacity without capital has been near average for our industry. Our progress improving product characteristics and quality has been better than industry average for a few years, but is still less than our goal rate. There are significant differences in the success of both these capabilities among our several product families. We have recently deployed several new manufacturing technologies which should increase our capabilities. Early experience with those technologies has been good.

Measurements
For the plant as a whole and for each major unit within the plant we will measure capacity as total tons produced in the best seven consecutive days of operation.
For the plant as a whole and for each major unit within the plant we will measure capacity utilization each month by comparing actual production to capacity as described above using the method known as Overall Equipment Effectiveness Ratio.
For each product family we will measure product quality using the method of the process capability index (Ppk).

Performance Targets
- By year end 2010:
  — The total capacity of the plant will in metric tons will increase by 50%.
  — The capacity utilization (OEER) of the plant will be 95%.
  — The average Ppk of all products will be 2.00.
- By year end 2007:
  — Total capacity of the plant in metric tons will increase by 10%.
  — Capacity utilization will be 89%.
  — Average Ppk for all products will be 1.50.
  - By July 2007:
  — The total capacity of the plant in metric tons will increase 5%.
  — Capacity utilization of the plant will be 85%.
Average Ppk for all products will be 1.20.

Figure 2.3   Sample goal combining customer needs and owner needs into a single goal of improved manufacturing operation.

With those memorable phrases as a starting place, most people will be able to do a creditable job of recalling the full content of each goal as it applies to their particular work or team. They will certainly recall enough details to make directionally correct decisions and have useful conversations with management or team members.

Note also that all the visions of the future open with a comment on the rationale of the business need underlying the goal:

- Figure 2.1: "Our business needs to demonstrate that our operations are absolutely legal, safe, honest and ethical."
- Figure 2.2: "The best companies in industry improve through the combined efforts of all the people."
- Figure 2.3: "Customers constantly demand new or different specialty products and greater consistency in commodity products."

Those opening sentences will be among the strongest invitations to early dialogue about the goals. Managers who publish these goals need to be prepared to make a compelling case for change that is consistent with the opening statements.

Conclusion

In most businesses, the current state is neither wonderful nor terrible. Some middle ground is the truth, especially as you look toward the future. The situation today is good, but looking out a few years, there are changes that will be needed, or at least changes that will be of great benefit.

> **Key Idea:** One strongly held personal belief of mine is that a business does not have to be bad in order to get better; it just needs to get better. Talking with people about becoming better than they are has a much different motivational impact than trying to convince them that they are currently bad.

I personally like to set horizon strategic goals that give direction to the enterprise for the next five years. Within that period, I like to have very specific performance expectations for each of the first four six-month periods. Sometimes, as in the examples, you can get that effect by setting a two-year performance target and requiring ratable progress each six months. Other times, it is acceptable to set more specific independent targets for each six months. Normally you would do this if you anticipate that your capability to make progress will vary with time. In such a case, you might set a slower pace for early periods, with a more aggressive pace in subsequent periods.

The purpose of interim targets, however, is to avoid the trap of letting goal achievement slide into the future until it becomes impossible to catch up with your initial expectations. Recognizing accelerating capabilities is OK, but do not let the early periods slip by without truly significant performance improvement. Often, the early opportunities are so apparent and ripe for action, and the new technical tools of improvement so attractive, that early and easy progress occurs at about the same pace as later progress that is more difficult but achieved with greater capabilities.

The next chapter continues to establish the basis for your new culture by describing the process for translating these management goals into local goals and actions for each of your operating teams.

Summary of Chapter 2

- Strategic goals are the organizing start to an ongoing communication that will provide both *direction* and *focus* to the actions of the entire organization for an extended period into the future.
- Strategic goals do not need to be *precise*, but they do need to be *directionally correct*.
- "Northwest to the Pacific" was a usefully correct strategic goal for Lewis and Clark. It enabled an immediate commencement of travel and years of *successful tactical actions*.
- By setting one strategic direction, you define all other directions as nonstrategic, and that provides *organizational focus* to all activities.
- Business strategy is the responsibility of the *most senior manager*.
- You can usefully employ strategic goal setting and improvement for the part of the business that you lead if you are the most senior manager for a *discrete portion* of a larger entity.
- Setting goals requires a close look at the future needs of the *business-critical stakeholders*, including customers, competitors, employees, owners, and communities.
- Setting goals requires an equally close look at *existing capabilities* to meet the future requirements of your stakeholders.
- The *gap* between the future needs of the business and the current capabilities defines the goals for change in the next few years.

■ Be careful not to confuse the means or method for making improvement with the needed *result of improvement*.
■ To make strategic goals useful for ongoing communication, the *written goal statement* should include five elements:
   1. A memorable short phrase that describes the needed change.
   2. A short few sentences describing the future needs of the business.
   3. A short few sentences describing existing capability to meet future needs.
   4. Objective measures of the desired performance.
   5. Specific performance targets to be achieved in the immediate future.

Chapter 3

Making Your Cultural Values Personal

> **Key Idea:** Before most people can act to help you achieve the strategic goals of your business, they need to receive specific tactical goals that are within the normal capabilities of their team. Before individuals can adopt the cultural values of your enterprise as their own, they need to understand the meaning of those values in a personal way.

Once you have established the strategic direction that your business needs to follow over the next several years, and once you have created (at the highest level of your organization) a set of goal documents that communicate that direction, you need to get your message out. When you translate your strategic goals into tactical goals and actions throughout the enterprise, you initiate the ongoing communication that's needed to create a culture of rapid improvement.

Strategic goals are a management work product that defines the areas of *focused importance* and the *direction* for change. Starting with that strategic direction for the business as an entirety, you need to take the next step toward action by making the goals intellectually accessible and tactically useful to individuals and teams throughout your enterprise. The strategy gets everyone facing in the proper direction. The tactics set the group in motion, with everyone doing his or her part to make the trip successful.

The two most common problems that prevent strategic goals from usefully permeating an organization are

- When senior managers do not disseminate the goals in any manner, and
- When senior managers disseminate goals in a format that is not meaningful to most team members.

Most team members (especially those on the front line) cannot look at a senior management goal such as "Improve the capability and capacity of the plant with new investment less than depreciation" or "Maintain our license to operate" (which were described in the examples from Chapter 2) and understand the way in which they can contribute to the attainment of those goals within the normal scope of their work. People simply cannot help you succeed when they do not know how to help.

> **Example:** Since retiring, I have become a director and now chairman of Energy Capital Credit Union. The credit union board meets once each month, and our meeting includes lunch. Just as with most lunches that occur in a conference room, the board's lunch historically consisted of a platter of miscellaneous sandwiches, some chips, and condiments.
>
> Beginning with my second meeting as a director, there was a platter of sandwiches to be shared among most of the board members, and a Styrofoam box with my name on it containing a Rueben sandwich or a meatball sub or something else just a little more interesting than the standard fare. The rest of the board members quickly realized that the president's secretary was getting me special meals, but they did not know how or why. It soon became apparent that they believed I was getting more interesting food because she liked me, and this resulted in a variety of amusing efforts by other board members to get her to like them as well.
>
> When that did not work, some of them finally broke down and asked me how I got the special meals. The answer, of course, was simple: each month before the meeting, I simply call and tell her what I want. The president's secretary is a wonderful person and is glad to make the small effort needed to get me a special sandwich. What she is not willing to do is to guess what the other board members might want. A standard platter of sandwiches has been safe practice

for years, and that is what you get unless you specify something else. This may seem like a trivial example, but it is a serious lesson in business culture: most people will not behave in a new way at work until a leader tells them clearly what new behavior is appropriate. (As a follow-up to this story, I should say that with time, we returned to all sharing a common fare, but began to have fried chicken, pizza, and other foods that are both better tasting and less expensive than the standard executive sandwich platter. We got this outcome because we all told the secretary that we wanted something different.)

The goal translation process is all about telling people, clearly and in detail, exactly how they can help. Most of your employees are similar to the credit union secretary: they are honest, hardworking people who are glad to join with management to help the business succeed, but they are unwilling to decide for themselves what actions that might require. This is especially true in a case where the new work is noticeably different from the work that has historically been successful for them. As you create a culture of rapid improvement, you are dramatically changing the work people do by adding the new work of *autonomously improving* the business to the existing work of *operating* the business. To ensure that they join with you, you need to be careful to define the new work and tell them how to succeed at it.

The process to move from strategic goals to tactical action that is derived from and supports the strategy is called *goal translation*. Goal translation is literally that: just as in language translation, the translator hears a message in French and restates the same message in English. The message has not changed, but the restatement makes the message useful to the person who receives it. With goal translation, you are doing the same thing.

In goal translation, you take the strategic management goals that describe the direction of the enterprise in the context and language of management and you translate those changes throughout the organization until each individual or team has received the same goals in their own context and language. As you move through the organization and get increasingly close to the front line, the translation process also converts *enterprise strategic goals* into *team tactical goals*. At the completion of the translation process, each front-line team will have tactical goals representing actions they can achieve within their natural capabilities. In that way, as with language translation, you take the same message and make it useful to every person.

Also, just as it was unimportant to my sandwich selection whether the credit union secretary liked or disliked me, this translation simply needs to be clear and direct. Nearly every employee of every business wants to do a good job. Your first communication task as a leader is to make sure that your employees know what constitutes a good job. Similar to the discussion in Chapter 2 of the impact of facilities on performance, it is always good if people enjoy their workplace. And it is important that they have collegial relations with the leaders. But those attributes alone are not the elements that make change successful. At least at the beginning of goal translation, it is far more important to communicate clearly than to establish a new personal relationship with people. They already have friends—what they want and need is a leader who tells them how to succeed at their new work.

For example, consider the goal to increase the capability and capacity of a plant with new investment less than depreciation. As a management team, the senior managers who set that goal know without translation what it means and how they can help. But the meaning and implementation of that goal may be unclear to people just a little further down on the organization chart. For example, a front-line team operating a machine at midnight on Sunday may have no idea at all how they can contribute to such a goal unless management provides them with more information.

One reason that few chief executives devote adequate effort to establishing formal strategic goals is that few managers actively use the goals once they have been written. Of those few who do personally use their goals, a still smaller number use the goals as a basis for ongoing communication throughout the organization. When Exxon Chemical committed to improve the statistical process capability of our products (as described in Chapter 2), we automatically committed to establishing formal customer specifications—because without formal specifications, process capability has no meaning. The same logic applies here. When you seek to engage people to help you achieve the strategic goals of the business, you automatically commit to giving them tactical goals that they can achieve toward that outcome. Until your people truly know how they can help, obtaining the promise that they intend to help has no meaning.

> **Example:** I recently purchased some furniture in the Houston store of a regional upscale furniture company. As I paid for my purchase, I noticed that on the wall directly across from the cashier, positioned so that she looked at it all day every day, was a nicely printed and framed copy of the company's mission and values. When I asked her what it meant to her to be the "customer's friend in the furniture business," she responded that she was working as fast as she could.
>
> I assured her that I was not unhappy about anything. I was just interested in company goals. After a brief conversation, it became apparent that she had "never really thought about it." Certainly

she had never benefited from a conversation with any manager or coworker on that topic. I do not know what the president of that furniture company does with his mission statement, but at the front line, it is just a bad wall ornament.

If your experience suggests that time spent on setting strategic goals is wasted, then it is likely that you have not experienced using the goals as a basis to communicate common purpose and shared actions throughout the enterprise. Give strategic goals another try and follow the full process described here to make goals useful at every level. You will be amazed at the results!

A Three-Level View for Translating Goals into Actions

The translation process is the first and best guarantee that the tactical actions throughout your business and at the front line are all additive and compatible to achieving your organization's goals. The essential element of the process that ensures the intended result is what I describe as a three-level view. The concept of the three-level view is that, at each step in the goal translation process, the evolution of strategic goals into tactical goals and ultimately into tactical actions is checked against *input* to goals and actions received from above, *coordination* of goals and actions with peers, and *delegation* of goals and actions to those below. Those are the three levels. Here's a quick overview of each level:

- Level 1: Teams at each level of the organization receive input to direct their goals and actions from the level above.
- Level 2: They also coordinate goals and actions with their peers. This peer review includes both the details of actions that all the peers will take together as well as the separate actions that each member of the peer team will take independently.
- Level 3: Finally, each team decides on the details of the goals and actions that they will delegate as input and direction to the next level.

As you can imagine there is a little "to-ing and fro-ing" to this activity, but it is neither painful nor slow. Consider both how quick and how useful it would have been if the analytical laboratory manager (who was described in the Section I overview) had simply communicated in advance to his peers in research management about his intent to change the work flow in the laboratory that provided service to the scientists.

The input level of the CEO three-level view	**INPUT** The first consideration of goal translation for the Management Committee is the external input that describes the future demands on the business and the gaps between the current capabilities of the business and the future needs of the business's stakeholders.		
The peer level of the CEO three-level view	**PEERS** The peer consideration for the Management Committee is the gap between the external needs of the stakeholders and the capabilities of the business as a whole. The Management Committee needs to determine what they will do to achieve the goals when they all act together.	**INPUT** The input to determine the goals at the Division Manager level is the goals and actions that each Division Manager will share with Management Committee peers acting together to advance the goals of the business.	The input level of the Division Manager three-level view is the same as the PEER level of the CEO three-level view.
The delegation level of the CEO three-level view	**DELEGATE** The next level of the CEO three-level view is the goals and actions that each Division Manager will take to the several divisions that comprise the business.	**PEER** At the Division level the peer consideration is the goals and actions that Department Managers within each Division will take when they act together.	The peer level of the Division Manager three-level view is the same as the DELEGATE level of the CEO three-level view. This is also the INPUT for the Department Manager three-level view.
		DELEGATE The delegation at the Division Manager level is the goals and actions that each Department Manager within the Division will carry forward into the several Departments.	The delegate level of the Division Manager three-level view is the PEER level for the Department Manager three-level view.

Figure 3.1   The three-level view.

An example of this translation concept is shown in Figure 3.1 for the relationship between the three-level views of the chief executive officer (CEO) and the division managers who report to the CEO. Assume for this example that the business consists of a four-level organization within which you are creating your three-level view of strategy:

■ The highest level is a CEO with responsibility for the entire business.
■ At the second level, there are several division managers and a few senior staff people, all of whom report directly to the CEO.
■ At the third level are department managers, each of whom has responsibility for a subset of a division.
■ At the fourth level are front-line teams, each with a team leader.

The CEO and the people who report directly to the CEO normally have some formal relationship, such as a "management committee." Those are the folks who act together to create the original strategic goal set for the business. The translation process for the CEO and the management committee is shown in Figure 3.1 and described below. Figure 3.1 also provides a three-level view of the translation into each division shown on the other side of the CEO translation. Using this same format, you will create a three-level view of the goals at each level on the organization chart, as described in the following subsections.

The CEO's Three-Level View

At the CEO level, where the goals are created, you have the first three-level view:

■ Level 1: The highest level—the input level—of the original three-level view is the external world and the knowledge of what is required for the business to succeed in the coming years.
■ Level 2: The next level—the peer level—is the CEO and the division managers and senior staff acting together as a management committee that will decide what they will all do together and what each will do independently in pursuit of the goals.
■ Level 3: The final level—the delegation level—of that first three-level view is each of the division managers who receive the goals in their individual capacities with responsibility for the part of the business for which they are the senior leader.

The Division Managers' Three-Level View

Also shown in Figure 3.1 is the companion and overlapping goal translation process for the division managers. Each division manager also has three levels to consider during goal translation:

■ Level 1: Each division manager receives input to divisional goals: these are the goals that they helped to create for the entire business as a member of the management committee.
■ Level 2: Each division manager translates those goals into their own part of the business in collaboration with their peers on the management committee as well as the members of the divisional team comprised of their own department managers and staff.
■ Level 3: The division managers each complete the translation process for their individual divisions, as the division manager and the department managers of that division decide what goals and actions will be delegated

as input and direction to the goals and tactics of each department within that division.

A sample goal for a division, derived from the original business-wide goal of increasing "capability and capacity," is shown in Figure 3.2. The goal in Figure 3.2 retains for the division the same goal statement as was selected for the entire business. Compare Figure 3.2 with Figure 2.3. Retaining the original goal statement is a unifying mnemonic that facilitates interpersonal conversations and links this divisional effort with all other efforts throughout the business.

The divisional statements of the future vision and the current reality are different from the CEO's statements for the whole business only in that they are specific to this division's business segment. The measures are also specific to the detailed changes needed in this division, including a wholly new measure to track the portion of total output derived from new products.

The important result is that the strategic goals of the division are all consistent with and obviously in support of the enterprise goals as established by the CEO and the management committee. The few differences between the goal documents reflect two considerations:

■ First, the details of the divisional goals represent the increase in specificity as the translation moves closer to the operational interface with the external environment; and

■ Second, the differences begin to recognize the translation that is in progress from *strategic goals* to *tactical goals* and ultimately to *tactical actions*.

Despite the necessary differences that are required to reflect the translation to the division's business-specific objectives, wherever possible, the divisional goal document has adopted the same or similar language as the language used for the CEO's business-wide goals. Consistency and repetition are valuable in all forms of communication when the intent is to demonstrate belief and support for new ideas or plans.

Note that in this example, the division's performance targets are not adequate to meet some of the aggregate targets set by the CEO for the entire business. This recognizes that the mission of this division is to provide product variety and satisfy the customers who are demanding technically distinct products, many of which are evolving rapidly. As a result, the division management anticipates that efficiency, measured as the overall equipment effectiveness ratio (OEER) and product quality, measured by the process capability index (Ppk), will both be lower than the average performance that the CEO needs for the business as a whole. (If you are not familiar with these measures, there is a more complete discussion of them in Chapter 12.)

Strategic Goal:
Improve the capability and capacity of our plant with new investment less than depreciation.

Vision of the future
Our customers constantly demand new or technically different specialty products and greater flexibility in producing the full variety of possible products in our portfolio. Our business is both capital intensive and cyclical.

We must improve our ability to manufacture both high variety and high volume products without new capital. This will allow us to satisfy our customers and increase our market position throughout the cycle as well as making us more attractive for future investment due to our improved return on capital employed.

Today's reality
Customers are very pleased with our technical capabilities to develop and provide new products which appear to be among the best in our industry. Our ability to manufacture the full range of products is limited by constraints on our total capacity often related to unreliable equipment. Slow equipment transition among products reduces capacity and flexibility.

Measurements
- For our Division we will measure capacity as total tons produced in the best seven consecutive days of operation.
- For our Division we will measure the portion of total production derived from new products produced for less than one year.
- For our Division we will measure capacity utilization each month by comparing actual production to capacity as described above using the method known as Overall Equipment Effectiveness Ratio.
- For our Division we will measure product quality using the method of the process capability index (Ppk).

Performance Targets
- By year end 2010:
  — The total capacity of our Division in metric tons will increase by 50%.
  — The portion of new products produced will be 30% of total output.
  — The capacity utilization (OEER) of our Division will be 90%.
  — The average Ppk of all our products will be 1.65.
- By year end 2007:
  — Total capacity in metric tons will increase by 10% with 20% new products.
  — Capacity utilization will be 80%.
  — Average PpK for all products will be 1.30.
- By July 2007:
  — Total capacity in metric tons will increase 5% with 10% new products.
  — Capacity utilization of our Division will be 75%.
Average Ppk for all our products will be 1.00.

Figure 3.2 Sample goal document illustrating the business goal from Figure 2.3 after it has been translated to an operating division.

This shortfall in performance needs to be resolved as part of the three-level view. The other division managers are peers of this division manager on the CEO management committee. Acting together, the CEO and the other division managers will need to accept and accommodate this shortfall in one division that produces primarily specialty products by achieving even better performance against the standard measures in the other divisions that manufacture primarily commodity products. Also, by recognizing that this division has a problem with achieving some of the performance targets, the CEO and the division manager are alerted that in order to make a contribution of equal value to the other divisions, this division may need to offset that shortfall in efficiency by excelling at other performance targets, such as profit or growth.

Individual Department Managers' Three-Level View

At the next level of the organization, individual department managers take the division's goals (which the department managers helped create) and move them forward to their separate operating teams and translate them once again. The final three-level view in the company consists of the department manager, the team leaders for the front-line teams, and the products that are delivered externally to satisfy the original goals. This final translation is shown in Figure 3.3.

As shown in Figure 3.3, the team leaders receive as input the goals that they helped to create as members of the department manager's staff. They collaborate with other team leaders in this department as peers to decide on the goals and actions that will be delegated by the department to the several front-line teams. Finally, the front-line team leaders delegate for the last time. Just as the CEO team received the first input from the outside world, the output from the front-line teams is the work itself or the improvement actions taken in response to the goals.

At this point, the translation is complete. Everyone throughout the organization knows what the goals mean to them and how they can contribute to goal attainment.

A Case Study of the Three-Level View of Translating Goals to Actions

Figure 3.4 is an example of the goal of "capability and capacity" as it arrives for action at a front-line team. The front-line team has adopted as much consistent language as possible from the higher levels to maintain the link to the goals of the entire business. This time, though, the vision of the future is quite specific

The INPUT level for the Department Managers is the PEER level for Division Managers as shown in Figure 3.1.	**INPUT** Department Managers receive as INPUT the goals and actions that they helped to create as part of the Division Managers staff.		
The PEER level for the Department Managers is the DELEGATE level for the Division Manager goals as shown in Figure 3.1.	**PEERS** Department Managers collaborate with their PEERS as well as with Team Leaders in their own Departments to determine the translation of goals and actions as it applies to the specific work of each Department.	**INPUT** Team Leaders receive as INPUT to their goals and actions the goals and actions that they helped to create as a member of the Department Managers staff.	The INPUT level for Team Leaders is the same as the PEER level for Department Managers.
The DELEGATE level for Division Managers.	**DELEGATE** Department Managers delegate goals and actions to each Team Leader within the Department.	**PEERS** Team Leaders collaborate with other Team Leaders and with individual members of their own teams to determine the translation of goals and actions as it applies to the specific work of each Team.	The PEER level for the Team Leaders is the same as the Delegate level for Department Managers.
		DELEGATE In the same manner that the original input to the CEO three-level view was the external world, the output of the three-level view at the team level again touches the external world.	The DELEGATE level for Team Leaders is the work itself, both the work product that is delivered to customers and also the improvement work that is conducted in response to the goals.

Figure 3.3 The three-level view in translating goals from a department manager to a front-line team.

and very tactical. The strategic goals of the enterprise have become tactical actions as they have arrived at the operating interface.

This team will improve its equipment, specifically extruder 4, by taking some very specific actions that they know of now and by searching for more specific actions consistent with the goal and consistent with the natural capabilities of the team. It is recognized by this team that there are other peer teams who are taking similar action on related equipment.

The evolution of the goals from the CEO level to the operating level does not appear to be very profound at each incremental step. Intentionally there is a great deal of common content that is passing directly through the process. However, the culmination of this process results in a substantial translation of strategy into tactics while maintaining commonality and consistency throughout the enterprise.

Strategic Goal:

Improve the capability and capacity of our plant with new investment less than depreciation.

Vision of the future
Our Department's customers constantly demand new or technically different specialty products and greater flexibility in producing the full variety of possible products in our portfolio. The Department needs to increase capacity through improved equipment reliability and increased speed in making the transition from product to product.

Our team will improve the reliability, flexibility and quality of extruder 4 using owner operator maintenance practices, SMED, statistical process control and other new methods such as Reliability Focused Maintenance as they become available. Other Departmental teams will address other specific equipment.

Today's reality
In current operation we lose time waiting for maintenance to perform routine repetitive work that is well within our capability. We have just learned about SMED and used it with some initial success. We can improve both of these losses with our own resources.

Measurements
- For our Team we will measure capacity as total tons produced in the best seven consecutive days of operation.
- For our Team we will measure the speed of product to product transitions.
- For our Team we will measure capacity utilization each month by comparing actual production to capacity as described above using the method known as Overall Equipment Effectiveness Ratio.
- For our Team we will measure product quality using the method of the process capability index (Ppk).

Performance Targets
- By year end 2010:
  — The total capacity of our Team in metric tons will increase by 50%.
  — The time required for product transitions will decrease by 90%.
  — The capacity utilization (OEER) of our Team will be 90%.
  — The average Ppk of all our products will be 1.65.
- By year end 2007:
  — Total capacity in metric tons will increase by 10% with 20% new products.
  — The time required for product transitions will decrease by 30%.
  — Capacity utilization will be 80%.
  — Average PpK for all products will be 1.30.
- By July 2007:
  — Total capacity in metric tons will increase 5% with 10% new products.
  — Capacity utilization of our Team will be 75%.
Average Ppk for all our products will be 1.00.

Figure 3.4   Sample goal document illustrating the department goal from Figure 3.2 after it has been translated to a front-line team.

As described above, the important characteristic of the translation is that the three-level view ensures that, at each level, there is recognition of the broader needs of the business. Each level starts with input that is more strategic from nearer to the enterprise level. They also coordinate with peer goals and activities. And each level delegates input and direction that is more tactical to the next team that is closer to the front-line interface with the external world. At each level, each team describes their own best contribution within the complete context of the enterprise.

At the CEO level, the original business need was defined as improving "the capability and capacity of the business with investment less than depreciation." No operating team could have received that goal and known with any certainty what was expected of them. Following the goal translation process, the team in this example knows very specifically that they are to improve the reliability, flexibility, and product quality of extruder 4 using new methods that are within their existing capabilities and resources. This team now understands exactly what to do, and the team members have quite specific performance targets and schedules so that they also know when the first increments of improvement need to be completed. Of equal importance is that their goals are linked to the business as a whole and also to the work of their peers.

The common language that permeates the translation process draws this team together with all the other teams. The consistency and commonality enable every team to have an understanding of strategic and tactical linkage throughout the enterprise. In such an environment, the analytical laboratory manager described in the Section I overview would never have been in doubt that his task of improvement was linked more to the effectiveness of the scientists than to the efficiency of the lab.

In similar ways, all of the original enterprise goals of the CEO are translated into actionable reality for each individual and team throughout the organization. When the process of goal translation is complete, every team should know how to contribute tactically to the strategic goals of the business. Every person should know how his or her personal goals contribute to the goals of the business, and every action by anyone should be compatible with the goals and actions of all the other people and teams operating the business as a whole.

> **Example:** In two different assignments, I found it useful to compile the original goals at the highest level of the organization as well as the first increment of translation and then publish them all together as a booklet that could be used to communicate our intent as a unified business. I was the manager for Exxon's large chemical complex in

Baytown, Texas, for seven years. During that time, we developed our original goals, and we also refreshed our goals twice. So we had a total of three booklets describing our shared goals and demonstrating our joint progress. This documentation became a very powerful communication device to demonstrate constancy of purpose and progress both internally and externally.

Keeping the Whole Team on Board

Chapter 11 covers in more detail the organizational and communications problems that typically arise when some individuals are excluded from the improvement process. Oddly, one of the first groups that is often excluded during the creation of an autonomous workforce is the middle managers. Sustaining a consistent three-level view of the goals and tactics of the enterprise throughout an enterprise-wide translation process ensures that all these critical people are included. Far more is at stake during goals translation than may be apparent. As you communicate with your people, never forget that managers are people too, and they require the same engagement and attention as everyone else.

Refreshing Your Goals

As discussed, the strategic process should commence by looking outside of your company to determine the needs of your business for the next five years. And as it progresses, measures should be set and performance targets established for the first four six-month increments. As a result, you should have business goals that represent a five-year strategic horizon; in addition, through translation, you should have specific tactical action and performance expectations for the first two years.

So what happens as you approach the end of the first two years? The strategic horizon has now moved closer, and most of the performance targets that you set originally should be achieved or surpassed. Therefore the two-year mark is time to refresh your goals.

As you refresh your goals, you should do another formal review of the future needs and expectations of your external stakeholders and also of your current internal capabilities against those needs. Ask the following questions:

- What are your critical constituents—that is, your customers, competitors, employees, community, and owners—going to be demanding of you next?
- What new capabilities do you have?
- How much progress have you made?

Even if you have kept empirically current with your constituents, a formal review of your future needs and capabilities is valuable. There is a notable difference between knowing what is of current interest to your stakeholders and understanding their future needs. The formality of a strategic review and documentation of what you find out is also beneficial in order to be certain that every member of the management team has the same understanding of each of the several elements of future importance to the business. This formal review is especially valuable if you will be pursuing new products, new customers, or new geographies, which implies that you may need information from contacts that are not a routine part of your ongoing business.

Refreshing goals should be just that: a refresher. In other words, update what you have, but do not start over unless the external environment has changed substantially from what was anticipated or unless you were simply wrong in the first instance. Continuing to use the analogy of traveling to the northwest from Houston, it would be appropriate as you refresh your goals to recognize the progress that has been made and to reset performance targets in light of that progress.

For example, the new current state could recognize that you are already in Santa Fe. So the new interim goals and performance targets would talk about Denver and points further northwest. You might add precision to your strategic horizon. After two years of moving northwest, it is now clear that you are ultimately going even further north than originally thought. The destination will be either Vancouver or Seattle: Portland is no longer within the strategic scope. You might also update your capabilities: you started out walking and along the way you have acquired a bicycle, so future progress should be more rapid.

Remember as you refresh your goals that one critical purpose of having goals is to enable communication that unites everyone in support of the business. When you publish your refreshed goals and translate them to the organization, it should be apparent to everyone that the organization is now, and has been, on the right track and making good progress.

There will be new challenges described in your refreshed goals, but they should be clearly related to the old challenges. If the world has really changed, or if there was originally a mistake, you may have to recognize that situation and substantially change direction. But once you have a strategically engaged workforce, it is important to avoid "starting over" unless it is truly justified.

Key Idea: If you are careful in your goal setting and goal translation process, then improvement actions should be apparent. When a team makes one improvement, then the next opportunity is obvious. In this environment, I have never—not even one time—experienced the effect described as "diminishing returns."

> In fact, my experience has been quite the contrary. The most common experience with well-translated strategic direction is that the front-line teams accelerate their rate of progress because they become better at producing improvement, and they tackle more important initiatives.

A Final Word on Translating Strategic Goals into Tactical Goals and Tactical Actions

The mindful and detailed translation of strategic goals into tactical goals and actions appears in theory to be slow and possibly painful. In practice, however, it proceeds smoothly and quite rapidly. The only truly slow and painful part is describing it and reading about it. Goal translation is not really difficult or cumbersome, and it is truly valuable. By carefully translating, you really will establish the basis for your new culture:

- Everyone is aligned toward the shared values as expressed in the strategies of the business.
- Everyone knows their own role, understands the roles of others, and understands the interrelation of their role as part of a group of peers.
- Goal translation makes the organization stronger by engaging everyone, including middle managers.
- The big team of the enterprise and the small teams at the front line are truly united in the shared understanding that ultimately will become the values of your industrial culture.
- Finally, goal translation avoids all three of the major problems that unprepared managers routinely experience with autonomous improvement:
  1. It prevents people from doing nothing because they do not know what to do.
  2. It prevents people from taking nonstrategic action that consumes time and money but does not contribute to the success of the business.
  3. It prevents people from taking local action that detracts from the overall effort.

As I have discussed before (and will continue to discuss throughout this book), great progress at a world-class pace of improvement only occurs when nearly all the people in your business are working together to make it happen. The detail and coordination needed to allow that effort to succeed is not possible with only the general direction provided by enterprise-level strategies. Teams at the front line need more detailed information and more precise instructions, and they need it in their own context.

The strategies originate the values and beliefs of the culture. Goal translation makes those values and beliefs more personal and provides the detailed tactics that are needed for front-line action. Chapter 4 reviews the creation and use of quality stations at the front line to make goals and actions at the front line visibly apparent.

Summary of Chapter 3

- Before people at the front line can act to help achieve the strategic goals of the business, they need to *translate the strategies into specific tactical goals* that are within the normal capabilities of their team.
- Few managers devote *adequate time* to the creation of strategic goals because few managers make the goals useful after they have been written.
- Strategic goals only become widely useful when they are *translated into action that many people can support.*
- During goal translation, start with a *three-level view* at the highest level:
  1. External world.
  2. President and direct reports.
  3. Direct reports in their individual roles.
- Sustain the three-level view throughout until, at the *front-line level,* you have the final three-level view:
  1. Front-line supervisors as a leadership team along with their second-line supervisor.
  2. Front-line supervisors along with their work groups.
  3. The work or work product itself.
- Make certain to keep everyone, especially *middle managers*, involved in the goal translation. Do not allow the middle of your organization to be excluded.
- Goals need to be *structured* so that they can be *refreshed* periodically, as the strategic horizon moves closer, without abandoning the original goals or starting over.
- A good goal translation should ensure that *people have the information* needed to
  1. Be certain that all people know what to do and how to help.

2. Avoid unfocused or nonstrategic improvements that cost time and money without contributing to the overall effort.
3. Avoid contrary improvements that enhance performance in one place, only to diminish performance in other places.
4. Achieve great strategic progress.

Chapter 4

Quality Stations: The Rituals of Your Culture

> **Key Idea:** In an industrial culture, just as in any social culture, people will generally behave in conformance with the norms of the culture, as a means of obtaining peer approval. For social purposes, behavior that receives peer approval is often sufficient, but for industrial purposes, more precision is needed to achieve detailed performance to very specific expectations of quality and timeliness.
>
> In addition, some physical or systemic changes may need oversight to ensure against technical errors that may not be foreseeable or identifiable at the front line. The cultural mechanism for prescribing behavior that needs to be specific and certain is ritual.

Rituals at Work

Management does not want to interfere with the practice of autonomous improvement once it has been initiated, but management must have some oversight to ensure that all activities of the business conform to expectations. The answer to this need for unobtrusive, but precise oversight is *rituals* that establish and retain consistency among the widely distributed activities of many small groups. A ritual is defined as

> Any practice regularly repeated in a precise manner established by tradition or prescription so as to satisfy one's sense of fitness.

When the industrial culture prescribes rituals of action, communication, and visibility, the work of autonomous teams can be subject to oversight that does not unduly constrain the activity.

Autonomous action is not *unmanaged*, it is just not closely *supervised*. In fact, autonomous improvement needs to be a *very carefully managed* process. There are many reasons for this. Although teams act with independence and initiative, management still needs to ensure that each team achieves sufficient progress and that all teams produce results that are additive and compatible to the work of others. Of great importance, management must avoid problems with safety or technical considerations that may exceed the vision or knowledge of the team. In businesses such as the chemical and food industries, and many others, there are potential consequences from mistakes in autonomous improvement practices that are far worse than loss of improvement.

> **Example:** Famous in the lore of the chemical industry is the disaster at Flixborough, England, in 1974 at the Nypro plant, a joint venture of Dutch State Mines and the British National Coal Board. Very briefly, employees undertook a series of physical changes to increase the throughput of their plant. These changes occurred over a few days and each one, in its turn, appeared to the people making the changes to be quite correct and logical, especially in context as an extension of what had been done before. Unfortunately, the cumulative effect of the several changes caused the plant to explode, killing 28 people and seriously injuring 36 others.
>
> Obviously, such an outcome is not acceptable. Even when you want to create an environment of autonomous improvement, some limits on the possible actions of improvement teams and some form of prior technical review of changes are essential if your business has the potential for unexpected consequences that may exceed the capabilities or understanding of the improvement teams, and a great many businesses do. When I related this event at one of my seminars, a manager from the sausage industry had exactly the same concern. He could not allow any autonomous changes that had the potential to produce bad sausage that could harm his customers.

Management can ensure sufficient progress and maintain safety by establishing rituals of practice to make the conduct of autonomous improvement visibly apparent and constrained by established limits. This visibility will enable an unobtrusive, but formal, management and technical review process that will ensure appropriate oversight of the changes without getting in the way of progress. There are four *basic rituals* of improvement that must be practiced to ensure that teams achieve at least certain minimum expectations of performance and safety. In addition, there may be other rituals that you develop to fit your people or the needs of your business, but here are the basic four:

- Show the tactical goals of the team.
- Show the projects in progress.
- Measure and communicate results.
- Make ideas for the future visible and interactive.

Each of these four basic rituals are described in more detail in this chapter. These rituals will be practiced by each team using a physical device known as a *quality station*, which is described in detail. The focus of this chapter is the use of quality stations as a way to communicate and to ensure management oversight, while still providing employees with autonomy.

Using Quality Stations to Implement the Four Rituals of Improvement

One approach to answering the companion needs of oversight and autonomy in industry is by using quality stations. A quality station is a physical device that allows each team to openly display the four basic rituals of improvement, as described in the following sections.

Ritual 1: Quality Stations Help Show Tactical Goals

Each quality station needs to show the tactical goals that are being progressed by the team and the derivation of those goals from the strategic goals of the enterprise. This ritual of quality station practice visibly represents the three-level view established during goal translation and ensures at least logical alignment among all the autonomous teams. By keeping the team goals and their derivation visibly apparent, managers and engineers can adopt a routine of unobtrusively reviewing the work of each team, so that there is less likelihood of any team initiating action that would be nonstrategic or counterproductive.

Ritual 2: Quality Stations Show Activities in Progress

Each team needs to show what project they are working on at this moment and the anticipated cost, schedule, and benefit of that work. This ritual of quality station practice ensures that each team is actively engaged in meaningful work to advance the goals. By keeping current actions visibly apparent, it is clear that teams are engaged in the improvement process. By communicating exactly what is currently happening, any unforeseen issues of compatibility or safety can be identified during the reviews of Ritual 1 before they progress too far.

Ritual 3: Quality Stations Show Projects Completed and Measure and Communicate Results

Each team needs to show what projects it has already completed and the results it has achieved. This ritual of quality station practice is in the form of an "after-action review" to ensure that the actual outcome of the work of the team is the same as the intended result. By accumulating the measured results of completed work, the team demonstrates not only that it is actively engaged in improvement, but that it is successfully engaged, which is also important. By displaying the measured outcome of its projects, the team also demonstrates the compatibility, safety, and effectiveness of its actions as completed.

Ritual 4: Quality Stations Show Ideas for the Future

Finally, each team needs an interactive section of the quality station where ideas for future action are proposed and developed. This ritual of quality station practice often enables simple ideas to initiate consideration by the whole team in a way that ideas mature into better ideas before implementation, and it also provides the visibility for effective management and technical oversight before any physical change is undertaken.

Details on the Four Rituals of Improvement

These four basic rituals of practice require that teams make their actions and results visibly apparent. These four rituals are enterprise-wide, and all teams must practice them. Because all teams are meeting the same basic expectations, the practice of these rituals should receive social support within the culture of your business. These rituals, combined with other operating standards or rules of practice adopted by the organization for all teams (such as establishing the minimum time between the first posting of an idea and the initiation of work to progress that idea) create a very solid foundation for autonomous action in a well-managed environment. Further detail on each of the basic rituals will make this concept clear.

Ritual 1: Show the Tactical Goals of the Team

To ensure that progress occurs at a world-class pace of improvement, all improvement activities need to be focused toward the strategic goals of the enterprise. The first basic ritual is the tool for maintaining the necessary alignment among the dispersed teams.

This alignment of actions throughout the business will be initially obtained using the goals translation process described in Chapter 3. But in the nature of things, the tactical goals of front-line teams have a shorter life than the strategic goals of the business. As a result, the tactical goals at each quality station will evolve, perhaps several times, during the life of the original strategic goals. The results of the original goal translation are a good start toward alignment and compatibility across the enterprise, but they are not sufficiently enduring.

At the completion of the original goals translation, each team has received specific tactical goals. As the teams make progress, they will need to periodically refresh their goals. This is not the same as refreshing the enterprise goals as was described in Chapter 3. When a front-line team refreshes its goals, the principle things that have changed are the current state and capabilities of the team itself. Essentially teams are constantly refining their tactical goals and actions to recognize that they have made progress, not to recognize changes in the environment within which the team operates. The requirement of the ritual is that this ongoing process of establishing tactical goals that are compatible with, and additive to, the strategies of the enterprise and the work of other teams is just as formal and visible as it was the first time.

Normally the requirement to show the goals of the team is satisfied by posting the goal statements that the team produces during the original or subsequent goal translation process. These goals should be clearly and directly responsive to the larger goals of the enterprise. Sometimes the teams show both their local goals and also a copy of the original enterprise or divisional goals to reinforce this connection.

If it ever occurs that the evolving tactical goals of any team have lost alignment with the enterprise goals or that any team has lost the connection with its peers, then the visibility provided by the quality station will allow management to help the team members get back on track before they waste their time or possibly detract from the overall effort. The three-level view process should continue to be practiced as each team refreshes its goals, but nothing is quite as certain to retain team alignment with the rest of the organization as the ritual of hanging the goals on the wall for everyone to see.

Ritual 2: Show the Projects in Progress

Each team should have an improvement activity in progress at all times. In a culture of rapid improvement, practicing improvement is not an option and it is not to be deferred until a later time without an excellent reason and clear approval. The second basic ritual ensures that teams demonstrate that they are actively engaged in improvement.

At each quality station, there should be a clear communication of what actions the team is taking at each moment. That display should include a description of the changes intended, the current status of the work, and an estimate of what the improvement result will be. Normally a schedule or an anticipated completion date is also included. In general terms, this review of work in progress should satisfy the needs of project management appropriate to the small-team environment.

This visibility is an excellent opportunity for unobtrusive yet close and consistent oversight of the improvement effort. When a team commences physical action on a project, then exactly what they intend to do becomes certain. At that point, it is often valuable for management and engineering (who reviewed the project originally as an idea) to take another look.

If a team does not have a project in progress or is not meeting its posted expectations for completing the project in progress, then there is room for some valuable communication. In fact, a team of 6 to 10 people probably should have several things in progress at any time if it intends to achieve world-class performance. If a team has no active project, or if the active project does not move forward for a reasonable period without a very clear reason, management should treat this as a failure of the team leader and initiate some more formal intervention to get the team back on track.

Ritual 3: Measure and Communicate Results

The only purpose for establishing a culture of rapid improvement is to achieve rapid improvement through the joint activities of nearly all the people. The third basic ritual of quality station practice requires that each team demonstrate that they are truly contributing to the effort.

Specifically, the third ritual of quality station practice requires each team to document the improvement activities that it has completed and the measured result of those achievements. This includes a description of the completed activity that would be sufficient to allow a peer to recognize a similar opportunity (if one exists), as well as enough detail to permit managers and engineers to conduct the after-action review to be certain that the activity was correct and successful.

For example, using the team goal shown in Figure 3.4, the team could report that in the first month of autonomous improvement, the team assumed responsibility for changing the oil and changing the filters in the hydraulic system of their equipment. As a result, those routine owner-operator maintenance tasks were done opportunistically during product transitions, as opposed to requiring a separate period of downtime for maintenance access. As a result of that action, 1 hour of production time will be saved during each month, resulting in the monthly ability to produce 10,000 extra pounds of product. Chapter 12 provides a detailed discussion of measurement, but for the purposes of this ritual, teams need to know, measure, and communicate the results of their work.

Using the team goal in Figure 3.4 as an example, that team is improving extruder 4, and the team members recognize that other peer teams are improving other related equipment. With recognition that they are mutually supporting the same departmental and enterprise goals in similar operating situations, it is easy to see that visibility of a successful project in one team can be very useful to stimulate other teams to take the same or similar actions. It is quite common to see members of one team perusing the quality stations of other teams for good ideas.

Obviously there will be a point where too many activities have been completed to keep all the details on display. Each of the quality stations will need to develop some algorithm to manage removal of old news. This is representative of several local rituals of practice that each team will want to adopt for themselves. As a starting place, until teams and managers get comfortable with the quality station process, the more information that is displayed, the better the results you will get.

Ritual 4: Make Ideas for the Future Visible

The best opportunity for unobtrusive but effective oversight by managers and engineers occurs when proposed autonomous activities are reviewed before any team effort is expended on implementation. The fourth basic ritual requires that each quality station provides an interactive section where the team members, and others, propose and develop new actions for the future.

Creating new proposals for action is always an exciting and interesting part of the work of any team practicing autonomous improvement. Team members, and others, can suggest ideas for action and consider them together. This is an amazingly powerful tool. Whereas traditional suggestion programs are largely invisible, with ideas disappearing into a box for remote assessment by some unknown person, the quality station process for idea creation is visible, local, and interactive. Suggestions are offered by people close to the work for discussion, development, and selection by all the team members who share the work.

This is one of the best examples of using the team's specific knowledge of the work and improvement opportunities to make really valuable and rapid progress. In fact, because each suggestion is reviewed and discussed by the people most familiar with the situation before any work is started, it is quite normal for a suggestion posted in the interactive section of a quality station to change significantly before it is implemented.

> **Example:** One of my favorite examples of this evolution started with a suggestion to change the safety guarding on an exhaust fan. This particular fan was roof mounted and very large. It was part of an array of many fans intended to ventilate an entire building that was constantly flooded by steam arising from a high-temperature hot water process. In south Texas, especially during the summer, the fans were a critical part of making the building comfortably habitable for the folks working there.
>
> The fans were on the roof and the drive motors were located on the top of the exhaust pipes. Both the drive motors and the drive belts linking the motors to the fans were protected by safety guarding, constructed much in the appearance of a large dog house made of solid sheet metal. Because of the size, weight, and position of the guarding and the motors, whenever a motor needed to be changed, it was necessary to bring in a light set of rigging equipment to lift the safety guard and the motor down for repair. The total repair task might involve a rigger, a mechanic, an electrician, and one or more helpers for several hours.
>
> The first suggestion to the mechanical team that was responsible for this repair was to convert the dog house safety guard from solid sheet metal to expanded metal. (This is like the open-diamond steel sheets often seen on top of barbecue grills.) The initial thought was that if the safety guard were lighter, the mechanics could start the repair before the riggers arrived with their equipment, by simply lifting the guard down. That started the team thinking seriously about improving this routine operation that had been in existence essentially unchanged for decades. Then the suggestions poured forth:
>
> - ■ The motor did not have to be on top of the exhaust pipe, it could be on the side. That took the motor from nearly 10 feet above the roof to about 4 feet off the deck, a convenient height to work.

- The motor did not need to be guarded; the only exposed moving part was the drive belt. That took the safety guard from the size of a dog house to the size of a toaster oven.
- The fan blades did not have to be steel; they could be fiberglass, which greatly reduced the weight of the fan and consequently reduced the size of the motor.
- This process continued until someone observed that the roof was not an electrical hazard or explosion zone so the motor could be plugged in rather than hard wired.

At the end of the discussion, before any work had taken place, the initial simple suggestion to reduce the weight of the safety guard had evolved into a change that enabled a single person to go to the roof alone and replace a bad motor in just a few minutes. In fact, the task was simplified to such an extent that the production operators could do it themselves, allowing prompt repairs on nights and weekends, when most mechanical crafts were not on duty. Because the original simple idea was suggested to the group who knew the most about the task, a big, routine job that regularly required special equipment and three crafts for several hours essentially disappeared.

Culturally Appropriate Small-Team Leadership

In addition to the four mandatory basic rituals of a quality station, there are several new practices of team leadership that will help teams achieve detailed action that is both autonomous and consistent with enterprise goals. Generally these new practices are companions to the basic rituals, and they are often described as "rules of practice" because they are mandatory for all teams, but not so exhaustive or visible as the rituals.

For example, an enterprise will likely establish a minimum amount of time that an idea must reside on the quality station as a proposal before it can progress to physical action. This "residence time" will allow management and technical review prior to the first expenditure of resources. In most situations, after the residence time has elapsed, the team is then free to progress the idea at their convenience. Rules of practice such as this adapt the basic rituals to the specific business situation of your company.

It may also be appropriate for the business as an entirety, or in part, to have very specific rules of practice that prohibit any autonomous action without prior formal approval in certain situations. For example, in a petrochemical plant, engineering approval and participation could be absolutely required for any changes to the "hydrocarbon containment envelope" that separates the hot flammable chemicals from the air and the people. Such a rule would likely have avoided the Flixborough disaster described earlier in this chapter. Typically the senior management will define the intent of such a rule for application to the whole business. The details of applying the general rule to the work of each team (such as defining the local scope of the hydrocarbon containment envelope) are developed by team leaders and supporting engineers.

> **Key Idea:** Before a business launches quality station practice for the first time, senior managers and technical experts should define the rules and limits of practice that will apply to all teams. Those limits and rules should be rigorously enforced and regularly updated. In general, you do not want to initiate autonomous action and then tell teams one at a time that they lack authority for the projects they have selected. That will only re-create the uncertainty that stops people from acting. And you certainly do not want to create rules of practice after something bad has already happened.

In addition to the rituals of quality stations and the universal "rules of practice," each team should adopt its own local rules of practice for such things as considering project proposals and selecting the project that will be promoted from idea to action. The folks at the front line who have their own budgets for autonomous activity are some of the best stewards of corporate spending that I have ever seen. They worry and work the projects to get real value for each dollar spent. Improvements at the quality stations routinely produce real returns on spending that are greater than full payback within the first year. That is far better than the results from most capital project improvement efforts. With that experience in mind, I have generally allowed teams to develop their own practices for project selection and budget management. Management, of course, still sets the budget.

Establishing and following the basic rituals and rules of practice, combined with other team interactions, is a significant part of culturally appropriate leadership of small-team improvement. Initially the team leaders will continue to provide specific direction for routine local work in much the same way that they always have done. Despite the intent to improve, the organization needs to operate the fundamentals of the business successfully each day. As described in Chapter 8, there will be a future role for autonomous teams that have matured in specific ways to participate in the conduct of routine work where the standards are clear and well known. For the practice of improvement, the team leaders collaborate with their teams in the local details of quality station practice to help ensure that improvement occurs in a safe and certain way. Team leaders are also responsible for representing management in providing the teams with the objective and subjective elements of engagement, as described in Section II.

Communications at the Quality Stations

Essentially a quality station is a communication device. In the presence of a quality station, there is always a lot more communication than normal within the team, with visitors to the quality station (such as with members of another team), and between the team members and the managers and engineers who support the team's efforts. It always comes as a surprise to people who initiate quality stations when they recognize that they previously did not have very much meaningful conversation within their own team and had effectively no conversation with other related teams.

Conversations between the teams and management become much more valuable. In large organizations, it is often difficult for senior managers to know the details of each operation sufficiently well to have really meaningful detailed conversations with the folks who are conducting the work. This is especially true when the organization is so large or so dispersed that senior management may only be at each work location infrequently. Often the people who are conducting the work at the front line have a lot that they would like to talk about during these management visits, but they need some support to help structure their conversation.

Many front-line people think that informally telling management about the good things they have done is a form of bragging, so without a quality station, they avoid doing it. Many just lack confidence in their ability to discuss details with a senior manager, or they think that the work the team did together should be described by the team as a whole or by another person who made a bigger contribution. There are many reasons that important communication from the front line to management simply does not happen in a traditional industrial environment. The result is that field visits by senior managers are either uncomfortably quiet or they evolve into inconsequential conversations about the weather, sports, or news—when they might otherwise have been much more valuable business conversations.

Quality stations can help avoid this communications breakdown. A quality station opens the communication by making the detailed work of the team visibly apparent. Because that work is strategically aligned with the goals of the enterprise, it has a meaningful context for both managers and team members. It also contains the seed material for anyone who is present at the quality station to have a meaningful conversation on the improvement process as it applies specifically to that team. And because this conversation with management is a formal role of team members in representing the team, there is much less reluctance to participate in these conversations. I have seen the most remarkable presentations of status and progress made by people who previously would have scurried away without a word upon the arrival of a senior manager.

> **Example:** In Baytown, Texas, after we had received significant international recognition for both our performance and our processes, we frequently received visitors who were attracted to us by the many awards we were receiving and the articles and books that mentioned us as a great example of what is possible. On one such occasion, the CEO of a major corporation was visiting us, along with a team of his senior executives.
>
> I received them in the morning and sent them out for a tour of the facility and a review of our activities. At the close of their day with us, the CEO remarked that I was blessed to have so many good managers. He was very surprised to learn that, except for the opening and closing interviews with me, he had spent the entire day with front-line technicians. The descriptions and discussions that he had been so impressed by had all been provided by folks who in prior times might not have talked with him at all.

Using the information displayed at the quality stations and the conversation enabled by that information, engineers, managers, peers, and literally anyone interested in what is happening at any place at any time all have a good way to find out in detail. Any team member can, and will, have an easy time holding that conversation.

Appearance of a Quality Station

The essential concept in the basic rituals of the quality station is to make the goals and activities of the team visibly apparent. Within the limits set by the rituals and rules of practice, quality stations each have a distinctive appearance. Information that meets the practical requirements of visibility can be presented in many degrees of formality and beauty. The appearance of quality stations and the formality or informality of team interactions at the quality stations will vary widely, according to the personality of the team.

Figure 4.1 is one of the first quality stations that I saw during a 1986 trip to Japan. This area is an open "cubicle" with only two walls that is located literally

Figure 4.1   A very social Japanese quality station.

in the middle of a production operation. As you can see, this team has lots of data covering both of its walls. The team members are clearly meeting the basic rituals of quality station practice. They also have a lot of social content. The fish picture, the awards overhead, and some of the other surrounding material was described as "motivational." The generous space, the table with flowers and comfortable seating, and the general air of social informality all imply that some extended and collegial discussions occur here.

Figure 4.2 is somewhat of a contrast: this Japanese quality station that I saw during the same visit to Japan as the quality station in Figure 4.1 is all business. The information is posted on walls adjacent to the shop floor. The material appears to be formally prepared and quite precise. There is no place to sit and no extraneous material of any kind. The meetings here are probably shorter, more formal, and more disciplined than the meetings held at the quality station in Figure 4.1. This team obviously has a different personality than the team represented in Figure 4.1, but both meet the basic rituals of the culture and the needs of the business in their own way.

Figure 4.3 shows a North American quality station that belonged to a team of "third-party" contractors providing maintenance services to the site owner. The work of this team was very tactical and very practical. The team had acquired a Polaroid camera, and the majority of its quality station rituals included displaying annotated photos of work that the team was doing, planning, and had

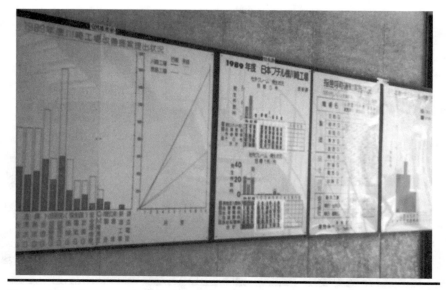

Figure 4.2   A very serious Japanese quality station.

Figure 4.3   A North American quality station.

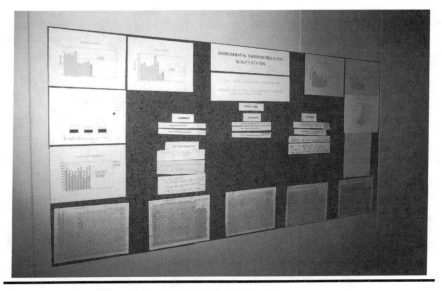

Figure 4.4   A quality station in the United Kingdom.

completed. The photos often included the image of a team member who was pointing to something or just smiling into the camera beside a project. Along with a few handwritten goals stapled to the wall, this format conformed to the personality of the team. The team complied with all the basic rituals for communications and visibility, but the social elements were informal, the compliance was easy to achieve, and the photos presented a very personal approach in keeping with the nature of the team.

Figure 4.4 shows a quality station for an environmental engineering group in the United Kingdom. Consistent with the personality of environmental engineers, they are using a lot of charts and graphs to describe their work. This quality station is located in the conference room that is normally used by this group for meetings of all types, including the quality station team meetings. Similar to quality stations on the shop floor, these engineers had put their data where they do their work.

The quality station for the maintenance team where the fan motor project described previously was created and matured was constructed entirely of handwritten sheets of yellow paper stapled to a cork board. The Japanese quality station that is shown in Figure 4.5 fits the definition of "functional but ugly," with several stacks of well-handled pages tacked on top of one another by topic.

The team that owned the quality station in Figure 4.6 was so concerned about appearance that it put their materials behind a locked glass door. Other

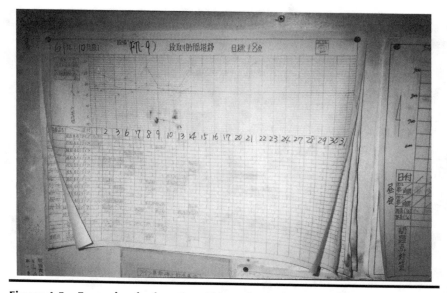

Figure 4.5 Example of a functional but ugly quality station in Japan.

Figure 4.6 A quality station behind glass.

than conversation with a team member, the way to interact with this team was by posting a yellow sticky note on the glass.

An instrument and analyzer team was making wonderful progress on a long-term project to improve the reliability and accuracy of safety and quality critical instruments. Its entire quality station was presented on top of a wall-size running graphic, showing the long-term trends in reliability and accuracy for the team's instruments.

The Staff Support Quality Circle (a team comprised of the executive secretaries throughout the site) had a quality station that was truly beautiful. Everything about it was attractive and perfectly executed. And the secretaries always had a good story to tell about improvements special to their capabilities. For example, they developed online procedure manuals for all the routine administrative tasks to improve efficiency and effectiveness through consistency and accuracy across the site.

In short, a quality station can have any appearance that the team desires and has the will to sustain. The appearance, character, formality, and maintenance of quality stations are some of the most important local rituals that teams create for themselves. So long as each team has all the mandatory rituals and observes all of the universal rules of practice of quality stations to satisfy the practical needs of communication and safety, I never worry about what the physical display itself looks like.

The Work of a Quality Station

Creating the original quality station is generally the last increment of the goals translation process. Teams often have a volunteer who wants to set it up and who does it according to personal tastes. Other times, such as with the Staff Support Quality Circle, team members decide together what their quality station will look like. But most often, the appearance simply evolves with time to fit the personality of the team. Some teams initially think that they want or need a quality station that is more formal than they are willing to support long term. Other teams start out requiring only the bare minimum of quality station formality and later grow into something more formal.

Despite best efforts to make the work of maintaining a quality station palatable to the team by allowing them to do the work in the way that best suits the team members, quality stations are, in fact, a new and separate task. Some folks will hate the extra work, while others will need to be limited in the amount of time that they devote to the task of the quality station as opposed to the task of making products or making improvements.

A good rule of thumb for the work of a quality station is that after it has been created and becomes operational, it is the responsibility of each of the team members to look at the materials on the quality station at least once a day.

This should be done at their convenience, in their "free time" either during the transition time at shift change, during a break, or whenever is best for them. Keeping current on the contents of the quality station is a work assignment that might require 5 minutes a day, but it generally should not be assigned a specific work time. For people who can carry the goals in their heads as a result of the mnemonic goal statements, a 5-minute daily review of the quality station is sufficient to activate their thinking and enable the ongoing discussion of goal focused improvement with teammates and others.

The time that the team meets together at the quality station should be limited to about 15 minutes each week. Throughout the week, the team members will talk informally among themselves and think about the projects or post ideas on the quality station for others to consider. Many will be actively engaged in the work of conducting an improvement project as an assigned task for which specific time is provided. During the weekly meetings, team members can review progress on current tasks, make decisions on the next tasks to begin, and do other related things. But the team leader should be careful that when the team is meeting, it does only those things that they must do together. Normally each front-line team already has an existing team meeting once a week, and this quality station review can become a part of that meeting. Some time is needed just to conduct the quality station activity, but that time should be small and carefully managed.

In addition to the time needed for routine maintenance of the quality station and to conduct team meetings, some additional time is needed periodically to update the progress summaries and the aggregate results of completed projects. Limiting formal updates of "reporting information" to a monthly frequency generally allows the time required for the update process to be largely invisible as a work element for one or more team members. Management does need to formally provide or schedule the time for performing this work, but if management is careful about selecting the right person, the right frequency, and the right amount of detail to be displayed, that care can limit this administrative work to a fairly modest level.

Management Quality Stations

It is certainly appropriate for the most senior manager and certain middle managers (division or department heads, for example) to maintain a personal quality station for the business or for the management committee that follows the same basic rituals as other quality stations. For example, I always personally maintained a quality station that showed the aggregate progress against the goals of the business and other measures of common interest. Moreover, as appropriate to my level as the leader of managers, engineers, and other professional groups, the activity sections of my quality station normally showed big-event improvements (such as capital projects, new information systems, or financial audits) or external events (such as customer, community, or owner interactions).

A Final Word on Quality Stations

Quality stations are certainly a visibly attractive form of engagement. Unfortunately, I cannot tell you how many times I have seen people who thought that the quality station was all that they really needed in order to practice autonomous improvement. These folks visited my operations and hurried home to immediately build their own quality stations. Let me say quite clearly: THAT NEVER WORKS!!!

The physical quality station is the visible form of a much more complex process to create and practice a culture of rapid improvement. The quality station is important, but no more or less important than any other attribute of the culture.

Summary of Chapter 4

- Autonomous improvement must be *very carefully managed* in order to ensure both adequate progress as well as safety.
- *Basic rituals* and *universal rules of practice* enable management to authorize autonomous activity with assurance that the outcomes will meet expectations.
- A quality station contains the following *four basic rituals*:
  1. Team tactical goals and their derivation from business strategic goals.
  2. A clear description of work now in progress.
  3. Team projects achieved to date and the results of those projects.
  4. An interactive portion to communicate proposed actions for the future.
- There are *formal rules of practice*, both *universal* and *local*, at quality stations to bring certainty and predictability to the actions of the team. Some generally adopted are
  1. Specify when engineering or management review and approval is needed before a project can proceed.
  2. Specify minimum criteria for a project proposal to be promoted from proposed to active.

3. Specify rules for managing team decisions, including selecting projects and budgeting activities.
4. Include any other rules that your team needs locally.

■ Quality stations provide a *framework* to support otherwise difficult communications internal to the team, between management and the team, and between the team and its coworkers and peers.

■ The task of creating and maintaining a quality station is *new work*, and management must assume the responsibility of providing people with the additional *time* needed.

■ Team meetings organized around the quality station are also new work, and management must *organize and budget for that work*.

■ Once the basic rituals of a quality station are satisfied, the *appearance* of each quality station should be at the discretion of the team. This is a good opportunity to show the personality of the team.

■ Management at all levels should create and maintain *their own quality stations* to make their objectives and results visibly apparent. This is also where the aggregate results of many teams and organizational units are reported.

ENGAGING PEOPLE IN YOUR NEW CULTURE

In Section I, you learned to create the first elements of your new culture: everyone shares the values, beliefs, and rituals of the business. Section I also opened the discussion of culturally appropriate leadership for small teams acting at the front line by describing the practice of leading a quality station.

Building on this base, the next step toward achieving rapid improvement is to provide the framework for people to engage with you to use their knowledge of goals and tactics to take autonomous action. In addition to quality station practices, you need team leaders to do other things that are required for small-team improvement to succeed. These are routine tasks that team leaders must perform in support of the team, so that their teams can successfully conduct the details of the business. This is special work that team leaders must do as representatives of management, not as members of the team. In the two chapters of Section II, I describe the work of engaging people to join with you to improve your business.

Objective Elements of Engagement

Chapter 5 describes five *objective criteria* that team leaders must provide before people can engage as full contributors to the success of your enterprise. These objective elements of engagement are

1. Tactical goals for the team to achieve.
2. *Resources* that the team can use at its own discretion.

3. *Time* that can be scheduled or spent to advance the improvements.
4. New *skills* appropriate to improvement assessment, planning, and execution.
5. A *framework* within which people can practice improvement.

Providing these elements of engagement is something that team leaders must do before people have the capability to engage and take autonomous action in support of the strategic goals of the business.

Subjective Elements That Disrupt Engagement

Sometimes a team may objectively have all that it needs in order to begin autonomous improvement, but improvement still does not happen. Normally, in those situations, some other thing is disrupting the ability of the team to coalesce or function. In those situations, the team leader must recognize that a subjective problem exists and must then identify and correct the problem, often with assistance or participation from other members of management or a subject matter expert who can help with human issues.

The *subjective elements* that disrupt teams are usually social or emotional. Often the problem is in one of two common areas:

1. One or more team members may disrupt the work of other team members. That behavior can occur on purpose when the disruptive team member behaves offensively toward the rest of the team or behaves inappropriately in some other way. Or the behavior can be inadvertent, such as when the disruptive team member is simply behaving in a way that the rest of the team does not understand. Both behaviors have the same result. When a team member behaves in a way that the team finds offensive, disruptive, or inexplicable, the team will not come together and effective improvement will not begin. Team leaders, perhaps with assistance, need to create or restore interpersonal harmony.
2. The other common area for a subjective disruption of team activity is that one or more team members do not trust management. After all, management has the power to reduce the workforce or otherwise adversely impact employees. Many companies have an actual history of doing just that. In some situations, third parties, such as unions, actively foment distrust. If the team believes that cooperating with management to improve the business will result in a loss of employment, then there will be very little improvement until management regains the trust of the people.

Chapter 6 describes management of the subjective considerations of teamwork and trust that are necessary for small-team engagement. In addition to these subjective elements that must be resolved in order for people to engage in the improvement process, there are other social issues that are important to the culture of the workplace. Those other social issues and the theory and practice of managing them will be discussed in Section III.

Chapter 5

The Objective Elements of Engaging People

> **Key Idea:** As you create autonomous teams to practice improvement throughout your organization, you need to provide those teams with the capabilities to succeed.

Even in a compelling culture of improvement, appropriate leadership of small-team action is required to ensure the precise and prompt performance that industry requires. The discussion of small-team leadership began in Chapter 4, as part of the discussion of quality stations. But there is still more to be done by management and team leaders if people are going to successfully operate your base business as they join your new culture and do things they have never done before.

Before teams will commence autonomous improvement, people want to be confident that management truly supports the effort. Creating this confidence among your people requires that managers genuinely engage personally in the new culture and do the things that managers do: that is, provide the policies, practices, and money that make autonomous improvement a formal part of the business. Informally "trying" autonomous improvement just to see if it is going to work may sound nice to management, but not to everyone else. This half-hearted approach to autonomous improvement often results in immediate efforts by a few enthusiastic people, but those efforts are generally short-lived and unhappy experiences for both the people and the company.

Managers who want to experiment with autonomy without committing to it often fall back on the slogan: "It is better to seek forgiveness than to ask permission." In this arrangement, management abdicates responsibility for leading autonomous improvement but encourages people to make their own changes, at their own risk. If the folks who try this are successful, they are lionized by management, in an attempt to convince more people to give autonomous improvement a try. If they are unsuccessful, of course, they are either "forgiven" or punished for taking inappropriate action. The management theory, apparently, is that the business will begin to experience the benefits of autonomous improvement, and management will not have to do anything initially except talk about it.

> **Example:** Exxon once had a consultant in employee engagement who had his personal slogan printed on the back of his business card: "An empowered person must come to work every day willing to be fired." For me, there has never been any day during the past 40 years that I was willing to be fired for trying to improve a business. In fact, in a serious business such as chemical manufacturing, there was never a day when I was willing to work with anyone who had such a casual attitude toward employment.

The problem, of course, is that for most people, the informal practice of engagement that forces them to guess what to do and how to do it is a bad bet. Rather than participating in the new behavior of autonomous improvement and attempting to calibrate their actions from the apparently random behavior of management's rewards and punishments, most people simply decide that it is better (or at least safer) not to participate. That is the best explanation for the amazingly low average rate of autonomous improvement in North America and Western Europe when compared to the rates achieved by the best companies. As detailed in Chapter 12, the best companies are achieving 40 or more improvements per person per year, while the North American average is less than 0.014. There really are very few situations in life where the leaders in any competition are 3,000 times better than the average participant.

When management fails to provide clear direction, there are both human and performance problems. The human issues are straightforward: when people are offered a chance to cause change at work but are genuinely uncertain what to change or how to achieve the change, then most people simply do not attempt to change. The performance problem with undirected autonomous improvement, however, is more complex: for management, world-class performance requires that each of the changes made by each of the many different teams must be strategically focused and additive to and compatible with the work of all other teams. When considering business performance, changes that are not additive to the strategic efforts of others, and changes that are contrary to the strategic direction, are either useless or bad. Unmanaged, or undirected, autonomous change has a huge potential to become either dissipated or counterproductive.

Further, a world-class pace of improvement requires that nearly all of the people will each make many improvements. As discussed in Chapter 12, the expectation is that truly engaged people will make 40 or more improvements per person each year. Recognizing that each improvement represents a change of some sort, that pace of improvement means that there will be a lot of changes. If a business is going to experience many changes without very much task-level supervision, then the process that produces those changes must be very carefully managed so that only the right changes are made in the right ways.

Initiating autonomous improvement requires both getting people to engage with you to produce 40 improvements per person each year and ensuring that those 40 improvements are the right ones, done in the right way. Both issues require specific management action for success. Certainly, meaningful engagement from the front-line people will never start until management has engaged first.

Key Idea: Although I spend most of this book discussing culturally appropriate leadership of autonomous improvement as a vehicle to cause more and better engagement, there is another reason for deploying careful leadership of the front-line teams: personal standards are different. Honest people who agree on the selection and nature of the improvement task can still disagree on whether a task was done properly and whether the outcome is correct. The team leader is responsible for clarifying these situations for the team by providing the business and management reference that ensures that the detailed actions taken to conduct and improve the enterprise are always appropriate.

The only effective method to engage people in the business and ensure that they take only proper actions and produce rapid improvement is to manage autonomous improvement as a formal part of operating the business. Management must develop and use a systematic, well-known framework of rituals and rules of practice that enables people to know for themselves that they are doing the right thing in the right way and further enables management to see that the results are conforming to expectations.

> **Key Idea:** When I think about managers who hope to benefit from autonomous improvement without actually committing themselves to formalizing the process for conducting autonomous activities, I recall one of my favorite quotations:
> "I am all for progress. It's change that I object to."
> **—Mark Twain**

Creating a Framework That Engages People to Help

Management must establish and team leaders must lead a knowable improvement process, including a framework that provides very specific formal support for autonomous action. The autonomous action that produces continuous rapid improvement is not unmanaged activity. Rather, it is management-directed and goal-focused activity that is not closely supervised. The framework provides the management direction and the goal-focused alignment.

Engaged people select projects based on both the general direction of management strategic goals and also the specific direction of management-approved local tactical goals for each team. Even then, the project proposals must survive rigorous (but unobtrusive) review as they pass through the quality station rituals. Projects that are not strategic may ultimately be done, but they are not authorized for autonomous action. Separate review and authorization is required for nonstrategic projects. The same is true of the tools for improvement. Engaged people use only management-approved methods and capabilities for autonomous implementation of projects. Additional capabilities may be used with approval or assistance, but they are not authorized for autonomous action.

Engaged people use the framework of engagement provided by management along with the rituals and rules of quality station practice prescribed by management to make improvements. As a result, all autonomous actions are visually apparent in a way that allows for thorough (but again, unobtrusive) managerial and technical review to ensure safety and in a way that ensures that each change is additive and compatible with all other changes.

There are seven elements of engagement that represent the responsibility of management and team leaders to provide this framework for autonomous team action. Each of these elements is part of the work of leading an autonomous team. There are five objective elements and two subjective elements. The five objective elements in the framework of engagement are

1. Clear *goals* that people can achieve.
2. New *skills* to do new things.

compare to Landles on "empowerment" - almost same, but Landler adds "accountability"

3. *Time* required to work on improvement.
4. *Resources* required to make changes.
5. A *structured system* (such as a quality station) with rituals and rules of practice.

Normally, if you give people the five objective elements of engagement, they will begin to practice autonomous improvement. When that does not happen, it is time for leadership to examine the two subjective elements that normally disrupt autonomous action:

1. A team does not trust management and therefore refuses or fails to participate.
2. One or more team members disrupt personal relations among the members of the team to such an extent that the team cannot function.

The rest of this chapter discusses the five objective elements in enough detail to enable you to practice them in your environment. The remaining two subjective elements of engagement are introduced in Chapter 6 and are discussed in more detail (along with other social issues) in Section III.

Element 1: People Need Goals to Achieve

The first element of the framework of engagement is providing people with clear goals to achieve. I have spent a lot of time already in this book on the topic of goals. It is important to always keep in mind that the direction you set for folks in the goal deployment process will ultimately determine their ability to do the right thing in the improvement process.

> **Example:** I once participated in a "wisdom in the woods" leadership program. Essentially the format for these is to take executives to a remote location where they conduct a series of exercises that are so different from their normal work that it becomes possible to experience pure leadership in an environment where no one has the advantage of possessing specific knowledge.
>
> At the completion of an event where the team of which I was a part had faired very poorly, I learned an enduring lesson. The team leader for that exercise stood somewhat dejectedly, looked back at the field where the exercise had taken place, and said: "It is really hard to be a leader if you don't know what to do."

That lesson is not just true for leaders. It is hard to do anything well if you have no idea what to do. It is not possible to overemphasize the importance of delivering to your people clear goals that they can achieve within their own capabilities. Fortunately, I believe that the time spent developing and deploying goals will not slow either your initial improvement efforts or your long-term establishment of a culture of improvement. (And the details supporting this belief—along with specific timing and a pro forma schedule for the first two years—are discussed in Section V, "Getting Started.")

One final comment on goals comes from the philosophy of Daniel Burnham, the Chief Architect of the 1893 Chicago World's Fair. Goals should not simply communicate minimum expectations. Do not hesitate to set strategic goals that are very aggressive—even goals that you feel may exceed your immediate business needs or the existing capabilities of your teams. Until you experience the power of an engaged workforce that is producing a world-class pace of change, you cannot appreciate the pace at which improvement is possible. Further, you should always communicate goals that people recognize to be worth the effort.

Key Idea: "Make no little plans. They have no magic to stir men's blood."

—**Daniel H. Burnham**

Element 2: People Need New Skills to Do New Things

The second element in the framework for engagement is providing people with the skills needed to assess opportunities and provide an appropriate response. One more reason that otherwise good leaders fall into the trap of empowering people to make unmanaged improvements, without direction or structure, is the conventional wisdom that "the people who operate a process are the people who know the most about it." That philosophy seems to lead managers to believe that if they simply authorize the people who operate a process to practice autonomous improvement, then the folks who know how to operate the business will somehow also know how to improve it. That turns out to be a serious error: many people who know a lot about the operation of a machine or process do not have any existing ability to improve it.

> **Example:** We once had a 75,000-shaft horsepower turbo compressor that was a real showpiece. It was a critical piece of equipment to our process, and the chief operator who ran the compressor had been

with it for nearly the full 10 years since it was first installed. In every way, that machine exceeded our expectations in both appearance and performance.

As we began to deploy the lean enabling methods to make the process visibly apparent, we believed that the turbo compressor would be a well-recognized and valued pilot project to demonstrate the use of that tool. So we asked the operator if he would mark the many instruments and controls of his compressor to visibly indicate the normal settings and operating range. The assumption that we made is that this would be a trivial exercise for a person with his experience and detailed knowledge.

The exercise actually consumed most of his discretionary time for months. It turned out that, although it was true that he knew far more about his machine than anyone else, it was also true that he could not initially look at the many instruments and know exactly what they were telling him. Until we helped him through this project, he certainly knew more than anyone else about the operation, but he did not know enough to bring the machine under very precise visible control.

Use of the methods of visible process control ultimately became more valuable than we had imagined. It became apparent that even with a highly motivated, highly skilled, and experienced operator, the performance of the machine reached a new level only after we gave him the task of making the machine's control visible. By providing the new skill that enabled the operator to run his compressor much more consistently, the intervals between maintenance downtime extended to several multiples of the manufacturer's recommendation.

The most knowledgeable people may know precisely how to operate the equipment or process and may even know exactly what the problems are, but may not know how to cause improvement. New skills and tools to analyze the opportunities for improvement and the further skills of creating and implementing an appropriate responsive change are critical to practicing improvement. Operators typically do not have those extra capabilities until management delivers them.

Focused goal deployment helps to narrow the range of improvement options for each team and also reduces the task of providing goal-related skills. Individuals and teams should only be given the skills that are appropriate for the improvements they will be making. And they should only be given the training in those new skills close to the time that the skills will be used. Early training that is forgotten before it is used and training that is inappropriate to the goals of the team are both examples of wasted time and resources caused by management.

For example, if the team is going to improve the reliability of its equipment by assuming responsibility for owner-operator maintenance, then you will want to give the team members the new knowledge of basic maintenance as it applies to their machinery. In the future, they may need other skills, but for now, they need only routine maintenance skills. More specifically, they need only the limited skills required to maintain this particular equipment. And it is likely that not all team members will need this skill immediately.

Many teams can attain new skills by borrowing them. For example, you could lend a team an engineer or an electrician or a statistician rather than taking the time to give the team its own skills in technically complex areas. This is especially appropriate if there is an immediate improvement opportunity that would be delayed by training, or if the need for a particular skill is likely to be a one-time event for this team.

The key issue is that management previously recognized the need to give people the skills to operate the process, and now you need to give them the further skill to improve it. It is of real importance in this effort to benefit from the focus provided by the goals translation. Each team has a few specific tactical goals. Focus the training on the precise skills needed by each individual or team to achieve their own goals.

I have previously discussed the problem of confusing the tool or method with the goal. Mass generic training is a very common indicator that this may be occurring. If you ever believe that you have identified a single course of training that everyone needs, then you have probably come to believe that deploying that particular skill has reached the same level of importance as if it were, itself, a goal. At that point, you should carefully reconsider before you require everyone to attend training.

Most businesses today are quite good at training. The two principle issues with giving people the skill that they need to make improvement are

- To recognize that people need specific training to practice improvement.
- To recognize that they need only the training that is specific to their task.

When people lack necessary skills, they cannot take advantage of improvement opportunities. When management consumes the time that people have to practice improvement with inappropriate training, then the improvement opportunity is lost before it happens.

Root Cause Analysis

Before I continue with the discussion of the need for skill to assess a problem, this subsection takes a look at the tool of root cause analysis. Many tools for causal analysis (such as statistical methods or reliability engineering) are complex and not immediately available to your improvement teams. A less complex way of understanding the source of a problem that your teams can use promptly is simply to ask a series of questions beginning with "Why?"

In this process, the team begins with the problem that needs to be resolved and they ask, "Why did this occur?" The answer to that question leads them to the *proximate cause.* That is, the answer to the first question "Why?" is the event or condition that directly created the situation that they are assessing.

Then the team asks, "Why did that proximate cause occur?" That inquiry leads them to whatever event or condition directly resulted in the proximate cause. Continuing in this method along the chain of cause and effect, the team ultimately discovers the initiating event, or the condition that set everything else in motion. This initiating event or condition is called the *root cause.*

In some situations, the analysis needed to discover the correct answer to the question "Why?" requires some serious analytical capability, but in many cases the only skill needed is the operating team's knowledge of the equipment and process, along with the discipline to continuously seek the next level of understanding. Think of this as peeling an onion: removing each layer brings you closer to the core of the problem. Here are the general rules for this simple, but effective process:

- Follow the chain of cause and effect by repeatedly asking "Why?" until you find the root cause.
- You have found the root cause when you can take "root action" to permanently correct the original problem that launched the assessment.
- "Root action" has the following characteristics:
    - Root action can often be taken within the normal capabilities and resources of the team that owns the problem.
    - The team that experiences the problem probably owns both the problem and the solution.
    - Root action does not add new expense, capital equipment, or routine work.
    - Root action to solve this problem does not create new problems in other areas.

Normally, if a team concludes that it cannot take root action to solve its problem, it is because the team members took a wrong turn as they followed the chain of cause and effect. Almost always, that wrong turn is the same one. The most common difficulty that teams have in practicing root cause analysis is that they decide that another team owns the problem and has responsibility for the solution. Typically this result occurs because the team asked "Why?" in the wrong way.

> **Example:** In Baytown, Texas, we had a team that operated an extruder with a small helical feeder for delivering a powdered additive into the extruder barrel. The feeder jammed when there were lumps in the additive. When the team asked "Why are there lumps in the additive?," they concluded that the problem was caused by failure of the warehouse to rotate stock. The additive, they believed, became lumpy as it aged. Having identified the warehouse as the cause of their problem, they proposed that the warehouse add a new task of tracking additive batches and rotating the stock to create a strict first-in, first-out delivery system.
>
> During a management review of that proposal, that did not appear to be root action. The solution did not belong to the team that owned the problem, and the solution required new work. Two expectations of root action were violated in that proposal. So we asked the team to try again. This time, instead of looking externally and asking, "Why are there lumps in the additive?," they looked at themselves and asked, "Why does our feeder jam when there are lumps in the additive?" With that version of the question, they promptly discovered a few modest changes that they could make to the feeder which resolved the problem with all the attributes of root action.

Simple causal analysis can be quickly deployed to most teams with very little training, usually training only the team leaders will suffice. I will refer to root causes and root action again in other examples.

Element 3: People Need Time to Work on Improvement

When we ask the people who operate the business to begin making improvements, we have added a new task to their day. Like all other tasks, the new task of improvement requires time. It is the responsibility of management to provide time for improvement. Management exclusively controls time at work.

If managers do not definitively provide time for the task of improvement, then people will know that you are not serious about making improvement a formal part of the work.

Except in the event of people who perform their work by attending a paced line, providing time to work on improvement is mostly a matter of management intent. The learning curve is real, and as people gain experience at their work, they naturally get better. In the process of getting better at their work, people create for themselves some discretionary time that can be used for improvement—if management does not take that time away by adding work or reducing staff.

Although it may not be apparent when you begin, most people (including those who work on a paced line) already have created the increased efficiency that will make time available for improvement. They have not let you know that they have become more efficient, because the normal management response to that news is to take their time away. Your folks do not want to give up the time they have created without receiving something in return. Fortunately for management, most people understand that they are going to be at work all day anyway. If they know that you are not going to make them work harder at their current task, and if they also know that you are not going to reduce the workforce, then most people can believe that receiving a new and interesting activity such as autonomous improvement is a satisfactory exchange.

If you are in this situation, the way that management "gives people time" is to schedule the time. For example, schedule a team meeting at the quality station for 15 minutes each Wednesday morning. After that quality station meeting (as described in Chapter 4), the more specific work of implementing the improvement projects becomes part of the routinely scheduled work of the individual team members, in the same way that they receive their other work assignments.

If your people attend a paced line, then you have a different situation, and more management effort is required to provide people with the time for improvement. The people on a paced line have become more efficient at their work just as other employees have. The problem that people on a paced line have is that the result of this efficiency gain is not available to be scheduled in one large increment because it exists in many small increments, each of which is contained within the tact interval (the time that each person "touches" the product as it passes the individual workstations) of the paced line.

Often (and if there is not an unfriendly relationship between management and the people working on a paced line or the union that represents those people), it is possible to negotiate a small increment of pace increase to accommodate the time needed for the team meeting. A 15-minute meeting in a 40-hour week requires a pace increase of about 0.5%. If you carefully ask for and receive nothing more than the additional speed needed for the team meeting, people will generally recognize that this is not a hidden attempt to get more output or harder effort. Following the team meeting, the individual work to progress the team initiatives will occur in the way that you normally release individuals from the line for other things, such as training or vacation.

> **Example:** While on the topic of vacations, even briefly, let me mention one other practice that I really value. Because management knows how to cover for vacations and people know how to be absent from their work for vacations, we created the concept of a "vacation team."
>
> Vacation team members come together and work on a significant project all day, every day, for a period of up to two weeks. At the end of that time, it is expected that the project will either be completely planned and organized or perhaps even completely implemented. Through this sort of intensive effort, we have achieved major initiatives such as consolidating five laboratories in three different organizations into a single central function.
>
> This is the sort of initiative that normally would have taken the same people months to accomplish on a part-time basis while they were carrying on their normal work. By undertaking a concentrated "vacation team" style of effort, the project was completed very quickly and no unusual accommodation was required for the team members.

In some cases, there simply is no time currently available, and management must add extra hours to the work group in order to "prime the pump" and initiate the improvement process. Sometimes it may be required to stop the paced line for a specified period without accommodating that stoppage with an increased pace. As a general rule, I dislike adding people or stopping the line just to practice improvement, but I understand that sometimes it happens. I truly believe that in a properly conducted improvement effort, there ought not be any time when the situation gets worse rather than better, even temporarily. This need to provide time for improvement is perhaps the exception that proves the rule. Without time, people cannot make improvement. Providing time, however you need to do it, is the responsibility of management.

Just be very careful. Provide extra time in very limited quantities and for a limited period specified in advance. You should always be certain that there is no expectation or practice that will permanently increase your costs. In the event that you need to prime the pump, then the first thing the team needs to do is find some way to make future time for improvement available within the normal capabilities of the team, or find some other prompt improvement that will provide the cash to fund the extra time.

As a suggestion, here are some places that I like to look for improvements that will promptly provide time or money to fund the improvement process:

- In capital intensive manufacturing, I often find that a reliability effort to resolve a chronic problem with critical equipment throws off a good amount of time and money.
- In other heavy manufacturing, it is often possible to improve the flexibility of a core machine in a way that will provide time for other improvement efforts.
- In light manufacturing, value stream mapping will normally lead to an appropriate change in work flow or practices that will provide the team with some time for other improvements.
- In offices or laboratories, I like to refer to Thomas Edison's description of invention as 10% inspiration and 90% perspiration. Even in research and other activities that do not appear to be closely related to manufacturing, there is a lot of activity that looks just like work. Identify that work and apply normal work improvement tools to it.

Chapter 14 includes a simple overview of several new tools that are appropriate to improvements of the type described here. If quality is not free, it ought to be at least self-financing. However you chose to provide the time, and however you chose to recapture the investment of the time that you provide, it is clear that management must formally organize the effort. Without assistance from management, people have no good way to make time for improvement within the workday.

Element 4: People Need Access to Resources

Time is one specific item of the corporate resources that are required for improvement, but there is also a more general issue. If physical change is required for improvement, and it often is, then all the resources that cause change are also required for improvement. In general, access to resources might mean that you lend the team an engineer, some craft expertise, or a statistician. Often, however, access to resources requires money.

I like to give each team a small budget of their own. I have used the word "small" to describe these budgets intentionally. Like time, operating teams already have operating budgets, and I prefer to see teams make improvements within their normal capabilities. But a little extra money to get the improvement process started gives the improvement effort, and management's commitment, extra credibility and makes the early projects easier to initiate. Often the practice of requiring teams to make improvements within their own capability or within the added capability of a small incremental budget has its own benefit.

Example: At one plant in the United Kingdom, we had purchased a pneumatic machine that made large boxes, about 125 cm on a side, for packing synthetic rubber. Unfortunately, the box-making machine regularly jammed. The team did a simple root cause analysis (as described earlier in this chapter) and determined that the cause of the jam was that some of the pneumatic valves would not activate when factory air pressure at the input to the machine dropped below 80 psi. The team's recommended solution was to communicate to the central mechanical group that factory air should never again drop below 80 psi.

This was a very large plant, so stabilizing factory air pressures near the top of the existing range would have been an enormous expense. Therefore we did not do that.

The team's second proposal was to buy an air compressor just to supply their machine. The capital project proposal also requested a spare compressor, spare parts for both compressors, and an operating budget to provide someone to be assigned full time to operate the new air system. Again, the message sent back to the team was that we wanted a root action solution that they could achieve with their normal capabilities and resources.

Ultimately the team did further root cause analysis along a different causal path. Instead of asking the external question, "Why does the air pressure drop below 80 psi?," the team asked the internal question, "Why does the machine jam when the air pressure drops below 80 psi?" At that point, they learned that the reason the valves did not actuate below 80 psi input to the machine was that the machine was inefficiently plumbed. When the input pressure to the machine was below 80 psi, some of the internal valves were experiencing air pressures below 60 psi, and at that level, they would not actuate.

The team finally proposed replumbing the few inefficient parts of the machine, which was a task that maintenance was able to implement for just a little money. The result was a solution that added no new equipment and no new costs or problems, and which the team achieved within its normal resources.

Providing Funds

At the beginning of a new initiative, it is common for management to provide some specific new funds as an improvement budget for the teams. This makes it clear to team members that they have a financial capability they did not have previously. Give the teams a small budget to seed the improvement process, with the clear expectation that you want the money back within six months. After the first six months, recover your initial investment, allow the teams to keep some of the savings beyond the initial investment that they have created in order to fund the next round of improvement, and capture any further additional savings as an improvement to the business. This self-funding requirement ("pay-as-you-go") is a real expectation. Autonomous teams truly ought to be able to take some initial actions that will fully return their investment within six months. Make sure that you expect that, and try to get that result as often as possible.

One relatively painless way to provide the funds that will start this process is to defer a capital project and divert the expense money from that project to share among the teams. When I have provided teams with seed money in this way, we have always demonstrated that we got an excellent return on investment. In a 1991 study of more than 100 autonomous teams from several different businesses and in several different places throughout the world, we documented a return of more than 5.4 to 1 during the first year. For each dollar that we gave the autonomous teams, we received back $5.40 of first-year savings.

Although this was a large and diversified study, even at the time that we made the study, we did not suggest that the result was either common or sustainable. It did, however, clearly indicate that early financial support for initiating autonomous improvement is justified. After you make that initial investment, you should measure the actual results achieved as we did and be sure that you are satisfied with the performance.

If we provided money in the first year by deferring a capital project, we would undertake our capital project in the second year. By the end of the first year, the teams had returned the seed money, so it could be used as originally intended for the deferred project. During the second year, the teams were spending some of the money they had saved in the seed year, and we were implementing the capital project. Within the span of two years, we had both a functional autonomous improvement effort as well as the deferred capital project.

Small-Event Improvements

If you carefully read the two examples of root action in this chapter, you will see that the original solutions proposed by both teams looked a lot like the sort of thing that managers and engineers often do:

- The extruder team proposed that someone receive the new work assignment to ensure that the problem would not occur again. That is a classic *management* response.
- The box team proposed a capital investment to solve their problem. That is a classic *engineering* response.

In the early days of autonomous action, people will tend toward one of two paths. First, they might assume that *small-event improvement* means that they are to work on only small, or even trivial, problems. Alternatively, they might want to work on significant problems in the way that they have observed managers and engineers working on problems. Neither is correct.

We want the improvement teams at the front line to take significant action. Trivial improvement is not worth the effort that establishing an autonomous environment requires. But we want the teams to take significant action in a way that reflects their intimate relationship with the equipment and process—for example:

- The extruder team ultimately installed a sieve-like device that broke up the lumps.
- The box team replaced about 10 meters of small-diameter tubing with piping that had a relatively large diameter.

Both of those actions are the sort of elegant solution that engineers often aspire to, but rarely achieve, because they do not have a sufficiently close relationship with the problem or do not have adequate time to achieve an elegant solution on relatively small problems. The teams that operated the extruder and the box machine each had several people who literally spent weeks looking at the equipment and thinking about the problem (as they operated the machine in normal production and as they made other, simpler improvements) before they came to their ultimate solutions.

With the proper framework for improvement, we can truly experience the effect that the people closest to the problem become the people who can best fix it. You should expect elegant solutions to meaningful problems and improvement opportunities, and you should manage in a way that achieves that result. The constant "awareness" of operating performance and improvement opportunities that people demonstrate when they create elegant solutions is one key indicator that the autonomous teams are maturing in a way that will enable them to contribute to routine operations.

Element 5: People Need a Structure for Action

People receive great benefit from working within a well-defined structure when they are starting something new, such as autonomous improvement. The quality stations and the rituals and rules of practice that you develop for the use of quality stations are both important. The use of quality stations was well described in Chapter 4; the important issue in this chapter is that your teams need the structure of quality stations as much as management does.

There will likely be some backlash about the effort required to construct and maintain the quality station. This effort is the team's version of the investment that management makes to create, translate, and sustain the strategic goals. It looks like extra work, but it is really the foundation for realizing enhanced performance in all the routine work that follows. The strategic goals organize the work objectives, and the rituals of quality stations organize the work itself.

> **Example:** I once worked with a maintenance technician who is a huge man and one of those people who never quite got over having been a Marine. Everything that he did and said had a strong "macho" component. One day he came up, put his arm around my shoulders, and said: "I used to hate my quality station, but now if you told me I couldn't have it anymore, I'd have to beat you to death."
>
> It was a strange conversation, but in his own way, he was telling me just what I wanted to hear. The quality station was now his, not mine, and he had recognized for himself the value that it brought to his work.

Summary of Chapter 5

- If people are going to become engaged to do things that they have not done before, then they need to be confident that *management* is engaged as well.
- Management cannot abdicate responsibility for autonomous improvement—it is not closely supervised, but *it must be well managed*.
- Unmanaged or undirected change has a huge potential to become *dissipated or counterproductive*.
- There are *five objective elements* required in order for people to become engaged in improvement. Each is required for improvement to begin, but each is a great investment:
  1. Clear goals that people can achieve.
  2. New skills needed to do new things.
  3. Time to work on improvement.
  4. Resources to make changes.
  5. A structured system and rituals of practice for autonomous action.

- *Root cause analysis* can be a straightforward and powerful tool for small teams to use as they begin the improvement process.
- *"Vacation teams"* can enable fast and focused improvement efforts without requiring special accommodation for team members dedicated to the efforts.
- Other places to seek initial improvements to prime the improvement pump are
    - Capital intensive manufacturing: try to find a reliability improvement for a critical process or unit.
    - Other heavy manufacturing: look for an opportunity to apply single minutes exchange of dies (SMED) technology in a core operation.
    - Light manufacturing: use value stream mapping to find the initial opportunity of greatest potential.
    - Offices and laboratories: apply work improvement methods to the part of the task that "looks like work."
- Make certain that *small-event improvement teams* do not practice trivial improvements or attempt to practice significant improvements in the way that managers and engineers practice improvement. That is, small teams should practice significant improvement in the way that is appropriate to small teams.

Chapter 6

The Subjective Elements That Disrupt Engagement of People

Key Idea: When a team apparently has everything that it needs in order to commence or continue autonomous improvement but it does not do so, then you are likely faced with a personal issue rather than an objective issue. Most of these personal issues are unique to the environment of an autonomous culture and do not exist at all in the traditional supervision model of management. Recognition and resolution of these issues almost always requires management intervention to help the team leader and frequently requires the assistance of a skilled professional.

When most people and teams are given the framework of quality stations and the capabilities provided by the objective elements of engagement described in Chapter 5, they actually engage in the improvement process. They tentatively, but promptly, begin to pursue their tactical team and individual goals with the time, skills, resources, and structure that you have provided.

But sometimes, that engagement does not happen. Everything objectively seems to be in place, but the team simply does not cause any improvement. In those cases, the team leaders need help. Once the objective elements of engagement are in place, you are clearly at a point where, if the team leader could have initiated autonomous improvement without assistance, that engagement would already have happened.

What if Improvement Does Not Happen?

Lack of progress at the quality station is the best indicator that a team is not functional. It is fine to have discussions with the team and the team leaders about the reasons for delay in initiating improvement. Perhaps there is a good reason in the form of another business need with a higher priority. However, if there is not a genuine good reason for delay, in a culture of rapid improvement each team needs to promptly commence autonomous improvement and make progress. If it appears to be acceptable to management for a team to opt out of this challenging new task, then some teams will surely do that. At the least, some teams will want to follow well behind the leaders. Therefore, if any team does not promptly make progress on its own, then management must intervene and help it get started.

Every time a manager goes to the field—and at the beginning, you should plan plenty of these visits—you should have a talk with people at their quality station. You should review with them the four basic rituals of quality station practice (which were discussed in detail in Chapter 4). Have them tell you

1. What their specific tactical goals are.
2. What actions they have completed and the resultant benefit to the business.
3. What is in progress now.
4. What ideas they are developing for the future.

It will quickly be apparent if a team is having problems with advancing each of those elements.

The first attempt by management to provide the team with help will be to review in detail the objective elements of engagement (recall that there are five objective elements of engagement; these were discussed in detail in Chapter 5). If the team lacks any objective element, then management should work with the team leader to fix that shortcoming before taking any other action. This may also be a good time to take a serious look at the team leader. If a team has gone through the same process as the other teams and the team leader has still not produced the objective elements needed for a team to commence improvement, that is often because the team leader is either weak or is intentionally obstructing autonomous action.

You may find that the team leader lacks appropriate skills for this new task of leading improvement through an engaged workforce. Or you may find a problem in middle management that is reflected in a team leader who is not able to accommodate a lack of support from his or her boss. Intentional interference with autonomous improvement by supervisors and middle managers is more common than you might expect. Often that becomes visible for the first time when assessing nonperforming teams.

The Subjective Elements That Disrupt Engagement

If you find that the *objective* elements of engagement are all in place, middle managers and team leaders are competent and on board, and the team is still not producing improved performance, then there is likely a *subjective* or personal problem with the team.

> **Key Idea:** As with all subjective problems, this discussion will not be as precisely structured as others are in this book. The best I can do for you is to suggest what you are looking for and where you might look. Your problems are likely to be of the same nature as the problems and examples described here, but the exact description of the subjective problem that is preventing one of your teams from succeeding will depend a lot on local factors that are unique to your people and business.

By far, the two most common subjective problems with building an engaged workforce are

1. A lack of trust in management.
2. Team members who are disruptive, including the possibility that the team leader may be disruptive.

These two causes are about equally balanced when considering many organizations, but within a single organization, usually one of these two is the predominant cause. The rest of this chapter discusses each in more detail.

Element 1: Some Teams Do Not Trust Management

By a very wide margin, the principle reason that people do not trust management is that management has the power to take away their employment or to otherwise adversely impact the terms and benefits of their employment. This lack of trust, or fear of management, may exist in any situation, but it is especially powerful if current or former management has a history of improving the business by taking things away from the employees.

A lot of industrial improvement takes the form of greater effectiveness or increased efficiency in operations. Without clear evidence of growing sales volume to absorb the improved efficiency, most people in manufacturing think that they know what efficiency improvement means to them. When people are afraid that the result of improvement will be that they (or their friends, relatives, or neighbors) will lose their employment, then there will be very little improvement. Before teams that fear management will make much progress, management needs to convince people that the improvement will not be bad for them.

Be careful at this point. Weak managers often fall back on the "burning platform" theory and attempt to convince people that the situation is dire and that improvement—regardless of the personal consequences for some people—is necessary to save the employment of others. If that is absolutely true, then go ahead and make your case to the people. However, if it is not true, or you do not have the facts to make the case in a credible manner, then you are well advised not to try that approach. Too many people have seen too many weak managers who have attempted to inspire action through fear. All you will get for your efforts is a loss of respect and credibility. The simple and positive approach is to convince people to help you because it will be good for them because their futures will be linked to a more successful, more competitive company. At the very least, you should be able to convince people that helping you will not be harmful to them.

Recognizing that the greatest source of fear is loss of employment or benefits, this is another place where the strategic goals of the business and the translation of goals into tactics for the small teams can help with communication. It is very rare if a business that intends to prosper has a single overarching goal of reducing the workforce. It is even rarer if the translation of tactical goals into actions at the team level focuses on reductions in workforce. When people raise the issue of loss of employment, either directly or indirectly, talk with them about the specific actions that they intend to take. It is likely that few, if any, of the actions planned by teams are actions that will lead directly to a reduced workforce.

The same is true of people who fear "cost reductions" that might impact them personally. (Fear or lack of trust in management is almost always personal.) Most industrial leaders understand that it is not possible to save your way to success. Even in businesses with cost problems, long-term or strategic success always requires something more than reducing costs. The only path to sustained success is to operate the business and to do that well. There are almost always goals other than reducing costs that need to be realized for successful long-term operation. And there are almost always other ways to improve costs beyond reducing staff or reducing people's compensation or benefits. Those other goals and the other ways to achieve them have already been identified as your organization established the goals for the business and the teams.

Focus your discussions with teams on the several elements of the team's own tactical goals. The team may have a goal of improving efficiency or effectiveness, but it will certainly also have other goals. Those other goals may relate to characteristics such as capacity, product variety or quality, maintenance, logistics, or overhead. Or they could address scrap, material consumed in production, or capital efficiency, including inventory and equipment investments. Unless the only immediate need of your business is improved productivity, there is nothing at all inappropriate about allowing a team that fears layoffs or reductions in benefits to commence autonomous improvement by initially pursuing another of your (and their) strategic goals. There is also nothing wrong with offering people a specific comment or two on the issue of employment as it relates to improved business success.

> **Example:** In a business where I was confident that we could grow sales and where we also had a significant flywheel of work contracted to people who were not employees, I actually committed at the beginning of the conversion to a culture of autonomous improvement that no current employee would lose his or her employment as a result of the improvements. As people experienced that the commitment I had made was true, improving the business for the future of everyone became a real bond between management and the improvement teams.
>
> One thing to consider as you practice autonomous improvement is that people (unique among all the assets of the business) have the ability to create continuing new sources of progress. This makes investing in your people uniquely valuable in the effort to make your business more successful. Every other form of investment provides a fixed benefit or a one-time change; in contrast, investing in your people (when they are acting as autonomous improvement teams) provides a continuing stream of new benefits.

It is indeed practical in many situations to make such a commitment. Most mature businesses have quite a few people who retire, die, quit, take a leave of absence, or leave the business for other reasons. As a result, even a well-run business with excellent employee relations might easily have a natural annual attrition rate of 8% or more. (This implies that the average of all employees stays with you more than 12 years. Even if you look around and see mostly people who have long tenure, there are always a lot of people you may not notice who stay only a very short time, and that effect greatly reduces the average.) Most businesses also have some overtime work that can be improved. In U.S. industry, this overtime is often 8% or more of the total work hours. In the United Kingdom, France, and other countries with labor laws or labor agreements that restrict overtime, there is normally a nearly equivalent amount of work performed that is rewarded by compensatory time off or other arrangements as opposed to overtime pay.

By reducing overtime, reducing the pace of backfilling normal attrition, and with modest organic volume growth, it is often possible to create and sustain productivity improvement at 10% or more each year, as well as double-digit product unit labor cost reductions, without a loss of employment for any of your current employees. Make sure that your people understand that the business has that potential, and make sure they understand that you have a personal goal to achieve that outcome. Even more important, make sure that you sincerely work hard and visibly to achieve that outcome.

As you discuss employment, never make promises that you cannot keep. There could be a general recession, or you could lose an important customer. Or an individual could need to be terminated for bad behavior. When I committed that no current employee would lose his or her employment *as a result of the improvements*, I specifically reviewed these other situations that might result in a loss of employment. Allowing in your communications for those situations that are obviously out of your control will be well accepted because it will be apparent that you have thought about the future before you made your commitment and are therefore more likely to keep it.

> **Example:** More than once, I have used my own employees at their own normal rate of pay to do work far different than normal in order to keep them employed. For example, I have temporarily had factory technicians cutting the grass around the plant. They cost me much more than the contract lawn service that we previously used. But at the end of the day, it was a highly visible (and thankfully temporary) demonstration that management would lead improvement to the business without hurting the people who provided the improvement.

I know of at least one business that has purchased the assets, but not the employees, of another business solely to ensure that there was sufficient work for its own people. Other businesses use contractors or part-time workers to manage variations in labor demand, so that regular employees can see the safety net of contractors between them and a layoff. Whatever you decide to do, it is certain that you will initially find some teams that will not make improvements because they do not trust what you might do with the result.

Recognizing that this lack of trust and lack of progress will certainly happen, you will have to be prepared for it. Three things are clear:

1. Because you know this situation is certainly coming, be prepared to address the concern without delay and without the initial misstep that is likely if you attempt to "ad lib" when the time for this conversation arrives.
2. If a team does not trust management, this is a problem that a team leader cannot possibly fix alone. Management—and possibly very senior management—needs to intervene and help get the team back on track.
3. This is a sustaining activity that needs to start promptly. If you plan to achieve a lot of productivity improvement, then you need to begin immediately managing your business in a way that is consistent with experiencing that improvement. Do not allow yourself to be surprised when your own plans come to fruition.

Fortunately this lack of trust is likely only at or near the beginning of the effort. Unless an external event, such as the loss of a customer, occurs that mandates a reduction in force, you will continuously build credibility as you demonstrate in practice that joining you to improve the business is safe for your people. Once you have established credibility for working to protect your people, even a mandatory reduction in force due to an external event such as the loss of a customer will not cause a loss of credibility for management if people believe that further improvement might prevent that from occurring again.

Element 2: Some Teams Have Disruptive Members

There is an almost unlimited number of ways in which an individual can disrupt the activities of a team:

- An individual can dominate discussions or refuse to compromise on honest disagreements.
- An individual can initiate bad faith disagreements.
- An individual can violate the norms of the group by talking too much or too little, treating the meetings as a coffee break, or simply not doing an appropriate share of the discretionary work.

The disruption can be intentional or unintentional; the following subsections describe the differences and how to handle each type. However it happens to occur, the problems caused by a disruptive team member may stop the team from coalescing and becoming productive. And disruptive personal behavior of one or more team members will sooner or later cause an initially productive team to become unproductive. Management needs to be alert to the possibility that this situation can arise at any time, not only at the beginning of the effort.

Intentionally Disruptive Team Members

Intentionally disruptive team members are often the easiest (or at least the most straightforward) to manage. Participation in the improvement activities is now a regular part of the job assignment. Refusal to participate, or intentionally disrupting the activities of the team, enables management to sit down with the disruptive individual for a standard chat about bad personal behavior. That conversation can, if necessary, lead to formal discipline and even discharge. Most intentionally disruptive people who want to keep their job soon straighten up when confronted by a deadly serious manager who will not tolerate the problem.

In fact, intentionally disruptive team members are often just testing the resolve of management, and they typically turn around quite quickly when confronted. However, there are three common exceptions to this expectation of a quick response to counseling:

1. Union members who are getting external support for their disruptive practices.
2. Team leaders (or other middle managers) who see autonomous action as destroying the leadership position that they have worked to attain.
3. Individuals who thrive on controversy or countercultural behavior.

Direct Relationships with Management

Both disruptive union members and disruptive team leaders are manifestations of the same core issue. Autonomous improvement implies a strong and direct relationship of trust between the company management and the people at the front line. As discussed previously, senior management should never bypass middle management in any form of communication or action, but there is always good value in having senior managers included in a direct relationship of trust. There is no objective reason for either unions or team leaders to fear this new relationship, but it may require a lot of conversation to get everyone to share that understanding. Supervisors in an autonomous improvement environment actually have a much more rewarding job. Rather than merely monitoring work for compliance to a standard, they can lead and facilitate change.

Have that conversation with any team leader or middle manager who is being disruptive or even unsupportive. Disruption by team leaders and middle managers during the early days of autonomous activity is quite common, and you should not overreact when you find that it exists. That being said, disruption by members of management that is not resolved promptly cannot be tolerated. After a reasonable amount of time and conversation, supervisors or middle managers who are disruptive or unsupportive must stop being leaders. At some point, you may need to tell them that they cannot be leaders if they continue the bad behavior. And if necessary, you will need to make that change happen.

Unions also have very little to fear from autonomous improvement. So long as people retain a natural suspicion of unchallenged power in the hands of management (especially some unknown future management), the union will surely be retained for the security it provides. In the minds of the people, the union may not currently be needed, but they might be needed at some later time. As union leaders and members reach that understanding, it is clear that the union's position is secure. It is then the decision of the union's leadership as to whether they become a positive force and join with you in creating a path to the future or act as an adversary to the business. In my experience, at the beginning of this effort, there will be uncertainty within the union leadership on which path to choose. This dilemma within the union is another situation that you must anticipate in advance. Early and frequent conversations with union leaders are a vital element of adopting a new culture for the business. Many businesses have chosen to include a union leader in some of the cultural design activities that are described in Section III.

> **Example:** Although most of my interactions with union leaders at General Motors during the 1970s were adversarial, in the 30 years since then I have found that union leaders are often very attuned to the needs of the business and quite happy to participate in making the future more secure for their members in many new ways, including cooperation in autonomous improvement. In Baytown, Texas, we had four unions. The presidents of three of those unions were outstanding supporters, practitioners, and leaders of the improvement effort. The president of the fourth union chose not to participate personally, but also never took any action that might have disrupted the effort.

Intentionally Disruptive Individuals

Unfortunately there are some people who just enjoy being disruptive. In some cases, these people are truly antisocial and take personal pleasure in being disruptive. In most cases, though, these are the people who think of themselves as the "class clowns" of the workplace. They are not trying to be disruptive; they are only trying to amuse or entertain their coworkers. In a supervision culture, these folks will have a well-developed skill for pushing the boundaries of acceptable behavior without getting fired. In the autonomous culture that you are creating, especially at the beginning, the boundaries of personal conduct are less certain and more fragile. When, for any reason, a disruptive individual refuses to "join up" in the new culture following serious counseling, management must act. All cultures have a means of correcting or excluding disruptive people. In an industrial culture, management must be the means for *formal* correction or exclusion.

Fortunately, in a culture of rapid improvement, an interesting transition takes place in the workforce that will provide you with some help as the effort progresses. In a supervision culture, the only person responsible for all forms of team behavior is the supervisor. Coworkers take no responsibility for and probably even take little interest in the disruptive behavior of others unless they find it amusing or offensive. However, if you follow the schedule proposed in Section V of this book, somewhere about 18 months into the process, your teams will be fairly strong and getting stronger. Teams at that point can still be disrupted by individual behavior, but it will happen less often. Teammates will be a good self-correcting mechanism to *informally* address people who are being intentionally disruptive. At the very least, team leaders can anticipate a strong base of support. The greatest danger to teams at that time will be team members who are unintentionally disruptive. That problem is harder to address because it is frequently not clear what to do about it.

Unintentionally Disruptive Team Members

The much more difficult problem for management to resolve is the honest, hard-working person who is disruptive in an unintentional way. This situation often requires the intervention of a skilled professional (much in the way that a marriage counselor restores harmony in dysfunctional families). Unintentional disruption is a good example of another situation in which management must help the team leaders. Most team leaders have little natural ability to provide the interpersonal counseling required to bring a team together in the presence of an otherwise good person and valued teammate who unintentionally becomes a disruptive force within the team.

Very often, unintentional disruption results from personal behavior of one individual that may or may not be offensive but is certainly inexplicable to other team members. This is likely when the team is comprised of individuals who, among themselves, have different personal cultures.

> **Example:** We once had an Asian woman engineer who in most ways was exactly what we wanted her to be. Unfortunately, as an Asian woman, her personal culture of communicating required her to be

very polite. She described this communication style as "rolling words seven times on the tongue" before speaking to be certain that she would not say anything offensive. The communication style of the other members of her team was fairly aggressive, with the result that, as a very polite person, she rarely got to talk during team meetings.

The interpersonal problem arose for the team because, as the engineering representative on a front-line team, she was personally very visible, and she was professionally very important to the success of the team. Her failure to participate in the team discussions caused her team to believe that she was not interested in them or in their work. In the personal cultures of the other team members, that belief represented a fair interpretation of her behavior.

The team members responded badly to the perceived lack of interest from their engineering contact. Soon the team was in some disarray and not making progress. After external intervention identified the true issues behind the engineer's previously unexplained lack of participation, a relatively simple solution was proposed. The team leader began to stop the discussion periodically and ask for her input.

This small accommodation provided her with an opportunity to participate in team meetings, but to do so in her own way. The team quickly came back together and became quite productive. It even turns out that by developing a more polite communication style, this team brought out more participation from other team members as well.

There are many ways in which one or more people can unintentionally disrupt a team and make it unproductive. First-line team leaders are often not prepared to manage that disruption when it happens, especially in the unsettled social environment caused by converting to the new culture of autonomous improvement. In the supervision mode, team leaders are much less dependent on team goodwill than when they are attempting to lead engaged people. In the supervision mode, they can frequently resolve modest interpersonal differences with specific instructions regarding structured behavior. In the engagement mode, however, team leaders need to receive some form of voluntary action from most of the people, and that voluntary behavior is often inconsistent with team leaders who are overtly prescriptive in directing other forms of personal behavior. Many team leaders will require either management or professional help to find and implement an interpersonal resolution for the team that fits the new culture you are creating.

Although unintentional disruption is not a direct threat to the activity in the same way that intentional disruption is, it is still a problem that needs to be corrected. No team can be allowed to refuse or fail to participate in the improvement process. The teams who begin to behave as a dysfunctional family behaves need skilled external help either to initiate autonomous action or to return to working closely together and become productive again after a disruption. It is management's job to identify when this need exists and to provide help. A front-line team leader is very unlikely to fix this type of situation alone. The creation of a skilled professional in industrial culture and other resources to help with these situations as they arise is described in Section III.

Summary of Chapter 6

- When management provides the *objective elements of engagement*, most people and teams respond by actually engaging in improvement.
- When engagement does not occur after a team has the objective elements in place, the likely cause is one of the two *subjective elements* that disrupt engagement:
    1. Teams or individual team members do not trust management.
    2. One or more individuals, including the team leader or another member of middle management, may be disruptive.
- When a team fails to deploy the objective elements at the same time as other teams, then the team leader may need *external help* to get the process started.
- When a team displays subjective problems with engagement, the team leader needs *specific skilled professional assistance* to bring the team back together.
- Frequently teams that do not trust management *fear* management will use the improvement to reduce employment.
- Use the strategic and tactical goals to communicate that the need for improvement is broader than the need for a reduced workforce. Make it clear that you do not intend to hurt the people who are helping you to succeed.
- You cannot *save* your way to success; something more is always required.
- Disruptive team members act either *intentionally* or *unintentionally*:
    - Intentional disruption is often the easiest to manage.
    - Unintentionally disruptive team members often signal a cultural difference among team members or between the culture of the team and the culture of the corporation.

THE SOCIAL DESIGN OF YOUR NEW CULTURE

In the earlier sections of this book, I described the objective or "engineering" aspects of a corporate culture. Because an industrial culture is different from a social culture in that it exists primarily for commercial purposes, establishing the business components of that culture first as we have done here provides an important foundation for the rest of the cultural transition. But, even in industry, culture is an essentially *social* concept. Therefore this section describes the social elements needed for your new culture.

As you create an industrial culture of rapid improvement, it is important to remember that the people in your business arrive at work every day with their own personal cultures. Those many different personal cultures will influence the social elements in the design of your corporate culture because they will determine how individual people will behave most naturally, relative to your work and in cooperation with others while at work. Remember that the variety of personal cultures among your people and the required corporate culture of your business are necessarily a unique combination.

That is the principle reason that each leader who undertakes to lead a cultural transformation must be prepared to design the new culture. At the end of the day, in order to succeed, you need to create your own culture. You cannot simply adopt an industrial culture for your business that either I or someone else has practiced previously in another business situation. You need a culture that is created specifically to fit the people of your organization, as well as the particular needs of your business. In many forms of improvement, but especially in the areas requiring a lot of personal engagement, leaders who simply attempt

111

to re-create exactly what they have seen elsewhere fail more often than they succeed. Singing the company song may be a great way to start the day in Tokyo, but do not try that in Baytown, Texas. Similarly, *Andon* (i.e., line-stop) may be a great technique for the auto industry, but it is more likely to cause an explosion than an improvement in the chemical industry.

There are four critical implications of managing the social elements at the interface between personal cultures and a new corporate culture. These will be discussed in the four chapters of this section.

First, management must understand the theory of cultural design as it applies to industry. In time, many people will participate in the evolution of the culture into one that precisely fits the needs of your people and your business. However, at the beginning, leaders (and those who advise the leaders) will start the process of creating a new culture with only the theory, some examples from others, and their personal knowledge of the people and needs of their business. When leaders understand the theory of industrial culture, there is far less chance that they will commit the serious error of attempting to reproduce a successful culture that someone else has created without first adapting it to their particular situation. The theory of industrial culture provides a basis for judging the applicability of other's experiences for use in your business. This is the subject of Chapter 7.

Second, the leaders must design an "on-purpose" corporate culture that allows their people from many different personal and social cultures to behave naturally and comfortably as they bring their full energy, creativity, and personal capabilities to work. Most industrial cultures today are nothing more than an informal adaptation of an external social culture. As a result, many people with different personal cultures are diminished or excluded from the culture at work. Those who are diminished or excluded from the culture of the workplace not only will be unable to help as you improve the business, but they will also be a visible reminder to others that the culture of the workplace does not fit your people and your business. The people who share the work with you must know and believe that they are all trusted and valued members of the culture that you create. This is the subject of Chapter 8.

Third, the new corporate culture needs to be inclusive. This is legitimately a subset of the cultural design described as the second requirement, but it is a subset that requires a lot of detail and attention. Designing an inclusive culture requires that you recognize the cultural differences that exist, provide your people a way to resolve interpersonal differences that arise as a result of cultural differences, and provide your people with support as they experience cultural change. This is all new and challenging work for everyone, and it is work that needs to be done very well in order to succeed. This is the subject of Chapter 9.

Fourth, as the culture of the workplace becomes more social and more inclusive, there will be a natural increase in the emotions that people experience at work. For most people, work has not previously been a truly emotional experience, and emotions in the workplace are uncomfortable. Management needs to prepare in advance for the arrival of real emotions in the workplace and must use the emotional health of the organization as an indicator of the extent of support that they enjoy for the pace and character of cultural change as it occurs. This is the subject of Chapter 10.

Chapter 7

Understanding the Theory of Industrial Culture

Key Idea: Always keep in mind that you are not creating a new business culture for fun or as a social experiment. You are creating a new industrial culture because you have the expectation that it will lead to improved business performance. If you are not able to understand the relevance of any cultural activity as it applies to your business and to your people, then you should wait or proceed slowly until you do understand it or until you have rejected it in favor of some alternative activity. I really cannot say this too often or with too much emphasis: You need a culture that fits your business and your people. There is no value at all in adopting the elements of some other business's culture if they do not apply to you.

As mentioned in the introduction to Section III, it is now time to get serious about designing the way that you will lead the human side of change for your business. The important point as you design your new culture is that if you want the people who work in your business to behave differently, then *you* need to behave differently first. As Albert Einstein said: "Insanity is doing the same thing over and over and expecting a different result." If you continue to lead your people in the way that you always have, and expect them to give you a different result, you are sure to be disappointed. Designing a new culture implies that management is prepared to change both the *formal* and *social* mechanisms for leading the human side of your business.

The three specific social objectives of any new business culture are

1. Create a business-wide culture that enables people from the many different social and personal cultures that exist within your business today to work with each other comfortably, capably, and creatively.
2. Create a culture that includes all the people who are part of your business as trusted and valued teammates.
3. Create a small-team culture within your business that lets people work closely together to achieve the detailed needs of your business.

Before considering the design of a new culture, there are several important theoretical attributes of human culture and business culture that need to be reviewed. Based on the understanding that you gain from that review, you will be equipped with most of the theory that you will need in order to undertake the practical steps to create a new culture that you design "on purpose" to specifically fit the needs of your business and your people.

Personalities and Personal Cultures at Work

You already know that each person who works with you has a unique personality. Typically the personality that an individual brings to work is a natural combination of race, gender, national origin, religion, and other heritage attributes of that sort. In forming an individual's personality, these heritage attributes combine with status characteristics such as education, wealth, health, sociability, family, and others. At work, these characteristics all combine again with attributes from the workplace, such as the type of work that a person does, the organizational level at which they work, the experience or seniority that a person has, and the way that the individual earns personal satisfaction, respect, or peer approval while at work.

Each of your people arrives at work with a complex personal culture that defines how each person would behave naturally absent the behavioral constraints of the workplace. Those personal cultures have not been designed for any purpose and certainly not for any business purpose. They simply occur naturally as a result of the heritage and environment of each individual. The many different personal cultures of your people will also define how each person will naturally interact with the other people in the workplace and with the industrial culture that you create.

Further, the personal cultures of each individual will determine how people interpret the actions and behavior of those around them. Behavior that is quite natural in one person may be inexplicable or even offensive to another person. As a result, personal culture often is a significant factor affecting business-critical social relationships in the workplace such as teamwork, cooperation, trust, and friendship.

On top of all that naturally occurring social cultural confusion, your people, with all their different personal cultures, interact with one another within the business culture of your enterprise. Although it is possible for businesses to have strong cultures, an industrial culture is not natural. If you want a strong industrial culture, it will be necessary to design and implement it yourself. As a result, few businesses today enjoy a culture that has any influence in shaping the personalities, interactions, and behavior of people while they are at work. This does not imply that your business lacks a culture, but rather that your business culture, as it exists today, is probably not strong or influential. But as you create a strong new culture, the environment within which your people interact will change substantially, and that is another important consideration in the design of your business culture.

Each Business Has a Culture That Defines the Workplace

Recognizing that your business consists of many people, each with a distinct personal culture, the first consideration in the design of your on-purpose culture will be the harmonious integration of those disparate personal cultures while people are at work. There has been a lot of research done on the interaction of different cultures, and that can be of real value to you.

A common finding from this research is that, in most situations, it is possible to identify a "dominant" culture that defines the environment of the interaction. Identifying a culture as "dominant" does not mean that the dominant culture is strong or influential, but only that for a particular environment, the dominant culture defines interaction among the several personal cultures. The importance of the concept of a dominant culture cannot be overstated in creating a new culture for a business. Although your current business culture is probably quite weak, the new culture that you create should have a great influence on the inter-actions of your people at work. The first lesson of dominant cultures in business is that, to the extent that an individual's personal culture is very different from the dominant culture of the enterprise, it is hard for that person to perform even normal activities comfortably and successfully. For routine operations, a person with a different culture can adapt somewhat with time. However, as new activities (such as autonomous improvement) are introduced the discomfort and lack of success that a person of difference experiences will increase.

If you want to test this belief about the difficulty of doing normal activities successfully within a different dominant culture, try this exercise. Identify a church, synagogue, or mosque in your city from your own religion where all or most of the members are people of another race. Attend services there one day. All the people will be gathered together for the same purpose, and you share that purpose with them. Because this is a place of worship of your own religion, the rituals of the service ought to be familiar to you. In many respects, this is very similar to a workplace situation.

> **Example:** I only propose this exercise because anyone can do it in almost any place. Many people in global businesses already experience this sort of effect at work. While I was with Gilbarco, I had responsibility for manufacturing operations in Greensboro, North Carolina, where I lived, as well as Canada, the United Kingdom, Australia, and Brazil. In all five locations, we were making effectively the same products for the same customers. Although I was perfectly at home in the plants in Canada, the United Kingdom, and Australia, I have to admit that I never really understood the Brazilian operations in the same way, and my contributions there were far less than in other places.

What you are certain to find is that in the new environment you will be distracted, uncertain, worried about fitting in, worried about appearing or doing wrong in some way, and truly not able to worship as you normally do. Even the *shared rituals* that are common to your religion will be surrounded by *local rituals* that are very different from what you anticipate. If you really want to experience the "fish out of water" effect, try going to a place of worship of a different religion or with people of a different socioeconomic group (or both of those) in addition to going to a place of worship of a different race. As you increase the number of differences between your personal culture and the dominant culture that surrounds you, you will become less comfortable and less effective.

If you were to attend a place of worship of a different culture regularly, you could adapt with time and begin to be more comfortable, but you would always know that you never quite "got it" like the others around you and that you were never quite as comfortable or successful as you previously were at your place of worship. More important for our purposes, you would find it hard to engage in the secular activities of that place of worship to the extent that you do today.

Even if you attended regularly, you would volunteer less and have less social interaction. When the dominant culture of any environment is very different from your personal culture, you can learn the formal routines, but informal and nonroutine activity will remain very difficult.

What you are experiencing is the effect of being in a dominant culture that is not your own. In that environment, even things that you have comfortably done all your life are harder and more uncertain. And that is the very human effect that some of your people experience every day at work.

> **Example:** You were probably very uncomfortable as you read the prior paragraphs describing an experiment that involved religion. The reason is that we have all been taught that we do not talk about religion or politics in business. If you add to that prohibition on conversation the "protected classes" specified in civil rights legislation (race, age, gender, national origin, sexual orientation, and others), you will generally describe the culture of many workplaces.
>
> People need to discuss and resolve interpersonal differences, large and small, before they can work together as trusted and valued colleagues. Most work cultures lack influence on social interactions because they either prohibit those discussions or "dumb them down" to such an extent that they are effectively useless. Such bland dominant cultures may appear to create or preserve a superficial harmony, but what they actually achieve is the permanent isolation of individuals or groups who are different in some way and without resolution always will be.

Social Cultures at Work

It is important to recognize that few businesses today have well-designed industrial cultures. The dominant cultures of most workplaces are simply informal adaptations of an external social culture probably with the addition of a prohibition against any discussion of cultural issues. For that reason, it is possible to provide a general description of the culture of most businesses today—for example:

■ In a family-owned and operated business, the culture of the business is normally the same as the personal culture of the family that owns the business.

- In a publicly owned single-nation company, the culture of the business is the social culture of the community where the business operates, mixed evenly with the personal culture of the most senior managers.
- In a large multinational company, the culture of the workplace is an even mix of the social culture of the country of operation, combined with the business culture of the country of ownership.

> **Example:** I learned a great lesson in this regard in Japan. Our Japanese managers often held business discussions in English, even when there were only Japanese natives present. They explained to me that when they spoke the Japanese language, they felt constrained by social limits that did not fit the business conversations they had learned to have within the culture of our company. By speaking English, they declared to each other that Japanese social norms were temporarily suspended and they were acting principally as employees of a U.S. company. At other times, they spoke together in Japanese and it was understood that the cultural norms at that time were local.

Because most industrial cultures today exist as an extension of social cultures that have been brought informally into the workplace, the culture of most workplaces has few business attributes. Even more important for the purpose of the social design of a work culture, the most common business culture today is not an inclusive culture. Most existing work cultures do not have any structured capability to include individuals who have a personal culture that is different from the social culture that has been adapted to the workplace. As previously mentioned, some (even many) businesses formally or informally prohibit the discussions that would lead to inclusion. The workplace should be inclusive, but it just is not. The rituals of work should be natural, but some people just do not get it. People should resolve interpersonal differences, but they are not allowed to do so. When the dominant culture of the workplace is created informally by extension of the social cultures of management or the community, there is an excellent chance that the society of the workplace excludes or diminishes those workers who are not part of the dominant social culture outside of work.

Three Typical Responses to a Dominant Culture

When the dominant culture of the workplace contains few if any business elements and is largely defined by the social culture of just some of the people at work, then the other people have to adapt to work much as you might have done if you had tried the experiment of visiting a new place of worship or as you actually have done while working in a country with a very different culture. Unfortunately for business, none of the likely adaptations produces a good result.

A common finding from the study of different personal cultures as they come together at work is that people who have a personal culture that is similar to the dominant culture of the workplace tend to enjoy the experience and prosper. For example, if a business is owned and managed by white male North American Christians, then the most likely spontaneous culture for the workplace will be that of white male North American Christians. As a result, they will be the people who will behave most comfortably and naturally, and they will get the most personal satisfaction from work. In some extreme cases, they may be almost the only people who get real enjoyment from the work experience.

White males will prosper in the workplace not because they receive favored treatment (although that is possible), but rather because they are comfortable, natural, and creative in their actions and in their relationships. They will easily join in nonroutine activities, and they will function well in small teams at the front line. The people who have a personal culture that is very close to the dominant culture enjoy work, they succeed at work, and everything is relatively good for them.

In contrast, people who have a personal culture that is very different from the dominant culture at work will not easily or naturally receive as much intrinsic value or personal success from work as will members of the dominant culture. They will not easily participate in the nonroutine activities or small teams of the workplace with the same comfort, enthusiasm, and personal enjoyment. These people with a different personal culture will typically take one of three paths as they interact with the dominant culture. These are described in the following sections.

1. People of Different Cultures Will Appear to Fit the Dominant Culture at Work

The first type of response is that a person with a different culture may adopt a personality and behavior that emulates the dominant culture while at work, then return to his or her own personal culture at other times. By adopting a behavior that is not natural to them, people of difference may appear to "fit in" at work, but they commonly do so with some effort and discomfort that detracts from their energy and creative ability to do other things. This cultural "protective coloration" is often quite successful for routine activities, but it becomes strained and less effective for the nonroutine actions of autonomous improvement and small-team activity. As a result, they are less productive and successful than they otherwise could be due to the personal capability and creativity that is consumed in adapting and due to the diminished success of the adaptation, just when the business needs it the most. They will volunteer less and have fewer close personal or team relationships while at work.

2. People of Different Cultures Will Adopt a Neutral Behavior while at Work

The second typical response is that a person of a different culture may become culturally and personally neutral while they are surrounded by another social culture that has been adopted as the dominant work culture. They conform to the work culture just enough to meet the minimum standards of behavior required by the dominant culture, but they never even attempt to conform or adapt to the values and beliefs of the dominant culture, either partially or temporarily.

Often this means that they do not bring the fullness of their own personality to work, and they do not adopt an adaptive personality during work. Unlike the first group, these people do not consume their creative abilities and energy in adaptation. Rather, they generally leave their creativity and energy at home. These folks may be competent at routine repetitive work, but they rarely make any form of special contribution. They are not engaged with the business or their coworkers. They have no social basis for successfully participating in either the creative aspects or the teamwork of autonomous improvement.

3. People of Different Cultures Will Resist the Dominant Culture at Work

The third typical responsive behavior is that people with different personal cultures resist the dominant culture by emphasizing their differences. For example, a French manager who is considered culturally moderate in France might affect behavior that he or others consider to be extremely "French" when he begins to work in an American company or in an American venue. Similar to the people in the first group, the people in this group consume their creativity and energy with unnatural behavior. Unfortunately, often nothing collegial or collaborative results from this form of unnatural behavior that emphasizes personal cultural differences.

Another common manifestation of this response of emphasizing differences to the dominant culture is demonstrated by people whose personal culture includes seeking peer approval by cultivating a "bad boy" image or other countercultural behavior. They consume their energy and creativity by constantly abusing the system and challenging authority. A less disruptive form of the "bad boy" culture is the "class clown." These people seek peer approval by entertaining their peers, often with disruptive antics of some sort. Although they will not be quite as disruptive as the bad boys are, the class clowns also consume their personal creativity and energy in nonproductive pursuits. Both the bad boys and the class clowns often also consume the time and energy of others in nonproductive ways.

What to Do about These Three Responses to Your Dominant Work Culture

The business implication from this assessment is that most of your employees who are not naturally members of the dominant social culture that has been adapted for your company expend or lose capability and positive creativity in order to behave in a way that is not natural for them while they are at work. To address this situation, you need to move away from the spontaneous work culture that simply mirrors an external social culture. You need to create an "on-purpose" culture for the workplace that brings all your people together and supports a shared cultural (and business) value of collaborative autonomous improvement.

> **Example:** The Asian woman engineer I mention several times throughout this book once told me that she fully understood that to fill her role as an engineer in our company, she should communicate differently from the communication style that she had been raised to practice. In her words, she had to choose each day how she would fail: that is, she could communicate our way and fail as an Asian woman, or she could communicate her way and fail as an engineer. Whatever choice she made was emotionally draining and distracting to her personal life and to her business mission every day.

In addition to diminishing the personal capabilities of individuals, a further concern is that unresolved interpersonal or intercultural relationships can greatly diminish the capabilities of multicultural teams and, through that, diminish the results of all the team members, including those team members who otherwise would perform well because they are members of the dominant culture. For example, recalling the Asian woman again, because of her cultural issues with communication style, her entire team became unproductive until we resolved that issue.

As you ask people to go beyond compliance with specific supervisory direction and engage with you and their teammates to improve your business, then that extra part of themselves they lose or consume in adapting to the society of work may be just the extra capability that you need, or the extra teamwork and cooperation in nonroutine work that is not possible for them and their team-mates may be what you need.

> **Example:** As I began to understand these issues and to discuss them with people, several friends volunteered stories of their personal adaptations. Some of those people have a specific regimen each morning of "transforming" from the person they are at home into the person that they feel they need to be at work.
>
> No one reported that they believed they became a better person as a result of this transformation. The transformations never added to personal engagement, creativity, and capabilities, they always subtracted.

Situational Cultures

A final finding from the study of merging cultures is of great value when designing the social elements of your culture of rapid improvement. Social differences among individuals in one situation might be very unlike the social differences between the same individuals in other situations. For example, the professional behavior of a black woman engineer at work might be very similar to the professional behavior of white male engineers at work. Outside of the workplace, the behavior for black women and white men might be very different, but at work, individuals from both groups can behave very naturally as engineers. In the same way that people can be culturally comfortable in professional roles, they can learn to be comfortable in other roles, such as when a person becomes comfortably fluent in a second language and happily enjoys the society associated with that language.

This is described as a *situational* culture. It is not an individual's personal culture, but it is a culture that an individual can embrace without discomfort or loss.

The concept of a situational culture suggests a path for the design of your on-purpose industrial culture. You can create a situational work culture that is based on the shared values and prescribed behavior of your goals and rituals. Similar to the behavior of professional engineers (which does not define all behavior of those engineers), you still have many social elements to consider, but it is a good start. As you design the social elements of your culture, try to understand and satisfy the theory of interpersonal relations within an industrial culture as it applies in your situation. The details of such a design are discussed in Chapter 8.

Essentially you will want to build a workplace culture that is purposely created with the following four characteristics in a way that is unique to the needs of your business and your people:

1. The foundation of the business culture is the commonly shared values, beliefs, and rituals that you create.
2. The social elements of the organization-wide business culture are designed by you and your people to uniquely fit the needs of your people and your business.
3. The formal practices and society of the business include and value all the people of the organization as trusted colleagues.
4. The local norms of the small teams enable all people within the business to work comfortably, creatively, and naturally with their teammates.

Key Idea: Ultimately this is the result you are seeking: a carefully designed industrial culture that engages all your team members in natural personal and professional behavior in support of your business while they are at work.

Summary of Chapter 7

People bring their individual cultures to work with them. These individual cultures are created for each person as the result of merging elements derived from their heritage, their societal status, and their role in the workplace.

■ When cultures interact, a significant factor in the outcome is the *dominant culture* that defines the environment of the interactions.

■ In most businesses today, the dominant culture of the workplace is the *social culture* of the owners or the community in which the business operates.

■ It is possible for you to experience the effect of being a person of difference in a dominant culture that is not your own by attending a place of worship other than your own, which has a different dominant culture from yours.

■ Dominant cultures at work that have evolved from an external social culture naturally *exclude or diminish* some of the people who work at your business.

■ In response to a dominant culture that is not theirs, people adopt *unnatural behavior* at work. This normally diminishes their capability or creativity.

- It is possible to create a *new culture* for the workplace that is designed "on purpose" to comfortably include all your business and personal issues.
- People within this on-purpose culture can act naturally in the same way that professionals learn professional behavior or in the way that people become comfortably fluent in a second language.
- This is the basis of our intent to design a *special culture* that is appropriate to your business and to the needs of your people.

Chapter 8

The Social Design of a New Culture

> **Key Idea:** Today, people often work in close proximity, but the work does not benefit from collaboration. They act as a *work group*, not as a *team*. As you transition to true team-based activity, your need for strong, interpersonal relations will increase greatly. In order for this transition to happen uniformly and quickly, management needs to lead the way with clear direction and expectations.

It is possible to design a situational culture that is especially appropriate for your own particular needs in bringing people together to share the goals and work of improving your business in a very natural and comfortable way. Most of this book provides the technical, practical, and administrative details for design of a new culture. This chapter describes design of the *social*, or *human*, elements.

Fortunately and unfortunately, there will be few specific details in this chapter that you might be tempted to copy, because "R&D"—in this case meaning *replicate and duplicate*—does not play well in social design. Instead, you need to design the social elements of your own corporate culture in a way that is unique to your business and your people. There is very little value in adopting or adapting social elements from a culture that someone else has designed. If all that you learn from a book or a benchmark visit to a successful organization is the exact ritual of their practices, then that implies that the working model of cultural theory that you plan to use as you design your own culture is a behavior-only model. As described at the time I introduced the three-part model of culture

127

that I have been using here (in Chapter 1), if your understanding of culture is limited only to behavior, you are more likely to do harm than good.

In fact, one of the biggest regrets that I have is that so many people have visited my operations through the years and copied only the rituals of our quality station practices without understanding or attempting any of the other cultural elements that made quality stations so successful for us. Visitors often returned to their own businesses and worked very diligently to reproduce what they had seen at our site. And they often sent follow-up teams to check the details. But without the culture to support it, quality station practice is just another technical initiative that depends largely on people—and without an appropriate culture, it will not be as successful for you as it has been for me.

Most industrial practitioners who write about or teach industrial improvement only tell you about the experiences, practices, and rituals of their successes; those rituals normally do not travel well without all the other elements of the specific culture that made them possible. That is the principle reason that adoption of Japanese manufacturing techniques is still in relatively early stages more than three decades after the Western world discovered their value. Rather than adopting the technology in a way that is consistent with our culture, far too many Western companies attempted to simply reproduce the practices that exist in Japan. Rituals grounded in someone else's culture become increasingly inappropriate and increasingly ineffective as the differences between the two cultures increase. Therefore I will describe here only the social elements that you need to consider and accommodate as you create your own design on the basis of the theory of industrial cultures. The actual design of your unique culture is up to you and your understanding of how the theory of culture applies to your situation. There will, of course, be examples from my own experience, but you should use those examples as illustrations of the theory, not as models to replicate.

Social Design in Industry

The social design of a new industrial culture begins with changing your expectations for social behavior at work in a way that is consistent with the values and beliefs that you have adopted for unifying the workforce and achieving the goals of the business. When I say "social" here I am describing the human interaction component of life at work. This may include informal social aspects such as personal friendships and lunch companions, but it also specifically includes establishing the formal social expectations for how people work together as individuals and small teams.

With the exception of prescribed rituals of conduct that are required when certain uniform and precise outcomes are needed, you will not manage these social interactions at work directly. Instead, you will create an environment where people will change their own behavior to be consistent with the expectations derived from the society of the workplace. This means that you need to create a social environment at work that encourages people to form strong autonomous teams that vigorously pursue attainment of business goals and improved performance. Therefore you need to create a social basis for each of the following characteristics of people working together:

- You need carefully prescribed behavior that meets the detailed business expectations of *precision* and *timeliness*.
- You need individual and team behavior to be *collaborative* and *inclusive*.
- You need *autonomous* behavior that is consistent with expectations, even in the absence of management oversight.
- You need organized and focused behavior that *advances your corporate goals*.
- You need to recognize that different individuals may contribute to success in different ways.

This list of the social characteristics of a collaborative and productive workplace is not surprising. Most managers today would easily recognize this list as descriptive of the sort of workplace that they aspire to create. However, similar to establishing the goals of the business, there is little value for managers to carry an informal list of aspirant social characteristics in their heads. The value of this list only comes to fruition when management formalizes its understanding of the social aspects of its intended culture and begins to take specific actions to turn those aspirations into reality for everyone.

The cultural attributes of autonomous work and strategically focused work have been discussed previously. The remaining social considerations can be considered in three categories:

1. Precision and timeliness: change the way your teams get the work done.
2. Collaboration and teamwork: change the way small teams form and communicate.
3. Inclusion and contribution: change the way your business values and includes individuals.

Social Consideration 1: Precision and Timeliness

The *operating* behavior of people and teams within a new industrial culture should be generally directed by the formal objective elements of the culture, including the unifying goals, prescribed rituals, and the rules of practice that apply to all people (as described in Section I and Section II). To that operating behavior you need to add organization-wide *social* standards or norms of group and interpersonal conduct that will also apply to all people. These social standards will describe your expectations for the way that people work together. These will not be merely a business adaptation of the social norms of an external, nonbusiness culture. These will be new social norms that you create to specifically address the need to unite your people into a single high-performing team that is appropriate to the conduct of your business. You want the common or group interpersonal behavior of your organization to be generally directed by social support for the people who uphold the norms of the new culture, balanced by peer pressure directed toward the people who do not.

Obviously the most important part of any consideration of behavior at work is the part where the work gets done. I said in Chapter 2 that even a great strategy will not matter if you lose your customers as you execute the strategy. The same sort of reasoning is true of behavior. Behavior that leads to a world-class pace of autonomous improvement becomes unimportant if you cannot get the routine work done, so let us talk first about the social elements of getting the work done. The basic work of the business benefits from social change when you organize the work to enable autonomous teams to make their own special contribution to routine work as well as improvement.

Key Idea: In most Western industry, although improvement is often practiced in small teams, most of the basic work is done in the traditional mode of individual work assignments. There will always be a need for individual work assignments, when the task is only appropriate to one person or only one person is appropriate to the task. But as your people and managers gain familiarity and competence working in teams, allow the teams to do more. People like working in teams, and when teams can be effective, they can often perform better than individuals acting alone.

If you organize the work so that all you need from your people is strict compliance to objective instructions, then you will not benefit from autonomous teams, and you do not need to consider the social aspects of work. The supervision model of compliance to instructions is largely independent of the several personal cultures that people bring to work because in that model, personal cultures are suppressed. I certainly am not being disrespectful to the supervision model of management. During the post–World War II era, this militaristic or industrial engineering approach was in place for some of the most impressive industrial success in American history, and it is still the management model that is most widely practiced.

> **Example:** When I joined General Motors as a first-line supervisor (called a "foreman" in those days), General Motors was clearly the preeminent automotive manufacturer in the world. My job as a foreman was difficult, but it was not complicated by social considerations. Each person in my group had a clearly defined task that had been well documented by industrial engineers. My job was to be certain that each of them knew the task and the standards and that each one did the task as instructed, without any variation, for as many minutes of each shift as possible.
>
> We were efficient according to our standards, in the way that had made General Motors a great company. But the work was impersonal, and it rarely improved or changed in any important way. Certainly the work almost never changed as the result of input from the workers. Behavior was uniform, but it was also uncreative and uninteresting. Personal or cultural variations in social behavior on the job were largely not visible or not tolerated. Although we were successful to the standards that had made us great, Toyota and others who had different standards began to overtake us.

It is now quite clear that world-class performance cannot be achieved by supervising compliance alone. Without considering the need for improvement, the precise and timely performance required for basic industrial operations today is greater than what can be attained by supervisors monitoring compliance. Autonomous teams are not only useful for improvement, they can be a big help in routine work as well. And the new social expectations that develop within the team will make that help a reality. The first step to obtain this benefit is to subdivide the work of operating the business into the routine, repetitive work and the special work.

How to Handle Routine Work

For routine and repetitive work, where the expectations for performance are well known, it will be possible for the members of mature autonomous teams to assume the primary responsibility to make the work happen. Previously precision, timeliness, and efficiency of routine work were the sole responsibility of the supervisor. Although most team members followed the instructions of the supervisor, most did not overtly support the supervisor beyond that. Certainly very few people supported the supervisor by making independent value judgments about the work or the process, or by addressing the behavior of teammates who did not cooperate. The reason for this lack of support is that in an adaptation of an external social culture into the workplace, there are few business considerations that drive work-related behavior for most people. In an environment of supervision to compliance, there is also a lack of responsibility. People do not have either a social or an objective reason to do more than follow instructions. In contrast, as you move to an autonomous improvement culture, many of the new team rituals that your people will develop and practice do support the supervisor and the business with both social and objective reasons to do more.

The lean practice of *Andon*, or line-stop, is a perfect example. Following this team ritual, when a problem is detected in production, the person who detects it is authorized to stop the production line until the team corrects the problem. Similarly the many techniques of *Poka-yoke*, or mistake recognition and avoidance, enable team members to detect quality problems and respond immediately. These practices and many others keep improvement at the forefront of routine operation by providing opportunities for "instantaneous" or very small event improvement continuously throughout the day.

When Andon, Poka-yoke, and other similar practices become part of the social expectations and rituals for team behavior, many details of routine work can be managed by the team without intervention by the supervisor. Many teams can find other great ways to conduct and improve the routines of industrial work. The social standards of team behavior—including shared expectations, social support, and peer pressure—are the secret to successful practice of these rituals.

Key Idea: The rituals of Andon and Poka-yoke are great examples of behavior that managers frequently observe or study and then attempt to reproduce without first establishing the culture to support them. For example, authorizing people to identify and correct the mistakes of coworkers, as required by Poka-yoke, can be a social disaster if you do not have a strong team culture. Allowing people to stop the line without clear expectations and a strong team response can be both a social and a production disaster.

How to Handle Nonroutine Work

Once the small teams have assumed responsibility for most of the basic production work, then supervisors or team leaders can focus on detailed management of the aspects of the team's assignment that are nonroutine, including those that become nonroutine because of an event of some sort. This is another opportunity to develop synergy between autonomous teams and management. When the details and expectations of operations are certain, the team can use the social rituals of team practice to conduct routine production more successfully than the most attentive supervisor. And if they will do that, then the supervisor can audit the routine work to ensure consistent business oversight and can focus more intently to manage the details of nonroutine work more successfully than before.

When to Begin

I wanted to review the applicability of small-team work to the issue of precision and timeliness in production operations first because those activities constitute most of the work in industry. Autonomous teams can have a very beneficial impact on routine production work. But that is not the place to start your autonomous activities. You should allow your teams to form and mature before you expect them to assume responsibility for the core of your business. Starting first with the hardest and most important aspect of the business is another trap that unwary managers often fall into.

It is best to retain your existing supervisor practice (or whatever practice that you currently employ) to ensure precise operation as you begin to form autonomous teams. Concentrate initially on building strong teams that experience working together autonomously while conducting improvement projects. The success of the team at small-event improvement will determine the ability of the team to later expand their scope to the nearly continuous activity of routine production. Once your teams are really good at autonomous improvement, extending them into autonomous operation is straightforward.

There are three characteristics that will help you to know that your improvement teams are ready to assume a greater role in routine operations:

1. The team functions well as a team. All members are valued and included, and the team has good experience and communications for making decisions and resolving interpersonal differences.
2. The team is providing team leaders with active social support, including exercising personal influence on the behavior of team members who are not cooperative or collaborative.
3. Team members are constantly "aware" of improvement opportunities and projects. Initially this will appear as an increase in the number and quality of proposals for team action. Later it will evolve into the elegant solutions of small teams resulting from extended observation and consideration, as has been described in the discussion of root cause analysis.

Social Consideration 2: Collaboration and Teamwork

Small teams are critical to the success of the organization in an autonomous environment. This is where people spend most of their time and do most of their work. Variation in personal behavior among the members of a small team is one of the most common causes when people do not engage with each other or when small teams fail to perform. This issue was introduced in Chapter 6 as one of the subjective problems that arise during the practice of autonomous improvement. Your teams need to develop the ability to discuss interpersonal differences in a way that is intelligent and inoffensive so that they can create their own local social rituals and practices for team actions that will serve to unite the particular members of each unique team.

> **Example:** This sort of individual small-team discussion and response is represented by the team of the Asian engineer (from Chapter 6 and Chapter 7) that agreed to periodically stop discussions in order to enable her to communicate in her own very polite way. The practice they adopted was important to their team, but it would have been clearly burdensome and inappropriate for most teams.

Key Idea: Autonomous action is the new environment for teamwork that you are creating, and it must be established and nurtured with great care as any truly new aspect of the business would be. Do not assume that your people know how to work in small teams with coworkers who may not be friends just because they know how to play in small teams with people who often are friends. And do not assume that they will spontaneously create social standards for team action that will be effective and inclusive. Management and team leaders have an important role in forming and sustaining high-performing teams.

Although you will be planning to migrate your autonomous teams into broader responsibilities, the first step is to form and develop cohesive teams where all individuals are included and where there is strong collaboration in performing work within the team. As you give teams a formal role in improving the business, you need to establish a formal expectation for the conduct of teams, including the social behavior within a team. Five attributes of personal and team interaction are critical. Sometimes you will develop these five attributes as standards to apply broadly to all people in the enterprise. You will also allow teams to establish additional standards (such as holding very polite meetings) that will be applicable only locally within a particular team. In some situations, there may be a general standard that applies to the entire enterprise and a similar, more rigorous standard that a team chooses to adopt for its own behavior.

The five social considerations of work in small teams are:

1. How do individuals conduct themselves in interpersonal relations with coworkers?
2. How do people form and sustain teams, and how do individuals behave as members of a team?
3. How do people collaborate and conduct work that is not closely supervised?
4. How do people communicate about differences in behavior or expectations?
5. How do people work together to create and implement improvement?

As you establish your teams, management will need to consider and address each of these in a broad sense for the enterprise and team leaders will need to consider each in a local sense for the several teams. Some of these questions are fundamentally answered in the rituals and practices of quality stations. I describe these considerations as social standards or social expectations, but it should be clear that I am addressing the interpersonal and team relations that arise as your culture is applied to the people who are doing the work of the business. Each of these considerations is a business issue as well as a social issue. Management can define how people work together without entering the truly personal areas of social conduct.

As often as possible, management should address each of these considerations by creating rituals of practice or rules of conduct that will be shared equally by all people, broadly across the organization. This will include the basic rituals of quality station practice (described in Chapter 4), as well as other rituals that you find are most appropriate for your situation. Local rituals specific to individual teams will later be derived from, and consistent with, the general practices. You should use the quality station as a core around which you can build a new society of collaboration within each team. Rituals are very powerful ways to prescribe appropriate behavior that also reinforces membership in the culture. "We do it this way" is an important statement for a group to share.

Including the rituals of the quality stations, management must formally establish social standards that apply to all people in the five areas listed above. This formality ensures uniformity of conduct and expectations throughout the business, and it avoids the potential that someone will view the standards of conduct as optional. Interpersonal relations that make the small teams inclusive and effective are far too important to be optional. However, you do not need a general standard for every possible variation of every consideration described above, and certainly you do not need a comprehensive standard for every possible permutation of behavior around those issues. Many of the detailed standards derived from the general standards will be handled in the small teams on an "as needed" basis. You also do not need to do all of this at once. But, following the schedule described in Section V, you should have many of these social standards in place by the start of the third six-month phase of implementation, so that as your small teams develop, they can establish their local practices to be consistent with the general practices.

As soon as you have teams beginning to form, you need to promptly begin visibly treating the social part of work (interpersonal and team relations) as important and begin adopting formal standards that support your aspirations for a collaborative and inclusive workplace. In the early days, the simple fact that you have begun to create social expectations for your workplace will go a long way toward establishing the company as a place with its own situational culture. As you do that, do not hesitate to experience the beneficial impact of social support for your efforts. Your people know that successful teams have standards. If they accept the standards that you set, they will help management maintain the standards within their teams.

Key Idea: I have said that management needs to establish the standards, but in practice, I should have said that management ought to review and approve the standards. Many senior managers have never personally worked on the shop floor, and those who have will often be fooled by their own outdated experience. The first time that I formally began to adopt social standards to describe our expectations for people working together in small teams, I had several well-respected first-line supervisors do the work, and the management team reviewed and approved it. Later I used the cultural design team named "Diversity Pioneers" (described in Chapter 9).

When people accept your standards and behave according to the expectations of the team standards, they will receive social support that will reinforce that behavior. Using well-respected supervisors or your cultural design team to help you in this effort will earn you a lot of early acceptance and support among the general population.

Communicating about Differences within a Team

When you begin to work in collaborative small teams to advance the corporate goals, it is clear that you need to find a way to enable each person to make his or her own best contribution. Individual contributions may be lost in the details as a senior manager considers the entirety of the organization, but individual contributions are very apparent and important in the environment of small teams. Teams need to accept all contributions that are appropriate to the business, and when team actions are unsupervised, these contributions can come in a wide variety. Fortunately, collaborative small teams are really quite good at accommodating differences. As individuals, we literally make value judgments to accept and respect the varied contributions of other individuals every day away from the job. The new part of accepting variations among people at work is a fairly simple extension of that personal experience for everyone except management. It is often managers and not others who most expect that everyone will behave in a consistent and predictable way.

For small teams, contributions in any variety that are clearly additive to, and compatible with, the values, beliefs, and rituals of the organization and are also inoffensive to colleagues and society should receive both management and peer support. Generally that is exactly what happens. The most common difficulty is that some individual behavior may indeed appear to be offensive. At the least, because autonomous action implies that people are no longer simply following uniform instructions, some individual behavior may be confusing to other people at work. When people take actions that team members do not immediately recognize or understand, it is not always clear that a person is collegial and working in support of the team goals. Very often the behavior in question turns out to be just fine; it is only perceived as inappropriate. All that is required is to resolve the misunderstanding.

Key Idea: The interpersonal relations on your new small teams are very intimate, and at that degree of social intensity, relations are both more fragile and more important than people are accustomed to experience at work. You will want to provide your teams with a new paradigm for people to communicate about social matters, especially about differences in behavior. Bringing new teams and diverse team members together requires that people resolve issues of interpersonal behavior that appear to be either offensive or inexplicable to other members of the team.

As discussed in Chapter 7, people behave differently due to differences in personal culture, and personal behavior is interpreted by the cultural standards of each observer. Behavior that may objectively be entirely appropriate may still require some discussion before team members accept it. By a very wide margin, the most common source of interpersonal problems among good, honest, hardworking people is when behavior that one person considers to be normal is misinterpreted by another person as either inappropriate or offensive. When such a misunderstanding occurs, the difference in understanding or perception will hold those individuals and their team apart until there is a resolution.

For example, recall the Asian woman who was too polite to speak when others were speaking. This personal behavior was disruptive to her team's performance because her team believed from her behavior that she was uninterested in their work. Her team members came to believe that she was uninterested because, for most of the team members who observed her behavior, that is the principle reason for which they would not speak during a team meeting. They interpreted her behavior through their own cultural beliefs, and as a result, they assigned to her a bad motive.

> **Example:** When my daughter was in college, she worked one summer as the hostess at a local Mexican restaurant. One evening, my wife and I went to her restaurant for dinner. During a break in the action at the hostess stand, our daughter came to our table to talk with us. My wife and I had both ordered chicken fajitas, and without any of us in the family thinking about it, our daughter ate a piece of chicken from my plate and shortly thereafter, she ate another piece of chicken from my wife's plate.
>
> Almost immediately, the woman at the next table said in an embarrassingly loud voice: "Miss, there is something wrong with our chicken, too."
>
> That woman had observed behavior that she did not understand, filtered it through her own values and beliefs, and had come to the conclusion that the explanation for the odd behavior that she had observed was that we had bad chicken. She, of course, did not realize that the hostess was our daughter, which was the only reason she was eating off our plates. The woman's first assumption, that we had bad chicken, quickly led her to the related belief that she probably had bad chicken as well. My daughter's natural but unexplained behavior led to a customer response that turned out to be very disruptive to the whole group of diners and to the restaurant management.

As you create a culture of rapid improvement through autonomous action, you need to focus on two new social aspects of communicating about behavior that did not exist in the supervision model of management. First, you need managers and other leaders to talk openly about interpersonal behavior as an expectation of the workplace, especially work-related behavior that is the product of your values, beliefs, and rituals. You want to formally communicate that it is appropriate for individuals to behave creatively and naturally so long as that behavior is in support of your business goals and inoffensive. Part of this communication from management will include the behavioral expectations and standards that are set by management for personal interactions in general, as well as the local expectations established within the several teams.

Second, because you will be achieving most of your improvement through small-team actions, you also need to establish a mechanism for all people within the small teams to have intelligent and inoffensive conversations that resolve interpersonal differences in personal behavior that might otherwise hold individuals or teams apart. Management needs to provide the structure for those discussions and positive examples of that practice. Use of the three-part model of culture as the product of values, beliefs, and behavior facilitates this conversation. Management should discuss the model of culture widely to help others to understand what they are teaching and doing. Managers as individuals should use the model as the basis for cultural communication to resolve interpersonal differences.

Encourage people to adopt the social practice of talking about the shared goals of your business. You literally want to create a social situation where all the people comfortably and frequently discuss the business and workplace that they share. This conversation tells you that the objective elements of your business culture are carried in their minds in a way that can effectively guide their routine thinking and actions.

Next, create an environment where people can easily have intelligent and inoffensive conversation about interpersonal differences. The purpose of this communication is to enable people to resolve interpersonal differences before they damage teams or diminish individual performance. Simple conversations of this sort should occur naturally among people without direction or intervention from others. Conversations of intermediate difficulty might be assisted by a team leader, who should have the benefit of some basic training in resolution of interpersonal issues. Still more complex conversations should be facilitated by a significantly capable professional. You will want to have all three levels of capability within your new culture. The following sections explore two quick examples of how a conversation might occur to resolve or avoid interpersonal differences.

Different Expressions of the Same Family Values

Example: My wife and I value our family, and that value led us to believe that it would be good to stay in one place. Accordingly, I managed my career so that I gained international experience through travel, but I avoided relocation. Other executives valued their families, but for them, that value led to the belief that their children would benefit from living abroad. They actively sought opportunities for international relocation. As mentioned before, it is possible for people with the same values to form different beliefs and practice different behaviors.

In a very global company, some of my colleagues believed that I had received a career advantage by staying near headquarters. In return, I believed that they had received an advantage from their experience abroad. In any event, if we had started and finished our discussion of international relocation with our different behaviors, there would be very little common ground. We each could have concluded that the other did not value his or her family in the same way that we do.

However, when we start the discussion with agreement that we share the same family values, there is a real opportunity for very interesting review of our different experiences. Perhaps we would resolve the apparent differences by concluding that both families had acted correctly, given the personalities of the children involved. What is also important is that even if we never resolve the difference, we will not misinterpret each other's behavior in a way that would damage our relationship and our ability to work closely together. People who share the same value but respond differently can have an interesting conversation but are unlikely to assign one another a bad motive. That is a common result of business conversations about personal behavior.

Most conversations that lead to improved understanding of behavior are not difficult or emotional, and they are not lengthy. They simply need to occur. The primary reason that so few explanatory conversations about behavior do occur is that people lack a basis to conduct such conversations in a way that they can be confident will be intelligent and inoffensive. Because everyone recognizes that personal culture is a sensitive topic, without a framework for conducting these conversations intelligently and inoffensively, the conversation often does not take place. In fact, in many businesses, the existing culture actively discourages people from having conversations about prohibited topics such as personal values and beliefs. The promulgation and ritual use of our simple model of culture as the framework for such conversations is an easy enabler for people.

Using the model of culture as a combination of values, beliefs, and behavior provides structure for conversation that can be intelligent, inoffensive, and very useful. Similar to some of the other structures provided in this book, there is nothing so new here that some people do not already do this naturally without the discipline provided by a formal structure. The value of adopting a structure is that, along with encouragement, support, and examples from management, it will enable most people to do something that otherwise only a few will do.

Different Interpretations and Assumptions of a Simple Task: Getting the Mail

Example: Normally my mail carrier delivers our mail about 10:30 each morning. Since I retired, I have gotten in the habit of reading the mail as I eat lunch. One day about 11:30, I went to the mailbox to check the mail and found that it was not there. A new neighbor was gardening and asked if I was expecting something important. I said that I was not.

About noon, I checked the mail again, and it was still not there. The neighbor was still gardening and watched me without comment as I did this. About 12:15, I saw the mail truck through the window so I went to get the mail. As I leafed through the mail while returning to my house, my neighbor asked if I had gotten what I was waiting for.

I realized then that although I had specifically told him that I was not looking for important mail, he believed from my behavior in visiting the mailbox three times in 45 minutes that I must be looking for something. In fact, I concluded that since I had earlier denied that I was looking for something special, my new neighbor probably believed that I was not only looking for important mail, but that I had misrepresented that to him.

So I stopped to reassure him. I was not looking for special mail. I was just hungry, and I was waiting for the mail to read before I had my lunch. This was probably an unimportant event, but this was a new relationship with a new neighbor, and an extra minute of conversation made sure that the unimportant event stayed that way—and that my neighbor did not believe I was misleading or lying to him about what was truly a simple task.

As you and your people gain greater facility with the relationship between behavior and beliefs, many small conversations will result in the resolution of many interpersonal differences before they mature into workplace obstacles.

All three of the examples mentioned in this chapter (chicken, relocation, and mail) were personal to me. Cultural conversations to resolve differences in behavior that are inexplicable or offensive to someone are always personal. And each of these examples was easily resolved (maybe less easily with the chicken episode). It is normally easy to resolve or avoid interpersonal problems if your people have a method and an example for conducting these conversations in a way that is intelligent and inoffensive. Even the more significant example of the quiet Asian engineer was resolved quickly once the team began to discuss it.

> **Key Idea:** As it turned out, the Asian woman had previously considered how to resolve the issue, but she waited to be asked before offering her simple solution. It is also important that after the team had formally acknowledged that she was a trusted and valued member by accommodating her communications style, her contributions became easier and more natural. In just a short time, although the team remained very polite, it was often difficult for an outsider to observe that they were acting differently from most other teams. Also, it is important to know that once she had reached a successful resolution with her first team, she was able to move to other teams and offer her proposal for polite team action without waiting to be asked. The interpersonal difference, once resolved, remained resolved.

How to Handle Aberrant Behavior

There are, however, behaviors that really are inappropriate and cannot be resolved by discussion. In those cases, management must establish formal standards for appropriate behavior, and management needs to enforce those standards. Social support and peer pressure are fine for modest adjustments to individual behavior, but behavior that intentionally disrupts the team or greatly offends the team members cannot be corrected by the team. Unfortunately in industry, the extreme social measures (such as shunning or exclusion from society) that might be employed to correct offensive behavior in social situations must be reserved exclusively to management. If management has the sole responsibility, then management must take action. The teams are counting on you to do your part.

Social Consideration 3: Inclusion and Contribution

In most industrial cultures today, management recognizes the value of people as a general concept, but it very rarely recognizes the value of individuals. In an inclusive culture of rapid improvement, individuals and the different contributions that individuals can make become important. Therefore, *including* and *valuing* individuals is essential to establishing a culture of rapid improvement. In this instance, your business needs to change both formal and social practices to ensure that all individuals are included and valued. No other element of the social design will unite your people if it is apparent that management allows some individuals within the group to be diminished or excluded from the society at work.

Including and valuing all of the individuals who work with you is, by far, the most difficult and comprehensive social change that you will undertake. The problem is that the existing concept of valuing "people" contemplates average behavior that is well within the expectations of management. "Individuals," on the other hand, often display a much wider range of behavior, especially in Western industry.

> **Example:** While I was representing the United States at the Japan Business Study Program, I was speaking with a very senior executive at a well-known Japanese company about comparative advantages between the United States and Japan. He surprised me by observing that the single biggest advantage he enjoyed was that all his people were Japanese.
>
> Further conversation revealed that he believed all his people knew how to work together; they naturally, routinely, and properly understood and responded to the subtle signals received from the behavior of teammates and management. The very homogeneous Japanese society naturally produced very homogeneous work teams of individuals who understood the social and corporate needs of collaboration.

In a very homogeneous social culture such as Japan, there is no difficulty translating a corporate value for people into a corporate value for individuals. There is not much difference between the average behavior of people as a whole and the natural behavior of individuals. There is a large body of social support that will assist management in sustaining normal behavior in the workplace.

> **Example:** When I first heard the Japanese industrial slogan "The nail that sticks up is quickly pounded down," I thought it was a statement about quality. I later learned that it is a comment on social behavior at work. Industrial behavior in Japan has strong social norms. And those norms are effectively regulated by peers, not management.

Most of us in North America and Western Europe do not experience such a homogeneous social or work environment. In fact, in comparison, the diversity of our society is enormous and appears to be growing daily. If you want to experience the benefit of a shared social culture at work within a very diverse society, then you have to create such a culture on purpose. More specifically, you need to create the social elements of a culture that matches your people. Where the Japanese industrial culture values homogeneous behavior and team consensus, we need a work culture that includes all the different people in our society and recognizes the importance and unique value of the different contributions that different people can make.

Key Idea: Let me say again that you need to establish a culture that uniquely fits your business and your people. The early adopters of lean manufacturing and other Japanese practices attempted to use the technologies as well as the rituals exactly as they had been developed in Japan. As a result, those early adopters often failed. In contrast, we began to have great success when we learned to separate the technology from the rituals, so that we could use the new tools in a way that suited our own people.

A starting place for including individuals into the corporate culture is for management to demonstrate objectively observable behavior that is consistent with valuing individuals. I am not suggesting that you value or even tolerate aberrant behavior. But good, honest behavior that advances the goals of your business and is inoffensive to coworkers should be acceptable in a wider variety than is common in industry today. Valuing individuals is the most complex and difficult of the three social elements of your new culture. Because there is a lot of content in both the theory and practice of including individuals, the full discussion of this consideration of social design is provided in Chapter 9, which is devoted to that topic.

Summary of Chapter 8

- Each company needs to design the *social elements of its own culture* in a way that is specifically appropriate to its own business and its own people.
- There are *three major elements* to designing the social elements of your new culture:
    1. Change the way your teams get the work done.

2. Change the way small teams form and communicate.
3. Change the way that the business *values and includes individuals*.

- To change the way your teams get work done:
  - Start first with team-based improvement and migrate to routine work.
  - Distinguish between routine work and nonroutine work.
  - Ensure that mature autonomous teams conduct most routine work where the standards are well known in the same way that they conduct other team-based activities.
  - Keep in mind that when teams are conducting routine work, the team leaders can focus on nonroutine work. This is an example of the synergy between autonomous teams and management. The existence of autonomous teams will make both routine and nonroutine work better than it has been.
  - Recognize when teams are sufficiently mature to move beyond improvement projects—specifically, when
    - The teams function well as a team.
    - The teams provide social support for team leaders.
    - Team members are constantly "aware" of improvement opportunities and projects.
- To change the way that small teams form and communicate:
  - Establish standard expectations for interpersonal behavior consistent with the values and beliefs of your organization and people for the following social considerations:
    - How do individuals conduct themselves in interpersonal relations with coworkers?
    - How do people form and sustain teams, and how do individuals behave as members of a team?
    - How do people collaborate and conduct work that is not closely supervised?
    - How do people communicate about differences in behavior or expectations?
    - How do people work together to create and implement improvement?
  - Establish expectations and practices for interpersonal communications to resolve differences.
  - Accept management responsibility to address aberrant behavior.

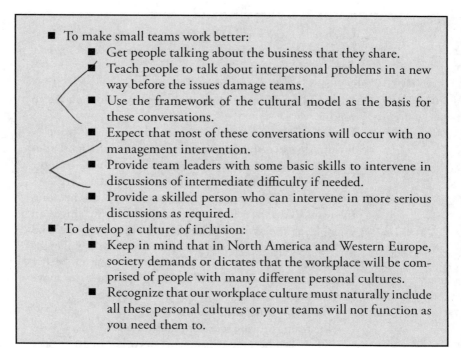

- To make small teams work better:
    - Get people talking about the business that they share.
    - Teach people to talk about interpersonal problems in a new way before the issues damage teams.
    - Use the framework of the cultural model as the basis for these conversations.
    - Expect that most of these conversations will occur with no management intervention.
    - Provide team leaders with some basic skills to intervene in discussions of intermediate difficulty if needed.
    - Provide a skilled person who can intervene in more serious discussions as required.
- To develop a culture of inclusion:
    - Keep in mind that in North America and Western Europe, society demands or dictates that the workplace will be comprised of people with many different personal cultures.
    - Recognize that our workplace culture must naturally include all these personal cultures or your teams will not function as you need them to.

Chapter 9

Valuing Individuals

Key Idea: The official policies and practices of most existing corporate cultures intentionally ignore individual differences. The expectation apparently is that people of different cultures will either adapt to the culture of the business or become culturally invisible in the workplace. The people who are diminished or excluded by these practices can never become full contributors to a culture of rapid improvement.

Of the three elements of social design described in Chapter 8, one requires a much more detailed description. Therefore this chapter describes the theory and practice of *valuing individuals at work* and especially the challenging practice of learning to value distinctive individual behavior.

Five Elements of Valuing Individuals

There are five elements to creating a corporate culture that obviously values individuals—each is described briefly here and in more detail in the rest of this chapter:

1. *Awareness.* People are inherently different. When management attempts to eliminate or suppress differences, or when people attempt to hide their differences, individuals who are different become *less engaged, less energetic,* and *less creative.* Management and others in your new culture need to be

actively aware of the differences among individuals and be prepared to discuss and accommodate those differences in ways that are intelligent and inoffensive while sustaining the work of the enterprise. Simply creating a general awareness of the issue of individual cultural differences and providing your organization with the model of cultures presented in Chapter 1 as a tool to discuss differences is an enormous benefit.

2. *Support.* Cultural change is an emotional event for many people, and some people will need specific emotional support during the transition. Management needs to provide early and specific support for individuals and for affinity groups of individuals with shared interests as they work to align their personal cultures with the evolving new culture of the workplace. This emotional support will enable people to join with you in the improvement effort prior to completing the entirety of the social change throughout the business, which is necessarily a slow process.

3. *Policies and Practices.* Talking about social and cultural change is fine, but everyone in your business understands that the cultural change is not sustainable until management changes the way it conducts the business to formalize and validate cultural change within the business model. As an absolute minimum, management needs to formulate and disseminate an official policy that prohibits harassment of any individual based on any of his or her personal attributes. Management needs to review the other policies and practices of the business to make formal, objective changes in the way the business values and includes individuals.

4. *Enforcement.* Cultural change that produces an enterprise-wide team of equally engaged and productive people also redistributes some of the joy and reward of work. Someone is certain to feel that this redistribution has resulted in the loss of a benefit to them that they previously considered as an entitlement. Such a person is likely to challenge or disrupt the changes. Therefore management needs to have a structure for enforcing appropriate behavior when the new policies and practices are challenged, in the same way that management would enforce compliance with other corporate policies and practices. Strictly enforcing the policy against personal harassment is the minimum step that is essential to demonstrating a new corporate value for individuals.

5. *Celebration.* Finally, management needs to provide a forum for openly celebrating cultural success. We celebrate success at reaching other business goals, and we ought to celebrate this as well. Celebration is more than an event. Celebration is an opportunity for you and your team to take a formal look backward to see how far you have come and an acknowledgement that you are successfully doing a good thing together.

The following sections describe how to develop each of these five elements, with examples from my own experience.

Element 1: Develop Corporate Awareness That Individuals Are Different and Valuable

The first step in creating a social culture that values individuals is as easy as developing a visible corporate awareness that individuals are different and that each is valuable. I have already discussed in some detail the loss of engagement, energy, and creativity that often results from hiding or ignoring differences. With that in mind, you have a business need to recapture that lost human capability for your improvement efforts. To create a corporate culture of rapid improvement, you need a social culture of inclusion. You need a culture where management and others acknowledge the value of individuals and the different contributions that can arise from those individual differences.

> **Example:** In Chapter 8 I described my conversation with the Japanese executive who believed that his greatest asset was that all his people were Japanese. In a society that places great value on consensus, that may be true: a team of very homogeneous individuals will coalesce quickly, and the consensus actions of that team will be quite effective.
>
> However, as mentioned in Chapter 8, North American and Western European businesses have teams that are necessarily comprised of different individuals. By respecting those differences, we can realize a uniquely valuable benefit. At different times and in different situations, any individual might step forward to make a valuable personal contribution that is enabled primarily because that individual is different is some way from others.

You want a culture that enables all people to acknowledge the existence of personal differences and discuss them intelligently and inoffensively. Awareness is the opposite of the corporate and military tradition of "Don't ask, don't tell." When behavior in the workplace is unexpected and unexplained (similar to my family's chicken fajitas incident described in Chapter 8), you and your people need to feel comfortable in asking about that behavior, and you need to have the capability for an intelligent and inoffensive discussion that makes the behavior understandable, in a way that keeps your teams together.

> **Key Idea:** This is not a social services program. I am not asking that you find the value in people who are not capable of working successfully in your business. Instead, I am suggesting that many of the people you have already selected to be part of your business have value far beyond that which you are allowing them to bring to work today.

Keep in mind the restaurant customer who believed that she had bad chicken and the new neighbor who may have thought I had misled him about the mail, both examples of unexplained behavior that I offered in Chapter 8. The point of these examples was that unexpected and unexplained behavior is naturally suspicious. If you are not able to talk about it in an intelligent and inoffensive way, then you are likely to conclude that the unexplained behavior is in fact bad behavior. That prejudice against unexpected and unexplained behavior works in several directions in the workplace:

- First, the behavior of management often offends people because it appears to be unresponsive to people who are different. Management is seen to reward only behavior that conforms to the expectations of management's personal culture. Possibly management ignores or even punishes behavior that does not conform.
- Second, teams and individuals often suppress or alter their natural behavior within a work culture that does not recognize differences, and thus some people do not contribute creativity and energy to support a manager or a business that inflexibly demands uniform behavior.
- Third, individual behavior that is unexpected or unexplained can cause interpersonal distrust or disagreement that will keep teams from forming or from operating effectively.

There are two management challenges in considering the issue of awareness:

1. Management must demonstrate that it is aware of individuals and that management is commencing to act in a way that values individuality.
2. Management needs to provide to team leaders and other people (who would not normally want to engage in a discussion of behavior) a way in which they can comfortably engage in such discussion.

Similar to the practice of improvement using the framework of quality stations (described in Chapter 4), providing a framework for the discussion of behavior is often the catalyst that makes that conversation possible for many people. The framework that I like is the values, beliefs, and behavior model of culture. The use of that model for cultural conversation is described in Chapter 8. With a framework such as this to support the conversation, it becomes possible for people to ask about behavior that they do not understand. Instead of quietly assuming that there is a problem, people who can comfortably ask about unexpected behavior often will do so. This is especially true if they understand that their inquiry has an obvious business purpose and is accepted as a social ritual of the business by management and by others. Discussion of behavior is the vehicle for keeping the teams together. In most circumstances, the discussions are easy, even superficial.

> **Example:** At the mailbox (the example I described in Chapter 8), I could have said something to my neighbor such as, "I know it appears that I am looking for something special in the mail, but I am not. I generally read the mail during lunch. Today the mail is late, and I am hungry. I have been waiting for the mail because I want lunch, not because I am expecting anything of interest."
>
> Similarly, in the restaurant example described in Chapter 8, instead of assuming that the chicken was bad and commenting disruptively on her assumption, the customer at the next table could have said to my daughter, "It is unusual to see a restaurant employee eating from customers' plates. Could I ask why you are doing that?"

Whether self-initiated or in response to an inoffensive question, the potentially disruptive event of misunderstanding someone's behavior can be avoided quite quickly. Unimportant events will remain unimportant. Encouragement from management and peers, a recognized business purpose, and a structure for the communication are the basis for the new conversations of cultural awareness and understanding among individuals.

In some situations, the interpersonal cultural issues are more complex or more emotional. In those cases, a more detailed discussion is required that uses more of the complete three-part structure of communicating about the cultural elements.

> **Example:** A teammate of the Asian woman engineer (first mentioned at the end of Chapter 6) might have asked her: "Engineering is a really valuable resource for our work, but you do not often participate in the discussion. Could I ask why not?"
>
> Following the cultural model, her answer could be: "I am an Asian woman, and I have been taught to value politeness. I believe that carefully considering what I say before I say it is a way to

ensure that I never offend anyone. But the discussions of this group proceed so fast that while I am considering what I might say about one topic, the discussion moves on to another, and I never get a chance to contribute. I would like to participate more, but I need you to help me."

It is important to recognize that the examples of the Asian engineer and my conversation at the mailbox are both a fair summary of the very simple conversations that actually took place. The Asian engineer already knew what the problem was and had formulated a way to resolve it. But consistent with her beliefs, she was not able to initiate that conversation until someone asked her about the issue.

> **Key Idea:** The most difficult part of most of these conversations to resolve potentially disruptive interpersonal misunderstanding is ensuring that they happen. Many small concerns such as these can clear themselves up promptly with a little private conversation.

For more serious or deeply emotional issues or for interpersonal discussions that stop being intelligent and inoffensive, there is a role for the team leader or even for a person who has special training or ability to lead the discussions. Often the team leaders will be the first to try resolving the interpersonal issues of the team. If they can achieve a resolution without outside assistance, that outcome is a great affirmation of the team's relationship with the team leader. However, if the interpersonal problems continue or worsen, then this is a classic situation where the leader of a nonfunctional team needs external help, and it is an obligation of management to provide it.

Recognize That Many Personal Qualities Are a Mixed Blessing

I like to use anecdotes from my own experience to discuss the ways that different individuals can bring different value to the business. Often I introduce these stories with a comment on the 1993 movie *Shadowlands*, because there is a great discussion of human values in that movie, which is the true story of professor and author C. S. Lewis. He led a comfortable but solitary life until he met and married poet Joy Gresham. After a brief period together, which completely changed his life, she was diagnosed with terminal cancer. Lewis was inconsolable with grief over the coming loss. At that point in the movie, Gresham tells Lewis that the pain of losing a loved one is just the other half of the joy of being together.

I have found that many people have some personal characteristics that benefit from a similar understanding. For most people in business, and certainly for many people who have a personal culture that is different from the current culture of your organization, there is some part of their behavior that is perfect; that is why you hired them. That aspect of each individual brings real joy to management and true value to the business. At the same time (or on the other side of the coin), there is another part of their personal behavior that you may want to be different. But often I find that the two halves are evenly matched and one characteristic exists because of the other. Consider the following two examples.

> **Example 1:** I was on a sales trip with a colleague when he got a phone call from his wife informing him that one of his sons had broken an arm at school. I told him to go home. I could finish the trip alone. He replied that his wife had the situation under control and there was nothing more that he could do. Besides, he added, he had seven sons, and if he went home every time one of them had an injury, he might never finish a trip.

> **Example 2:** At the other end of the spectrum is a woman who worked as our diversity coordinator. She had a wonderful intuitive capability to understand how people think and feel about changes in the workplace, and she therefore provided me with an invaluable service throughout a period of intense change. However, when the editors from *Industry Week* magazine were coming to assess us for designation as one of "America's Ten Best" plants, she was scheduled to make an important presentation, but she chose to stay at home that day with a sick relative. In her place, she arranged for a colleague to make the presentation.

Both of those people had personal cultures that provided real contributions in some situations, and they also had personal cultures that appeared as real weaknesses in other situations. If I needed someone to undertake a customer trip with some certainty that it would proceed as planned, I know who I would ask. But I would not ask that man to help me assess the emotions of the people in the plant. Or, if I need to know the emotional status of my organization in order to assess the health of the changes in progress, I again know who to ask, but I probably would not ask her to commit to a long round of critical sales calls. The *Shadowlands* observation is often true: the part of a person's behavior that might be a weakness in one situation is often just the other half of the personal characteristics that makes them a strong performer in another situation.

It is the responsibility of management to recognize and demonstrate awareness of differences among people, including both the strengths and weaknesses of each person. This demonstration will occur when management is present in person at the team level, at the quality station, and in discussions both private and public. At the corporate level, recognition of the value of individual differences will appear in the formal policies and practices that we adopt, the way that we lead change, and in the support that we give the teams of distinct individuals. This is not to imply in any way that people will just do what they are good at or what they enjoy. People have basic assignments, and those need to be done and done well.

In the second example above, although our diversity coordinator did not come to the office on the day of the presentation, she had prepared it and arranged a completely satisfactory substitute.

> **Key Idea:** The disappointment that our diversity coordinator was not there to make the presentation herself was my personal response to her actions. That response was part of my culture, not an objective result of the business outcome. The business outcome was fine, and although she was not there, she had ensured that the business outcome would be fine. I just needed to learn how to live with that.

Element 2: Provide Emotional and Social Support during Cultural Changes

Cultural change begins with communication. As you begin to talk openly about the social and operating changes inherent in valuing and including individuals, people will become interested. When you begin to talk about changing the policies and practices of the business to ensure fair and equal engagement of all people, then people will become very interested, albeit in possibly different ways: people will be enthusiastic, worried, or watchful. A critical consideration for management is to understand that many people, especially people of difference, will be ready for a cultural change long before you can put all the necessary changes in policy and practice uniformly in place throughout your organization.

As you begin to communicate about the changes that are occurring and those that will occur in the future, you raise expectations and you enhance consciousness of the current situation, which may not be as wonderful for everyone as you think it is. This effect will be especially true among people who receive formal training to help you facilitate the changes or who otherwise participate in the design and implementation of the changes. They are exposed to the coming changes in a very intense way. Therefore your business needs to provide emotional and social support during the cultural changes to enable your people to communicate more openly about the changes and their emotional response to those changes. The essence of the support is to provide people with a safe venue for focused conversation.

You want people to share ideas and experiences in a nonconfrontational environment. To facilitate this discussion, you will want to provide a discussion forum for sharpening the focus of their understanding on common issues. The principle reason for management to provide this support is that people have concerns about the cultural change, and the cultural change may highlight other personal issues that are either extremely important or deeply emotional. You want those issues to be discussed first among friends, rather than exposing those issues for the first time in an emotional or confrontational discussion with management or teammates. In a support group that shares common interests, the emotions are part of the discussion rather than a barrier to communication. This allows people and management to benefit later from the more focused and less emotional communication that is obtained when people have rehearsed their ideas prior to sharing them with others.

Dealing with "Heritage" Issues

Beyond improved communication on practical matters, there are many issues of cultural change that are purely emotional. There is no objective content to the discussion of these issues; they represent only an emotional response to the changing situation that needs to be discussed before the air is clear. Many of these issues and events are heritage issues, often from many years ago. There really is nothing that current management can, or even should, do to address these heritage issues. Often, though, the issues still feel current to those who were involved, and it is not apparent until after they have been thoroughly discussed that the event at issue really occurred, for example, during the 1960s and not last week.

Example: I would love to give you the details of how I came to this understanding. It is a great story. Unfortunately the individual involved would be too easily identified. What I can tell you is that at the time we were doing this work, he was a well-respected manager with a very successful career. Yet before he could be a full participant in leading cultural change, he needed to talk with someone about the fact that in his first job, his coworkers would not eat lunch with him. There was nothing tangible that he wanted or needed, but he did have an emotional need to share his experience with others who would understand.

Despite the impossibility of a current objective resolution, these heritage issues are an impediment to progress until they have been discussed and receive a subjective resolution or an emotional closure. Sharing the issues among similarly situated friends in an environment of optimism for the future is often all the resolution possible or needed.

Establish Affinity Groups

The most common way for management to provide this support is to enable people to meet in affinity groups. For example, there might be a group of women technicians, or a group of black professional men, or other groups who feel that they have something to discuss among themselves. It is best to allow people to pick their own groups. For example, I once attempted to start an affinity group for all women, only to be quickly told in no uncertain terms that the women technicians had very different issues from the professional women, who had issues that were also different from the clerical and administrative women, wherever they worked.

The support that my managers and I provided for affinity groups was quite simple:

- We offered a place for the group to meet.
- We formally and broadly announced the meeting so that all interested people had the opportunity to attend.
- We provided light refreshments.
- We provided a facilitator for their meetings.

The meetings were always scheduled outside of work hours, although lunchtime was an acceptable time to meet, and if a lunchtime meeting was selected, then the refreshment we provided was a simple lunch. By providing a place on our site for the meetings and by providing refreshments, we put our money where our mouth was. The meetings were understood by everyone to be officially sanctioned by management, because we paid for them to occur.

Facilitate Meetings of Affinity Groups

We always provided a facilitator for each meeting of an affinity group because we wanted to be certain that no affinity group discussion ever degenerated into an "ain't it awful?" complaint session. The meetings of the affinity groups had a business purpose to clarify understanding and proposals relative to current issues and cultural change. If necessary, a discussion to clear away the emotions of old issues was appropriate, but the facilitator always returned the group to the forward-looking objectives and retained the positive environment of optimism for the future. The charge that each affinity group was given was to help us make forward progress in defining ways for the new culture to become more inclusive and for the members of their group to become more engaged and more successful contributors to the overall success of the business. There is no benefit from looking back in anger, and we worked diligently and carefully to avoid that.

The affinity groups became surprisingly popular and productive. Several—including the group of black professional men and the professional women's group—spontaneously began community initiatives in the local schools, providing role models, mentoring, and specific help in math and science to local children. In the community close to our plant, many children had not previously been in contact with successful black and women scientists and engineers. This voluntary effort that the groups created was a great value to the children of our community—and a great value to the participating members of these affinity groups.

All of the affinity groups effectively filled their business role as described above:

- They provided group members a safe forum to share emotional discussion.
- They focused positive discussions for the future.
- They provided management with a test market for new ideas.

In more than seven years of close work with many different affinity groups, I never experienced a single disappointment because a group lost its focus or became more negative than positive.

Unexpected Affinity Groups

We had some groups that sprang into existence that were surprising to us. One such group called itself the "Eagles": this was the pronunciation they chose for the acronym of their group, which was the "Exxon Gay and Lesbian Employees" (EGLEs), although the group ultimately changed its name to ELAN, for "Exxon Lifestyle Awareness Network." It turned out that we had colleagues who lived a variety of alternative lifestyles. We became the first major part of a multinational corporation in America to meet with the group Parents, Friends, and Family of Lesbians and Gays (PFFLAG). Because our employees told us that it was needed—and this was several years before most other businesses recognized the existence of unique lifestyle issues at work—we were actively and productively involved in including our colleagues who shared those issues.

Establish a Group of "Diversity Pioneers"

Another way to provide people with emotional support during the cultural changes is to form a central entity that represents people in the details of the cultural design. The intent is for management to obtain the advice of people throughout your organization in a more formal way. This includes people of different personal cultures, as well as a fair cross section of the different businesses and occupations within the organization.

For example, I once had such a group of about 20 people who met with me for a half day or for a long lunch once a month; we called ourselves the "Diversity Pioneers." We candidly discussed the cultural changes that were in progress, including the policy and practice changes to be reviewed in the next section of this chapter. We discussed how the different individuals and groups felt about the state of the business. We discussed changes that were in progress and the new issues that were arising. I heard directly from them, and they heard directly from me. They represented their constituents to me, and they represented management to their constituents. This arrangement worked well for at least seven years, with not a single disappointment to me.

As we developed experience discussing important human issues, the pioneers became very close and very trusting. In one meeting, a member shared a personal secret that turned out to be an excellent contribution to advance a discussion in progress, but which the member wished to retain as a personal secret. To the best of my knowledge, 5 years later, when I no longer had routine contact with that group, not one of the 20 people in the room had broken that confidence. That sort of mutual respect and trust enabled us to do many things of great value for our business and for our colleagues. In addition to serving as a further layer of emotional support for people experiencing change, the Diversity Pioneers also served as advisors to management in the details of the cultural design.

Element 3: Establish New Policies and Practices for Your New Culture

Communications, strategies, a framework for discussion, support groups, and central representation all help get you moving in the right direction. But the people of your company all understand that real change that is sustainable occurs in business when something of substance changes in the way you conduct your business. As you lead cultural change, you will need to be prepared to make a substantive change in the way you conduct the formal business of managing people.

For example, to my certain knowledge, Exxon has always had a great internal and external reputation as a place where very real diligence and discipline went into selecting the best qualified person for each promotion. As managers, my staff and I were very proud of how diligently and well we worked that task. Unfortunately everyone but the managers understood that there was really a separate issue, which was: "How does a person *become* the best qualified?"

Among the qualifications considered for promotions were special assignments, training classes and training assignments, multiple-post qualification, filling in for an absent supervisor, making presentations to management, and many other things. What everyone but management recognized is that, although we were genuinely careful to consider all these things (and more) in order to select the truly best qualified candidate, we exercised almost no senior management control over how an individual became most qualified. Individual supervisors generally had personal discretion to decide whether a person on their team received any or all of these preparations for promotion.

As we began to consider the need for revisions to our policies and practices in support of our desired cultural changes, the issues related to promotional preparation were communicated to me through the Diversity Pioneers mentioned in the previous section. In response, we changed the formal policies governing personnel development. Most of the qualifying assignments and related training that led to promotion were soon covered by formal criteria, including management and peer review, to ensure that everyone who wanted to qualify for promotion had a fair chance to become qualified.

Key Idea: This was a real and visible change in the way that we conducted the human side of the business, and it was a very important step in convincing the larger population that we were serious about establishing a new culture of inclusion. I was very fortunate to find this opportunity. Although the change was very significant, it was almost completely noncontroversial. It provided a great boost to the credibility of our efforts with very little impact on the emotional health of the organization.

This particular change of policy happened to be fully within my personal authority. As time went on, there were other changes to policies and practices that were identified and implemented because we believed locally that they were needed and because locally we were authorized to make those changes. There were also some proposed changes that were far enough beyond my personal authority that I could not authorize them. That was probably the proper outcome. Those changes, had they occurred at my site, would have created an internal inconsistency with the rest of the corporation far beyond my personal ability to predict or manage the outcome. Just like the laboratory manager that I have mentioned several times in this book (beginning in the Section I introduction), a manager with less than complete responsibility for the enterprise always needs to consider the impact of his or her actions on the larger organization.

That limit on my authority meant, however, that there were times when all or most of my advisors, including the Diversity Pioneers, agreed that a proposed change in the policies or practices of administering people would be good for us, but I had to tell them that those changes could not be implemented. Although I usually believed that the proposed changes would be good for us, I could not allow us to do things that would be good for us but bad for others. Unless you are the CEO of an independent corporation, this dilemma will happen to you, too. As you engage others to help you in cultural design, be prepared for people to identify to you the policies and practices that they believe need to change. In many cases, as you begin the effort, the people who you enlist to help will already know of several situations that have bothered them for years. Use your own business judgment and the good advice of your culture design team to sort through the recommendations to find those of real value. Remember that the design team represents their constituents to you, and they should also represent the design team (including you as the design team leader) to their constituents. There will certainly be recommendations that you cannot or will not adopt, and the design team should help you communicate those decisions within the positive context of changes that do happen.

Finally, do not try to change everything that needs to be changed at one time. The social elements of culture change are much more of an evolution than other aspects of industrial improvement. Always change at a pace that most of your team can support and nearly all of your team can tolerate. The details of assessing and responding to the emotional health of your organization as it experiences change are discussed in Chapter 10.

Element 4: Enforcement of Your New Culture's Policies and Practices

Unfortunately for everyone involved, this topic is exactly what it sounds like. As you change your culture, and especially as you change your formal policies and practices, there will certainly be someone who wants to test the system to be sure you are serious. The principle reason to expect this challenge is that there will be people who perceive that they are losing an advantage or an entitlement that they have historically enjoyed. Before they give that up, someone will want to test your resolve. Other people may just challenge change as part of the act to preserve their role as the class clown of the workplace (as discussed in Chapter 7).

The management issue is that you need to be well positioned before this challenge happens. Prior to the first challenge, you need to communicate clearly that the new policies and practices of inclusion are formal expectations for the conduct of the business. Respect for the new culture is an expectation of employment. In other words, you need to communicate in advance of an occurrence that a serious violation of the new policies and practices will be treated with exactly the same dignity as a serious violation of all other work rules for your company. Hopefully this communication alone will head off most of the challenges, or at least make the challenger cautious enough that, when it comes, the challenge will result in counseling rather than punishment. Almost certainly, though, someday there will be a significant challenge. When that challenge comes, everyone who wonders if you are serious about making cultural changes will be watching closely to see what you do.

The first task of management is to make clear communications of formal policies and practices so that there is no uncertainty as to what is expected of people. After that, if a challenge occurs, you need to have a plan in place for responsive actions that convince your people that you have acted in a manner that they respect. This is usually simple: treat the new policies and practices exactly as you currently treat existing policies. Then, of course, you actually need to respond to the violation.

The policies and practices for the social elements of your new culture are needed to engage all your people in the business. They are a significant part of meeting the new performance expectations, not just a nice thing to do for people. As such, these new policies are neither more nor less important than the policies and practices that you employ to manage any other part of running your business. Therefore you need to be prepared to support them in that way.

Element 5: Celebration of Your Cultural Change

This topic is also just what it seems to be. There are a great many reasons to celebrate as culture change occurs. There will be specific changes of real importance, and there will be exceptional people who become heroes among their colleagues. Together, these will result in tangible benefits that improve the life and engagement of your people and make your business more successful.

I have always enjoyed formal celebration of achievements as a great way for teams to get together and look back with joy at what they have achieved. In a culture of rapid improvement, I often experience that the focus and speed of improvement means that as soon as one step forward is completed, the next one to be undertaken is readily apparent. As such, there is a tendency to constantly look ahead to the next task that needs attention. Occasionally stopping for a moment so that everyone together can take a formal look back, which recognizes and appreciates how far you have come, is truly valuable.

Formal celebration does not always imply a major event at an off-site venue. An organized pause in the activities of the day is often just right for the purpose. Maybe it is because I am married to an Italian, but I believe that this is normally better if there is food involved in some way. A practice I have followed with some success is to have a catered lunch brought to the plant for the team or the larger entity that has something to celebrate. At least here in the Houston area, it is possible to get a lunch steak, a baked potato, apple cobbler with ice cream, and a glass of ice tea prepared and delivered for about $10 per person. As another option, many of our teams enjoy doing their own cooking, so we acquired a BBQ pit on wheels that we haul around the plant for that purpose.

I like to tell people on Friday that at lunch on the next Wednesday, there will be a celebration of a particular achievement. That gives people time to think about their success and look forward to the celebration. Anticipation enhances the emotional value that they receive from the event. I always try to be very clear that we are celebrating a recognizable specific event or outcome. People derive very little real pleasure from unspecified recognition. The quality stations (described in Chapter 4) will help you achieve this goal of recognizing specific accomplishments. Through the quality station process, management can always be quite specific about identifying an achievement in detail. Your people can talk among themselves about what they have done from Friday until Wednesday. On Wednesday, management can say a few simple words, and then join the team for lunch. That is enough. This is a time for collegial interaction, not speeches from management.

Normally the team or department/division-level celebrations on site are focused on specific goal-oriented operating improvements. At least once a year I like to have a larger event that reaches broadly across the enterprise and is focused more specifically on culture changes. When we had such an event, we invited everyone to nominate coworkers who had made a special difference. As part of the nomination, it was necessary to provide some specific details of what had been done. The nominees were then invited to a dinner off site. Everyone who was nominated by anyone else was invited. The only limit on participation was that there could be no self-nomination. Our theory was that if someone thought that an individual deserved recognition, then that nomination was enough to secure an invitation to attend our dinner. In several years of following this practice, I was never once disappointed that an unworthy or disruptive person came to our dinner. While at the dinner, a few individuals who had made widely recognized contributions were given personal recognition in the form of a small trophy. The dinners were naturally more formal than the lunches, but still relatively inexpensive.

Both dinners and lunches were just for fun. People enjoy celebrating specific success, and I like to do it for large and small groups as often as we appropriately have a reason to celebrate. For example, I had a videotape made of our first annual cultural celebration. Whenever I watch it, I see that there was more pure human emotion at that event than at all prior corporate gatherings I had attended, combined. For the first time, many of us looked at each other and knew that together we had done—and would continue to do—something of great importance. We were creating a culture of inclusion that truly valued and engaged all people for their different capabilities and contributions.

Summary of Chapter 9

- The next step in designing a corporate culture of inclusion is *creating a corporate practice of valuing individuals*. This is an extension of the existing corporate practice of valuing people generally.
- There are *five major elements* of a culture that values individuals:
    1. *Awareness.* Management and others need to be actively aware of the differences among individuals and be prepared to discuss and accommodate those differences in ways that are intelligent and inoffensive, while sustaining the work of the enterprise.
    2. *Support.* Management needs to provide early and specific support for individuals and for affinity groups of individuals as they work to align their personal cultures with the evolving new culture of the workplace.
    3. *Policies and Practices.* Management needs to review the policies and practices of the business to make formal, objective changes in the way the business behaves toward individuals.
    4. *Enforcement.* Management needs to have a structure for enforcing appropriate behavior when the new policies and practices are challenged, in the same way that management would enforce compliance with other corporate policies and practices.
    5. *Celebration.* Management needs to provide a forum for openly celebrating cultural success.

Chapter 10

Managing
Emotion at Work

Key Idea: The last social element of designing our corporate culture is that we need to understand and manage how people think and feel about the changes in progress around them. As this chapter discusses in some detail, the emotional state of the people is the best indicator that you are doing the right thing at the right pace. You may need to modify what you are doing or adjust the pace at which you make changes in order to maintain the emotional health of your organization and the engagement of your people.

As you begin to make cultural changes, people will become more emotional. Increasing the state of emotions at work is not difficult. For most people today, coming to work is not an emotional experience. They know what to expect on the job, and they are well prepared to get through the workday with very little or no emotion. Most managers like it that way: emotion in a traditional workplace is a sure sign of problems. Once people have been around long enough to master their personal adaptation to the culture of the workplace, this nearly emotionless state at work is equally true for everyone, including those who are—and those who are not—members of the social culture that your business has adopted.

Within the range of workplace conditions and norms that apply in North America and Western Europe, it is also true that, once people have grown accustomed to the workplace they occupy, there is little real emotion, whether you work in a place that is among the best within that range or a place that is among the worst. I usually compare this to the young man who did not realize that his mother was a bad cook until he joined the army. People are very adaptable. Whatever physical or social work situation they have become accustomed to is generally treated as emotionally "OK" and does not cause an emotional response, until it changes.

Exploring Emotions at Work

Figure 10.1 illustrates this effect for a stable work environment. The horizontal scale represents the range of emotions from "feel bad" on the extreme left to "feel good" on the extreme right, with a midpoint of "OK" or "no emotion." The vertical scale represents the number of people who have each emotional state. When there is little change in the workplace, a few people feel a little bit good and a few people feel a little bit bad, but the vast majority of people have no real emotion about coming to work. The full range of emotions from the people who feel the best to the people who feel the worst in a stable work environment is very limited. Also, generally the people at work belong to a single unified population that shares the same general emotional neutrality in the workplace.

Figure 10.2 illustrates what happens to workplace emotions in an environment of real change that will impact people personally. When the situation at work begins to change, people separate into two very distinct and very identifiably different emotional groups:

- One group thinks the changes will be good for them, so they generally feel good about the changes.
- The other group believes that the changes will be bad for them, so they generally feel bad about the changes.

Further, there will be a fairly wide range of emotions within each group and an even wider range of emotions in the population as an entirety. Within the emotional range of the "feel good" group, there will likely be some few individuals who like the changes and yet, on balance, feel bad for some reason. A common cause for this emotional response is that people have gotten their hopes raised by the potential for good changes in the past and been disappointed. They are hopeful, but wary of committing again, until you convince them that the good changes will come to fruition this time.

In a state of heightened emotion, the net emotional state of a person in the positive group who feels bad may also be due to a personal response to some other thing that is happening in the workplace along with the cultural changes.

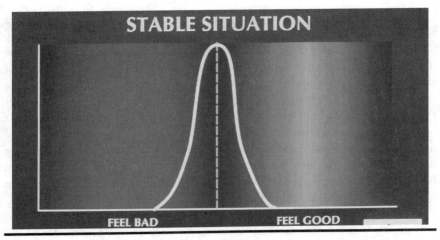

Figure 10.1 The emotional range in a stable business environment is very small and the workforce is unified.

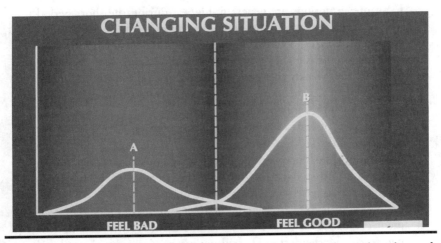

Figure 10.2 In a changing work environment, the range of emotions is much wider, and there are two clear groups with different emotional responses to the changes.

Once people begin to engage emotionally at work, they will experience more emotions, from more causes, than before. Not all of those emotions will be related to the intentional changes launched by management. As discussed in Chapter 9, the emotions may not even be related to any current event. But all the emotions that people experience will become a part of how they feel at work.

The other group is much the same, but at the other end of the scale. This group believes that the changes will generally be bad, at least for them. So they generally feel bad. Again, there will be a broad range of emotions in this group, and some individuals who expect to dislike the changes may feel good overall. The most common cause for the apparent dichotomy of emotions in this group is also the same as it was for people in the "feel good" group. People doubt that the changes they are concerned about will actually occur. The critical issue for management is that in place of a workforce that has historically been emotionally unified and demonstrated little real emotion, you now have a workforce where emotions are both strong and apparent and within this emotionally engaged workforce you have two distinct emotional groups. When you create real cultural change, you simultaneously create an emotional situation that requires careful management.

When your people begin to experience or even anticipate real change, you will greatly expand the range of emotions on your site. A few people at the extremes (both good and bad) of the distributions shown in Figure 10.2 will demonstrate emotions that are surprising and unexplained in their intensity.

> **Example:** Emotions are generally highest during the short period when the changes are still new but it has become certain the changes will occur. During one such period, I had a Bible study group send my boss a letter signed by about 50 people stating that they were opening their weekly meetings by thanking God for sending me to lead the plant. In the same month, an anonymous individual sent a letter to my boss denouncing me.
>
> My boss, of course, wanted to discuss with me which letter was correct. I said that they both were. The true message in both communications was that people had recognized that real change was in progress, and they felt strongly about the personal effect that those changes would have on them as individuals.
>
> Not surprisingly, in the conservative and unemotional environment of "headquarters," my boss thought that it was bad that he had received either letter. He had never personally experienced real emotion in the workplace, and he did not like any part of it.

Unfortunately a necessary early step in creating a future that consists of productive autonomous teams is the creation of two groups with quite different emotions. Most of that emotion is caused by the steps that you must take to include and value people who may have previously been diminished or excluded by their differences. Another significant source of emotional concern is the conversion of the work from closely supervised to autonomous. Many very capable people choose a career at the front line of industry specifically to avoid the decisions and responsibility associated with autonomy. Even if you have never seen emotions in the workplace and do not expect to enjoy the experience, management at all levels needs to be prepared to assess and manage the arrival of emotions in the workplace. If you are making real changes, real emotion must accompany those changes.

> **Key Idea:** It is often said that the world's most powerful broadcasting station is WII-FM. That means: "What's in It for Me?" In spite of your best efforts at inclusion and teamwork, most people will have an emotional response to your changes based solely on the way they understand the changes will impact them personally. As a result, during the times of greatest change, you will certainly have two different emotional groups within your operation. Right behind the concern of real emotion arriving in the workplace is the companion concern that the workforce will become emotionally divided.

Listen to What Your People Tell You about Their Feelings about Work

Obviously the graphs of Figure 10.1 and Figure 10.2 are theoretical. You will never know the emotional state of your people with anything approaching that kind of precision. The figures do indicate, however, the general characteristics of the emotional changes that you should be looking for in your workforce. That knowledge will help you recognize the changes as they occur—for example:

■ You need to know the extent or overall range of the emotions in the workplace: do the people who feel either good or bad, feel that emotion very strongly, or just a little? You can generally treat one or two people with extreme emotional responses as aberrations, but if a meaningful component of your workforce becomes very emotional, then you must respond to that signal.

■ You need to understand the balance of emotions: how do most of your people feel about the changes? The "emotional midpoint" needs to stay on the feel-good side of the scale.

■ You need to understand the dynamics of emotions: are people feeling better or worse as the changes progress?

With the theoretical construct illustrated in Figure 10.1 and Figure 10.2 as a foundation for your thinking, you can begin to look for these critical changes in your workforce.

You have many sources of data if you listen as people talk to you. When people become personally interested in the changes that you are leading, they will want you to know how they feel about it. This is another situation where large and small businesses both have capability that is proportional to their size. The managers of a large business will need more capability, and more formal capability, to assess the emotions of their people, but they will have the resources available to achieve that. The managers of a small business will have less formal capability, but a closer personal relationship with their people.

> **Example:** To cover a plant that is in continuous operation, most of the people who worked for me were on a schedule that called for working four days on and four days off. One of the front-line leaders called me in my office about once each month from his fishing boat on Galveston Bay. Superficially the call was just for fun between the two of us. He wanted to remind me that I was working, while he was fishing. But after that, he would begin to tell me stories about "funny" things that had happened in the plant. Most of his stories contained great nuggets of information about how people were feeling at that moment. Probably there were nuggets in all the stories if I had been smart enough to figure them out.

There are as many different ways to get information as you can imagine, especially when people want you to know. I guess that over the years I have used most of them at one time or another. I joined the local health club that most employees belonged to and established a predictable schedule for going there. I ate lunch in the cafeteria, normally with different people each day. I conducted some formal and informal surveys to periodically get a little "bulk" opinion data. More than anything else, I listened carefully for emotional content that I could fit into my understanding of the models shown in the graphs in Figure 10.1 and Figure 10.2. You will find your own ways to gather data that fit your personal capability to listen. The important thing is that people want you to know how they feel, and they will find some way to send you the message if you will receive it.

Everything Is Not Good When Real Change Is Happening

When I periodically meet with a manager who tells me that there is real change in progress at his site and everyone is happy about it, then I am certain that one of two other things is truly the case. Most likely in this situation, there really is no great change in progress. The manager believes that all the people are happy because no one is obviously unhappy. What is more probable is that people are not demonstrating any emotion in the workplace because they believe that nothing of substance is changing. I have seen more than a few businesses where the manager was describing major progress with great performance soon to follow and yet everyone there except the manager knew that nothing of substance was happening. That is the less harmful of the two possible options when management mistakenly believes that great change is in progress and everyone is happy.

The second option is that there truly is real change in progress and the manager does not know how people feel about it. This option is much more serious. When there is real change in progress, there is always real emotion in the workplace. And there are two clear emotional sides to most conversations. At that point in the change process, management needs to have good knowledge of exactly what people think and how they feel or you can easily lose control of the changes. You need to know how people feel about the changes because you need to manage the environment of change to accommodate these feelings. If strong emotions and negative thoughts begin to accumulate, either because people believe that you are doing the wrong things or because you are changing faster than people can accept, it is easy for progress to stop or for even more serious problems to arise in the workplace.

Interpreting the Emotions of Change

The way that I interpret the emotions of change is that there are five typical scenarios:

- *Scenario 1:* If nearly all the people have no real emotion, then there likely is no real change in progress.
- *Scenario 2:* If a large majority of people feel good about the changes and only a few feel bad, then you are likely doing the right thing, but doing it slowly. The emotional capability of your people could tolerate faster change.
- *Scenario 3:* If most people feel good, but not very good, and some people feel bad, but not very bad, then you are likely doing the right thing and doing it at about as fast a pace as your people can tolerate. This state of play is distinguished from the state where people have little to no emotion, because it is clear that there are two emotionally distinct groups watching the changes as they develop, and it is clear that the people are emotionally engaged as opposed to being emotionally neutral. The presence of the distinct groups and the emotional engagement is apparent because there is a lot of serious conversation about the changes.

■ *Scenario 4:* If most folks feel somewhat bad and only a few people feel good about the changes, then you might be doing the wrong thing slowly enough that people are not greatly disturbed. Alternatively, you might be doing the right thing faster than your crew can tolerate. In either event, if the emotional balance is negative, you need to reassess what you are doing, and how you are doing it, or you will lose your support. Positive cultural change cannot occur in an environment where most people feel bad about it. You may have an experience of forcing business changes that most people did not like, but the same thing is not possible for cultural change.

■ *Scenario 5:* If a large majority of people feel very bad about the changes, then you have lost the support of your people. Without the emotional support of the team, you will never lead a cultural change. It simply cannot happen. At this extreme, represented by a majority of people experiencing serious negative emotions, if you continue your current actions and pace, you will not only lose the people's support for your actions, you seriously risk having your workforce turn against you in other ways.

Example: Look what happened recently (2001 to 2007) at Home Depot when the new CEO attempted to rapidly reproduce the manufacturing culture of General Electric within a retail business. The folks in the stores rejected the change in ways that had significant impact on customer service. As a result, the customers went elsewhere, ultimately costing the CEO his job.

In fact, this experience represents two serious management errors. First, instead of creating a culture appropriate to the people and business of his new company, the CEO simply attempted to reproduce a culture that had been successful elsewhere. Second, as he did that, he ignored the emotional health of his organization.

If your intent is to create changes that lead to a culture of improvement, then the emotional health of your organization is a vital consideration in your task. In some situations, this knowledge is your throttle for managing the pace of change. If your workforce is generally happy, you should increase the speed of implementation to maximize the improvement. Or you may need to slow the changes to a pace that your crew can tolerate. If you find that people have stopped being generally happy and have begun to feel quite bad, then something is probably wrong.

In situations where most people are genuinely unhappy, the emotions of your people might be a "go" or "no-go" switch on the topic of creating a new culture. If you are making noncultural changes of substance, such as reducing pensions, moving work out to a nonunion shop, or assigning new customers to a Chinese joint venture, there may be very strong negative emotions in the workplace. That is likely not a good time to recruit your people to join you in creating a new culture. Generally I would recommend finishing that activity or at least allowing it to mature until it is no longer recognized as a current change of circumstance before attempting to lead cultural change.

But only you know your unique situation. With other changes in progress, it might be just the right time to give your people the opportunity to greatly enhance their performance by creating and supporting a culture of rapid improvement. If you can earn their emotional support for such an effort, you might succeed very well indeed. That is a choice for you to make as you design a culture that exactly fits your business and your people. Monitoring and managing the emotions of the workplace will let you make those decisions with a high likelihood of taking the correct path.

That is the reason that I refer to this process as "managing" the way that people think and feel. Understanding emotions in the workplace and responding to them is a great tool for making good decisions and improving performance. As you make the right decisions, people will respond emotionally. Unfortunately I cannot suggest that the happiest workforce is the most productive. The genuinely happiest workforce appears to occur in situations similar to the Hawthorne experiments described in Chapter 2. Continuous and insignificant change, such as changing the wall color or the lighting level, can be very satisfying to people. The changes are a sign that management is paying attention and yet there are no consequences and there are no responsive changes required from the people. People will respond very happily to such a situation with a small increase in productivity. But that increase is not sustainable and rapidly disappears once the constant attention stops. A culture of rapid improvement is very different. You intend to create substantial change, not insignificant change, with the companion expectation of greatly increased performance from the people, and you expect to sustain that new pace of change indefinitely.

The requirements for assessing and responding to the emotions of your people are simple. First, management needs to accept that this emotional change must occur in a situation of real change. Gaining that acceptance from management is often harder than you imagine. Few managers have experienced a lot of emotion at work, and most are uncomfortable with the concept. The ideal that a manager can make great changes and also make everyone happy is something that many managers aspire to achieve. Accepting the fact that such a situation is both unlikely and not optimum is really hard.

After that acceptance is gained, then you need to know in nearly real time what the current emotional balance is among your folks. Finally, you need to manage the content of the change or the speed of implementation so that the majority of the troops stay on your side. It is very dangerous indeed to introduce real change into the workplace and then ignore the emotional response that is sure to follow.

> **Example:** After I had become aware of the existence of the Exxon Lifestyle Awareness Network described in Chapter 9, I proposed to the Diversity Pioneers that we commence formal consideration of the needs of this group. At that time, I had almost two years' experience with the Pioneers, and together, we had addressed and resolved some human issues of real significance.
>
> But when I first proposed formal consideration of lifestyle issues, it became apparent that even this group was not emotionally ready. Some members became visibly nervous, some stopped participating in the conversation, some began to quote the Bible. I withdrew the proposal for formal consideration, and we discussed lifestyle issues informally for nearly another year before we finally began to include these matters as a part of our agenda for change.
>
> Ultimately, including lifestyle considerations was one of our great successes. But it had to occur later than I had planned in order to accommodate the emotional needs of my team. Forcing that issue before the team could tolerate it would have surely disrupted this valuable effort.

If You Cannot Interpret Emotions at Work, Find Someone Who Can

Because I understand the value of knowing the emotional state of people in the workplace, I have worked diligently to gain information about how people think and feel, and I have developed some skill at the mechanics of doing that. But in all honesty, it is not a strong point for me today, and it probably never will become a strength. I am not a naturally empathetic person, and I have not been able to develop enough skill even to simulate the behavior that a naturally empathetic person would display.

> **Example:** My wife and I once attended the funeral of a friend's mother. In honor of the mother's heritage, the service was conducted primarily in the Spanish language. Because I speak a little Spanish, I was busily trying really hard to understand everything that was being said. Then I realized that my wife, who speaks almost no Spanish, was sitting beside me crying. I had understood the words

that were being said, but my wife had understood the emotion of what was happening.

My approach to resolving this personal empathetic deficiency was to identify someone who could help me. In keeping with the pay-as-you-go mentality, I gave up an administrative assistant to fund this position. This is clearly a capability that I enjoyed as manager of a large business. If your business is smaller and cannot support a full-time position, you should at least identify the people in your operation who are naturally empathetic and make it a point to listen to them regularly.

This woman who helped me to understand the emotional state of the business is the same one described in Chapter 9, who had missed her appointment with the *Industry Week* editors. She had truly great natural empathy as well as a strong connection to the community of people in the plant. She was constantly and naturally engaged in trusted communication with people throughout the operation. Pretty much at all times, she actually knew how people thought and felt. She could provide me and other managers with a good assessment of the emotional state of the business along with some good details to support her opinions.

We provided her with in-depth training in cultural change as well as professional affiliations with several groups of people engaged in the same practice at other businesses. We gave her a position and a license to work broadly in support of the emotional health of our people. In essence, we took a naturally empathetic person with existing credibility among our people, and we created our own top-drawer subject matter expert in the human side of change. She also organized and facilitated the meetings of the several affinity groups, provided the training for our communication initiatives, described in Chapter 11, and recruited and facilitated the Diversity Pioneers. As a result of selecting and developing the capabilities of a naturally empathetic person who was already part of our organization, we enjoyed the benefit of a true subject matter expert for our cultural initiatives who was broadly accepted by the organization.

You may or may not need the assistance of such a person. Clearly that is for you and your advisors to decide. You do, however, need to have credible knowledge about the thoughts and feelings of your workforce, and you do need to act on that knowledge.

Interpreting Emotions Is Key to Implementing Successful Change

Most leaders assume that the emotions of the people throughout the organization are really of only modest interest to them because, in the past, the emotional state of the business has rarely been an important issue. That is often true. Although in times of real change, managing the emotions of the people who work for you becomes very important, most managers have never experienced that situation. The simple reason is that most managers do not truly cause significant change.

World-class performance is rare, not common. Managers, though, imagine that they are causing dramatic change and many are working very hard to do so. Many have been working hard for some time and are just waiting for the wonderful results to roll in. But when you talk to the people who actually conduct the business for these managers, it is common to find that they do not have any emotional response to the reported changes. When that happens, then you can be sure that the wonderful results will never roll in. The only reason that people do not emotionally respond to changes in the workplace is if they know that nothing will really change for them.

Key Idea: As a leader who intends to lead great improvement, you need to be prepared to manage the full range of emotions as they occur during the changes that you will lead. But the first, and by far the most common, lesson from managing emotions at work is that if there is not a significant range of sincere new emotions among the people that you lead, then you are not yet leading significant change.

Summary of Chapter 10

- Emotions at work are the best indicator that the *direction and pace* of cultural changes are supported by your people.
- When people know that *real* change is in progress, they develop strong emotions consistent with their beliefs of the *impact of those changes* on them.
- *Two changes happen* in the workplace when this occurs:
    1. There is *much more emotion present* and not all of it is directly related to the current cultural changes.
    2. The total population of your business will *subdivide into two groups*: one generally positive and one generally negative.
- It is *not possible to lead significant change* without experiencing this emotional impact. You must know that it will come, and you must manage it in a way that creates a positive emotional balance.

- I interpret the emotions of change in the following five scenarios:
  1. If nearly all the people have no real emotion, then there likely is no real change in progress.
  2. If a large majority of people feel very good and only a few feel bad, then you are likely doing the right thing, but you could be doing it much faster.
  3. If most people feel good, but not very good, and some people feel bad, but not very bad, then you are likely doing the right thing and doing it at about as fast a pace as your people can tolerate.
  4. If most people feel bad, but not very bad, and only a few people feel good about the changes, then you might be doing the wrong thing slowly or you might be doing the right thing, but doing it faster than your people can tolerate.
  5. If a large majority of people feel very bad about the changes, then you are likely doing the wrong thing. Alternatively, you might be taking appropriate but difficult steps to benefit the business, but those are not steps consistent with creating a culture of engagement.
- If your *personal capability* to know and interpret the emotions of your people is limited, you might benefit from the advice of a person who has good capabilities in that area.

MANAGING AND SUSTAINING CULTURAL CHANGE

Like everything else in industry, the work of designing and implementing a new culture is not the end. The next consideration is managing and sustaining the new culture. I have routinely included comments on managing and sustaining other cultural issues as appropriate to the prior material. The three chapters of this section provide some insight into three separate, but important, issues of sustaining your new culture: communication, measurement, and personal competence.

Chapter 11 covers communication, which of course is at the heart of any culture. People have to know the values and beliefs of the culture before they can join it and practice the rituals. They need ongoing information and instructions as they operate within the new culture. People also need a constant flow of encouragement and support as they experience significant change. As you lead a cultural change and as you sustain it afterward, people need to receive three different types of communication, each delivered in a different, but uniquely appropriate way:

1. The communication may be *news* that intends principally to inform, although there may be some subjective or interpretative content that passes along with the news.
2. The communication may be *statements of belief and support* intended to obtain understanding and intellectual commitment from the recipients.
3. The communication may be *instructions* where prompt and precise action is required.

Recognizing the distinct types of communication so that you can deliver each in the appropriate way is critical to leading and sustaining a culture of rapid improvement. Chapter 11 also describes a process for formally using the entire organization in the communication activities in a way that makes the communication more useful and more certain.

Chapter 12 covers measurement, which is the final arbiter of the success of any change. Because the new type of improvement practiced in a culture of autonomous improvement is small-event improvement, you will need to adopt a measurement practice that tracks small events without overwhelming them with the cost of traditional measurement practices. In addition, although culture change consists of many related initiatives and actions, measurement certainly is the element of the change process that is most likely to determine the details of what people will do. People always respond directly to measurement.

Leadership of the new culture needs measurement in order to be certain that the culture change is progressing and also that the culture change is producing quantifiable business results. Because measurement is so important, the system of measures and the practice of measurement need to be credible and consistent. The measurement system, once deployed, needs to be continuously managed and defended in the same way as any other important practice of the business.

Finally, Chapter 13 addresses *competence*. As we change our culture to become more dependent on the contributions of individuals and teams, we also become more dependent on the personal competence and the personal contributions of individuals. Assessing personal competence and the relationship of competence to organizational performance has been uncertain and has previously not yielded a definitive management practice that produces good results.

Fortunately a new practice of measuring and managing competence has been developed that you can deploy within your own organization. Competence that is measured in this way corresponds directly to organizational performance. More important, competence that is managed in this way is practical to achieve. Even if you do not have the time or inclination to deploy the whole capability of a competence measurement and management system, there is some valuable general knowledge that has been distilled from my experience with the practice that you can use with good results.

Chapter 11

How Communication Reflects Your Culture

> **Key Idea:** Many of the most interesting and valuable ideas covered in this book so far are associated with communicating in new ways. Communication is at the very heart of any significant management action, and that fact applies doubly to managing and sustaining a culture change. Throughout the culture change, management must be certain that its communications are received and understood by the people who will benefit from the information and act on the direction.

As you lead a culture change and even after the culture change has gotten a good start, communication demands special attention from management because you will be communicating with a workforce that is becoming (or has become) largely autonomous—and that will be a new experience for you and for them. This will require you to master a new set of communication skills. Most of the communication from management during this period of creating and sustaining an engaged workforce requires some form of translation before it is useful to the people who receive it.

> **Example:** I recently had this experience myself, though outside of the work environment. I was invited for an afternoon of sailing on a friend's boat. At one point, it became obvious that something had gone wrong: the sails had begun to flap, and we appeared to be at least a little bit out of control. Shortly thereafter my friend

confirmed that a problem existed by shouting: "HELP ME!" So I stood up and moved to where he was, at which time he shouted again: "NOT HERE!" I did not know what to do, and when that became apparent, he shouted again: "THE PORT JIB SHEET IS FOULED IN THE FAIRLEAD!"

Well, I know that "port" is the left side of the boat, and I understand what "fouled" means, so I looked around and found a rope that had looped in a way so that it would not pass through its pulley. Once I had found the problem, the correction was pretty quick and the trouble was over.

Later, though, I realized that I had been in the exact situation that we often put our people in when we communicate. My "skipper" needed help, and I wanted to provide it, but after three communications and two false starts, I had received only enough information to guess what could be done. The reason is that the first two communications had been truly useless, except to get me excited. The third had been in a language that would have been fine for a fellow sailor, but was very close to useless in communicating to me.

Senior management often cannot communicate directly because business conditions that are the basis for communications among senior management are often not apparent to others, and the language that senior managers use among themselves is often not useful in discussing the situation with others. As a result, senior management needs to learn and practice the art of delivering messages in a new, often indirect, way that allows people to understand and act on the information. Normally that requires *translation*, and translation requires that senior managers communicate through middle management rather than deliver the message directly. The middle managers will put the message into a *local* context and into the language of the recipients.

As soon as it becomes clear that senior management cannot personally deliver most messages, then it also becomes clear that senior management needs to create and operate a formal and auditable process to ensure that information and instructions reliably get to all the people. Even when you cannot deliver the message in person, you still need to know that the message was delivered. Moreover, the activity of communicating has significant organizational implications. For example, communicating directly from senior management to the front line is often done in a way that weakens middle management. Instead of weakening middle management, you need to conduct communications in a way that strengthens middle management by making certain that all managers throughout the enterprise are included in the communications.

This chapter discusses the three major types of communication that management needs to deliver to the organization and the theory of making that communication successful. The organizational implications of communication are then described. Finally, I describe a way that I have found to be very useful to ensure that indirect communications are received and effective.

> **Example:** Once a boss told about a meeting when he was a young engineer and the company president was making a presentation to his work group. The topic of communication was a major element of that presentation. Someone in the group asked the president what the difference would be between a good, competent senior executive who also was a good communicator and an equally competent executive who was not a good communicator. The answer stayed with my boss for the rest of his career. The president answered: "The difference is about $100,000 per year."

As you successfully change the culture of your business to obtain engagement from more people, it becomes important that you communicate with them often and that you do it properly. It also becomes more important that you remember as you engage people in communication that middle managers are people, too!

Three Types of Messages from Management

In general, there are only three message types that senior management should participate in delivering. The three different messages each have unique considerations for effective delivery, so identifying the type of message that you intend to communicate is the first step in getting the communication right. The three types of communication that are appropriate for senior management involvement are

1. Delivering news.
2. Providing statements of belief and support.
3. Giving instructions for action.

The next sections describe each of these types in detail.

1. Delivering News

The most straightforward type of communication from management is delivering news. People enjoy hearing news about the company and about themselves.

They especially value hearing the news quickly and from a respected source if the news has some impact on them personally. News in a corporate sense is the same as news in the media: that is, it always has the form of "something has happened" or "something is about to happen." After providing the headline of what has happened or what is about to happen, managers can add as many details as they are comfortable discussing or as many details as time allows. It is possible for the news to include the additional element of praise or recognition for the company as a whole or for an individual or team that is significantly related to the news.

Personal participation of senior management in delivering the news (instead of merely posting it on a bulletin board) requires that the news meet three requirements:

1. The news should be *truly important* to the entire organization. Senior management should personally deliver important news.
2. Another consideration requiring personal involvement of a senior manager is *timeliness*. If management wants everyone to get the news at the same time, then the easiest way is to have one manager tell them all.
3. The third consideration for the personal involvement of management is that the news has *emotional impact* that will be enhanced by the manager's participation. It could be that senior management has good news to which people will assign special value if they hear it from management before they hear it from anyone else. Alternatively, the news could be bad news, and senior management involvement serves to emphasize the seriousness of the situation or perhaps mitigate the damage.

> **Key Idea:** News that is not significant, time sensitive, or emotional can, and probably should, be communicated without the personal participation of a senior manager. That is what bulletin boards are for. Personally involving managers for delivery of the many lesser forms of news diminishes the impact of management involvement when the news is truly important.

The critical distinction between news and the other messages from management is that there is no requirement or expectation that the recipients of the message will take any specific action, or indeed take any action at all, in response to the message. The sole purpose for delivering the news is to inform. The recipients of news may elect to do something in response, but that is not a specific management expectation, and the action to be taken by the recipients is not under the direction of management.

In most cases, the person closest to corporate news who will deliver it with the greatest credibility is the most senior person available. It also turns out to be a communications success if people know that the most senior person cared enough to be certain that they heard the news. When a single person delivers the news to everyone at one time, the timeliness issue can normally be managed. However, if your operations are too distributed or your technology is not up to the task of a single announcement, then normally a time-coordinated announcement by the most senior local manager at each location is the solution. In all parts of the organization, your official communication needs to reach your people before the news reaches your people through any external sources. For distributed communications, this requirement also implies that your official internal communications should reach all your people before any unofficial internal source relays the same message.

There often are organizational implications that arise and continue as a result of the news. Corporate news concerning serious business or personnel actions may have a long life. However, beyond selecting the most appropriate individual to make the delivery, there are few organizational implications for the practice of communicating the news.

2. Making Statements of Belief and Support

The second type of message that management may want to deliver is a message of belief and support. This message either intends to convince people to accept a new philosophy, idea, or position or it intends to demonstrate management support for an action previously taken or soon to be taken by others. The message of belief and support takes the form of: "I believe that this is [true, good, valuable, etc.], and I would like you to believe it also." Alternatively, the message may be: "I support this action, and I would like you to support it also." I often think that this is a message of "intellectual sales." Management wants to influence others to "buy into" their ideas or actions.

As with delivering the news, along with providing the headline of the story, it is possible to communicate as many additional details in the message of belief and support as you are comfortable adding. The essence of a message of belief and support is that management is seeking to obtain a response, but the desired response is emotional or intellectual, not physical. Management participation is valuable to lend the dignity of the manager's position and the organization's personal respect for the manager to the credibility of the idea or action. The purpose of this message is to explain ideas or actions persuasively. People are then asked to agree with or accept or support these actions. They are not being asked by the manager to take any specific actions themselves. The intent of this message is persuasion, not instruction.

There may be a slight crossover from messages of belief and support into the realm of instructions (described in the next section) only if the responsive actions requested by the manager are quite general. For example, a senior manager may deliver a message of belief and support on the theme: "I believe that United Way is a great benefit to our community and a great way for us to show that we are a good corporate citizen. I hope that you all make a generous pledge to United Way this year." In such a case, the request for a physical act is actually not much more than a modest extension of the original request for intellectual belief and emotional support. People are not required to make a generous contribution to United Way in the same way they are required to carry out job assignments.

Fortunately there is not a time constraint on messages of this type. There is no other source of information that can make this communication redundant or late. This is the type of message that is often described in the adage that "people will not hear you until you tell them three times." That adage does not apply to communicating news because news is only news the first time; and it does not apply to communicating instructions because instructions normally require prompt response. But that adage requiring repetition does apply absolutely to communicating messages of belief and support. In fact, this is exactly the type of message that people want and need to hear as often as possible and from as many people as possible. Some people will want to hear that the most senior manager supports the new initiative. Some others will need to hear that their immediate supervisor believes the idea is good. Most people will require a constant stream of statements of belief and support from many members of management and other credible individuals as you initiate and progress significant changes to the work culture.

> **Key Idea:** You will not make the intellectual sale of a new culture or any other major change to all the people throughout your organization until most of them have heard most members of management openly and consistently support the new ideas for quite some time.

Although most people will promptly begin to *comply* with instructions related to culture change, the *initial acceptance* from most people for any completely new idea may require six months or more of constant and consistent communication. From that point forward, *ongoing acceptance* of a new concept will require repetition of the message of belief and support on a regular basis until the idea has matured and is no longer considered to be a new idea.

Management cannot tell people too often or in too many ways that it believes in what they are doing and supports their efforts. This is purely an intellectual exercise. If management fails to fully commit itself to the new idea and to communicate its commitment throughout the organization, or if it ever becomes apparent that the mind of management has moved on to other things, people are likely to stop believing before the new idea reaches fruition. This need for continuous and diverse communication also describes the organizational implications of communicating belief and support. This form of communication is truly an activity that requires the participation of the whole management team from the most senior executive to the newest front-line supervisor. It is clear, by a very wide margin, that the two biggest mistakes management makes in communicating belief and support are failing to communicate personally often enough and failing to include every manager in a disciplined plan of sustained communication. Management needs to develop and lead a plan for constant and consistent communication in support of your new culture.

Of those two, failure to include other managers in the formal communication plan is commonly the most serious mistake that senior managers make. Except in the smallest companies, the most senior executive cannot personally meet the organization's need for a continuous flow of statements of belief and support. Remember that middle managers are people, too. Middle managers also need to continuously receive the message of belief and support as well as continuously participate in delivering it to others.

It is important to practice this communication with a disciplined approach. Although statements of belief and support in corporate initiatives are part of the natural communications repertoire of senior managers, they are not a natural form of communication for most middle managers. As a result, most middle managers will not participate in communications of belief and support unless they are specifically called on to do so. Senior managers must construct and manage a detailed plan of structured communications that can be monitored and assessed to ensure that middle managers and others are, in fact, consistently and constantly participating in delivery of the message. This is not common practice for most people and, without structure, it will not happen or it will fade away far too early. Even more important, unless management launches the new initiative in a way that gives middle managers and front-line team leaders a clear role in the communications, conduct, and outcome of the initiative, the middle managers will have no basis for credibly making a statement of belief and support.

3. Giving Instructions for Action

Instructions are the final form of message from management. This type of communication is exactly what it sounds like: management intends to communicate specific instructions, and management expects that in response to these instructions, people will take the specific action as directed. Messages of this type take the form of: "Here is a new [task, method, or standard of performance]. I expect that you will carry out this task or adopt this new practice."

It is common to supplement instructions with either related news or with appropriate statements of belief and support, or both. The critical distinction in this case is that when a manager gives instructions to the organization there is a clear expectation that people will promptly act in compliance with the instructions. Understanding the news or accepting the concept is not enough. The only appropriate response to receipt of instructions is to carry out the instruction.

> **Key Idea:** Instructions are the most complex form of communication. The reason for the complexity is that you are not simply communicating information or ideas. When managers deliver instructions, they expect that people will act in response. If the communications as received are not precise, it is certain that the responsive actions will be equally or even more imprecise, often with an unacceptable outcome.

Senior managers often believe that the best way to get any important message out to the field is to tell all the people themselves. That is absolutely the wrong way to communicate instructions. In this case, credibility is reversed from the situation of communicating news. For delivering the news, credibility was assigned to the senior manager closest to the source of the news. In contrast, for the delivery of instructions, credibility is assigned to the person closest to the action described by the instructions.

> **Key Idea:** In most cases, the most credible communicator for instructions is the front-line supervisor or the immediate supervisor of the person receiving the instructions.

The reason for this inverse credibility is that, as they receive instructions, people do not want to hear from someone who knows what the instructions are. They want to hear from someone who knows the situation in which the instructions will be applied. Because instructions result in action, people want to hear from someone who will share the action with them and someone who will share with them the responsibility for the outcome. People want to receive instructions from someone they know, someone whose opinions can be calibrated against prior experience, and someone who they can personally trust. In nearly every situation, this implies that people want to receive instructions from the person who normally gives them instructions. Again, the front-line or immediate supervisor is the person most likely to succeed at delivering instructions.

That leaves us with the communication issues of timeliness and accuracy. Even if management must give up personally delivering the message, they cannot give up responsibility for getting the message (and the responsive action) correct and on time. As always, when management needs to be certain that something happens, it needs both a process for conducting the activity and a method for measuring the outcome. The details of creating a formal and auditable process for communicating instructions and other forms of structured communications, which I have used successfully, is described near the end of this chapter.

The inverted assignment of credibility associated with delivering instructions implies the same organizational issues that accompany the communication of belief and support. Senior management acting alone cannot meet the communication needs of the organization. All managers throughout the organization are needed to translate the instructions and make them locally meaningful and credible. All managers throughout the organization need to have a clear role in a disciplined communication process, and they also need to have a clear role in the performance of the initiative.

Organizational Implications of Communication: The Role of Senior Management

The analysis above of the three types of messages from management leads to an interesting conclusion: that the anomaly in corporate communications is in the delivery of news, not in the other forms of communication. For most purposes, other than delivering the news, senior management should not be the sole communicator or even the preferred communicator.

> **Key Idea:** I have found that a good guideline is that if a senior manager intends to talk directly to a large group of people who are more than two organizational levels removed, then that message needs to be limited to only two concepts. Senior management can personally deliver the news and senior management can participate in expressing belief and support.

As a senior manager, you can effectively tell people about actions that you are taking, but not about specific actions that you want them to take. You should recognize in advance that mass communication by a senior manager is often a horribly inefficient consumption of lots of time and that nothing tangible is likely to result. Your people might enjoy hearing from you, and most senior executives enjoy making presentations, but the situations in which this occurs should be very limited.

> **Example:** An American friend of mine had an assignment in Sweden. He truly enjoyed speaking to his people in mass assemblies and, as a result, he did it frequently. Although the Swedish people are all great linguists and generally understood him well when he spoke in English, after a few months in the country, he attempted to address a large assembly in the Swedish language. His language skills were much more limited than he believed, and it was generally reported after the event that no one had been able to understand what he was trying to say. It was also reported that most of the people in attendance listened politely and left the meeting without comment exactly as they always did. They were not bothered in any way that a senior manager had called them together and spoken to them for 20 minutes in a way that they had not understood. The assembled group believed that if the message required them to take action, they would hear it again from someone else. Finally, it was reported that some people had tuned out of the meeting so early and so thoroughly that they had not even noticed that the presentation had been attempted in the Swedish language! Clearly, mass meetings with the boss at the podium are often not at all what the boss hopes they are.

In the focused forum of a quality station, or as a visitor to a team meeting, senior managers can have very effective communications with an individual or a small team. The detailed alignment and information that enables such a conversation is one of the critical design intents of creating a quality station (as described in Chapter 4). Even in that venue, though, communications are best if the senior manager assumes the role of reviewing and commenting on information received from the team as opposed to initiating new directives or action-oriented content. Other appropriate communications from a senior manager at a quality station are comments on the general strategies of the business or the details of the quality station process: that is, the senior manager can use the opportunity to restate a prior delivery of news or to participate in making statements of belief and support.

The sole exception to this general limit on communication at a quality station occurs when the senior manager has personal expertise that is specifically recognized and clearly applicable to the details of the discussion. For example, I had been a practitioner of lean manufacturing and its enabling technologies for more than a decade prior to introducing them into the chemical industry. So I frequently made very specific comments about that technology as I visited quality station teams who were in the early days of practicing lean manufacturing. I have also seen other managers succeed at that type of detailed local communication when they were drawing on their own personal expertise. I once saw our president sketch the internal details of an ethylene cracker for the team that was operating it. It turned out that he had participated in the design of that cracker 20 years before.

In certain situations, it is possible for a very senior manager to effectively—but temporarily—assume the role of supervisor in directing very specific actions in very special circumstances. For example, General Patton (at least in the movie) demonstrated this effect when there was an intractable traffic jam of tanks at a critical intersection near the combat zone. He personally directed vehicle movement until the traffic jam began to clear. In that event, his personal authority was so much greater than the task at hand that he was able to compel instantaneous clarity in a very confusing situation. It is also important to note that he was not giving mass instructions or instructions of long duration. He instructed the tank commanders one tank at a time on instantaneous maneuvers to clear the jam. But an effect such as this is limited in time and scope. Generally, if a senior manager wants to give action-oriented instructions, then that needs to be done in some other way.

The critical communications issue here is that senior managers must immediately abandon any belief that they will incite the troops to effective detailed action through any form of mass instruction. With the exception of almost instantaneous and very simple actions (such as donating money to a religious leader), even the most wonderfully inspirational speakers rarely achieve more than exciting people emotionally and preparing them for future action to be directed in detail by someone else. This inspiration or excitement is really generated by a very persuasive statement of belief and support, not an instruction.

The Role of Middle Managers in Communicating

When a senior manager attempts to give people action-oriented instructions in mass communication, two separate, but serious, organizational problems arise:

1. The first problem is quite simple: people who are more than two organizational levels removed from the speaker often literally do not receive the message.

2. The second problem is that senior managers who communicate instructions by going around, rather than through, the organization effectively disenfranchise the middle managers.

Problem 1: People Do Not Get Your Message

When a CEO or other senior executive attempts to give people specific work instructions in a mass communication, the people experience true cognitive dissonance. The words that you are saying are so different from what they are prepared to accept that they simply do not understand you, and you cannot speak plainly or forcefully enough to make them understand. They know that you are speaking to them, but the words do not make any sense. As described in the example of the American manager in Sweden, people have become so accustomed to hearing senior managers talking but not communicating that it made no real difference when one literally talked in a way that people could not comprehend.

> **Example:** A consultant once described to me some work that he had done for a pizza delivery company. The CEO of that company had spent more than $100,000 to make a professionally scripted and produced video describing a new initiative that he wanted to launch in the way that pizzas were boxed and delivered. The video was shipped overnight to every store in the nationwide chain and every employee in every restaurant was required to watch it. When the communication process was completed, it appeared that not a single person actually made the desired changes.
>
> The consultant interviewed employees throughout the company, including employees who had just finished watching the video. Not one employee reported understanding that he had been asked to change the way he worked. At best, some of the employees understood that something would change at some time in the future, and they were awaiting local instructions that would arrive in due course.

Problem 2: Middle Managers Are Disenfranchised

As bad as problem 1 sounds—that is, that direct communications from senior managers are often ineffective—the second problem is even worse. When senior management initiates direct mass communication of instructions with the front-line teams, then the rest of the organization is effectively disenfranchised. This can happen in two ways.

First, when a front-line supervisor or a middle manager is invited to the mass meeting to receive new instructions in the same way as everyone else, then that supervisor or manager has been transformed, at least for the duration of the meeting, into just another person who happens to be in the room. The middle manager receives the same message at the same time as everyone else. That effect is unimportant when the message from management is news or support, but it is very important if the message is an instruction for action.

Middle managers cannot effectively support the senior leader's instructions in further communications with their teams because they have no additional information. If the instructions delivered by the CEO to the assembly are important or urgent or emotional or unclear in any manner, the people who report to the middle managers will naturally turn to them for explanation and interpretation, but the middle managers will not be able to provide either. This outcome is naturally embarrassing to middle managers. The most common human response in this situation is for middle managers to join with the rest of the troops in being generally negative about big changes that they do not understand and have not been prepared to support.

Key Idea: The effect of middle managers who "change sides" during the discussion of important events because they cannot adequately represent management is especially prevalent among first-line supervisors.

Team leaders operate at the cusp between management and the front line at all times. For supervisors who were promoted from the ranks of front-line workers, this conflict of loyalty is quite strong. First-line supervisors who do not understand management-led instructions or changes can easily move emotionally away from their alignment with management and toward their historical alignment with the front line.

The second way to disenfranchise middle management is demonstrated by what happened with the pizza company in the last example: the CEO made his video and sent it directly to all restaurants. Four levels of the organization, from senior executives to the several area managers, were not even in the room when the message was conceived or delivered. These important people were simply cut out of the process. Except for the CEO who initiated the changes, and the front-line teams who were expected to implement them, no one in the company had a clear role in the outcome. The CEO not only failed to prepare his middle managers to represent the changes, he took them completely out of the game.

As a result, the altered box materials that were needed to support the new packaging concept arrived after everyone in the stores had forgotten about it.

The detailed location-specific instructions to make the new delivery methods effective locally were never provided. In short, the contributions that middle management normally makes were not made because middle management did not have a stake in the game. A cynic could even suggest that in this circumstance, middle management did, in fact, have a stake in the game, because the important contributions of most middle managers was much better understood after the initiative failed.

The effect described in the pizza delivery fiasco also describes the expected source of one of the biggest problems that is uniformly encountered while managing significant change. In routine operations, middle managers are some of the best people in your company. These are the people who have advanced to leadership roles through many years of expertise and solid contribution. In times of great change, these same middle managers often transform into the "muddle in the middle."

Key Idea: A surprising number of initiatives to practice autonomous improvement fail because of intentional disruption or simple neglect by middle management. Middle managers are the critical communicators of change, but they are often left out of the process by senior managers who want to make the important communications themselves.

From the perspective of the middle manager, autonomous improvement apparently changes, restricts, or reduces the authority of middle managers and especially first-line supervisors to closely supervise their team. That change of responsibility is a great concern for individuals who have made a career of providing task-level supervision. Senior managers often add to this concern by cutting middle managers and supervisors out of the communication process. The result often is that some of the best people in the company become either neutral or negative toward important events that should demand their attention.

Manage and Measure the Communication

As mentioned at the beginning of this chapter, there is a disciplined process for using the organization to communicate and for auditing the outcome of those communications. The alternative to ineffective mass communication that creates a "muddle in the middle" is to use the organization to communicate.

Using the pizza company again as an example, the CEO would conceive the new packaging and delivery initiative and communicate the details to senior managers. Thereafter, level by level throughout the organization, the message would be passed from each direct supervisor to the people supervised. Somewhere along the line, one of these subject matter experts would recognize the need to coordinate the initiative with the availability of new boxes. Someone else would recognize the need for location-specific details to supplement the original general instructions. Middle managers would communicate the message and, in the process, middle managers would do what middle managers normally do.

At the end of the communications process, each delivery person in each store would receive meaningful instructions, with the local details and the materials to support the new initiative, directly from the local store boss in exactly the same way that instructions are normally received. Everyone in the organization would have made their best contribution, and the initiative would have succeeded. This is what was ultimately done on the second attempt to roll out the changes at the pizza company after the consultant intervened. By communicating in this way, the organization is stronger and the performance is better. Everyone is in the game and has a clear role.

A good way to achieve this result is very similar to the deployment of translated goals, except that this process occurs much faster because this task is much more focused. Here, we are not communicating a big concept such as strategic direction that will endure for years. We are communicating a specific instruction that needs prompt implementation. In this communication process, an initiative is conceived by management and, immediately, the essence of the message is reduced to a few salient points, perhaps four or five critical messages that are important to the overall communication.

Those few key messages are written down on the front of a small paper, such as a 3 × 5 card. Each key message also has some supporting detail or related facts. Those are also written down, normally on the back of the same card. Similar to the concept of using a mnemonic (as described in Chapter 2) in the formal statement of strategic goals, the purpose of putting the salient points of the communication on a small paper is to enable people to carry the message around with them. In this case, the small card allows middle managers to literally carry it around with them: a 3 × 5 card will fit in most shirt pockets. The purpose of this card is not to communicate detailed task instructions that are the same throughout the organization. The intent is only to establish the key points of the initiative in the same way for all people. The details of implementation actions will occur during the translation. Instead of spending a lot of time and money to create a video, management spends a little time to distill the message to its key points. Reducing big initiatives to a few critical elements is also good discipline for management to ensure that they understand the essence of the undertaking.

The communication cards are delivered sequentially to each level of management, along with some conversation on the details and the translation of the details to the specific work of each group. The key points of the initiative, as designated by management, are delivered on the front of every card exactly as originally written, but each succeeding manager also uses the back of the card to communicate the local details as they apply to the work of every particular team. In this manner, the message gets through the organization with the key points communicated exactly as intended by management. Each succeeding level of senior management, middle management, and supervision is cut into the process, and each level actively participates by translating the details of the task. The details are translated using a three-level view to ensure compatibility in exactly the same way as was described for the goals translation activity in Chapter 3.

At the end of the communication process, each individual throughout the organization has received the exact form of the key points that every other person has received. Each person has also received clear evidence that their own team has been specifically considered in the communication and that their own team leader has bought into the changes. Each person has received, along with the key points of the initiative, all the local details that are needed to implement the instructions effectively within the team. And each person has received the message from the individual who normally gives job instructions.

This method also provides an easily auditable process where management retains control of both pace and content. For example, a plant manager can communicate at the time that the first cards are delivered to the plant's senior management team that during the following week, senior managers will be walking among the front-line quality stations and during those visits the teams will be asked about the communication. The clear expectation created is that within a week, all the people will accurately know the few important elements of the message as well as the local version of the supporting details. And management will be on the floor checking to ensure that the message has been delivered and received. Any pace of implementation that is necessary to the task can define the time available for communication. If the need for action is truly immediate, then all levels of management need to stop other things and promptly make the translation and communication. This process of formal and auditable communication is not necessarily slow; it is simply thorough. As with most other activities in industry, getting the initial communications right is more likely to speed the task than to make it slower.

In the event that the management audit of the communication indicates that an unsatisfactory outcome has occurred in any location, then it is possible to review the communication cards, measure the extent of the problem, and cause the communicators in that chain of information and instructions to try again. This is a scientific activity. It can be learned, taught, and practiced with a predictable outcome. Instructions can be communicated usefully and rapidly, or the instruction process can be done over until it is done correctly.

Key Idea: By using a formal communications management process such as this, all levels of management can communicate to their teams in the way that is best for them, and senior management can be certain that the message has been received throughout the organization.

Summary of Chapter 11

- Many of the most interesting and valuable concepts of culture change involve the way that we *communicate*.
- There are *three principle types of message* that people receive from management: news, statements of belief and support, and instructions.
  - News
    - News is delivered in the form: "Something has happened," or "Something will happen."
    - News can include praise for the organization or for individuals or teams within the organization.
    - Senior managers are often the preferred communicators for news.
    - The critical issue in communicating news is to get the news out in a timely and credible manner.
    - Communicating news does not require or anticipate a response from the recipients.
  - Belief and support
    - Statements of belief or support are delivered in the form: "I believe this and I would like you to believe it also."
    - The intent of communicating belief and support is to create an intellectual or emotional response, not an active response.
    - Effective communication of belief and support requires constant and consistent communication from many people at all levels of the organization over an extended time period.
    - The two biggest mistakes of managing the communication of belief and support are failing to sustain the communication and failing to engage the entire management team in a process of disciplined communication.

- Instructions
    - Instructions are delivered in the form: "Here is a new task, or method, or performance standard. I expect that you will change to adopt the new practices."
    - Instructions clearly expect an active response.
    - Instructions are best delivered to each person by that person's supervisor. This implies that each level of management has a specific active role in the communication of instructions.
    - Communication of instructions needs to be timely and accurate.
- The role of senior management:
    - In most situations, senior management is not the preferred communicator, especially in the forum of mass communications.
    - Senior management should never attempt to communicate instructions in mass communication or to individuals more than two organizational levels removed from the senior manager.
    - Mass communication or communication to individuals more than two levels removed from senior managers should be limited to delivering the news and initiating the discussion of belief and support.
    - Senior managers may have interesting and valuable discussions at the front line in a limited forum such as a quality station or in an area where the senior manager has personal subject matter expertise.
- The role of middle management:
    - Communicating through middle managers is critical to defining their role in leading the changes.
    - Failure to engage middle managers or communicating around middle managers leads to neutral or even negative behavior which is often a major contributor to the failure of management initiatives.
- Manage and measure communications:
    - It is possible to use a process similar to goals translation to ensure that communications led by supervisors and middle managers are both timely and accurately received throughout the organization.

Chapter 12

Measuring the Performance of Small Events

Key Idea: Autonomous improvement often occurs as a result of many small changes or as a result of a big change accomplished through many small contributions. Small changes and small contributions to big changes need to be measured differently from the traditional big-event changes measured by existing measurement practices.

Measuring performance is a critical factor in establishing, managing, and sustaining a culture of rapid improvement. As business leaders, we may each have our own personal or individual motives for creating a new corporate culture that is more engaging and more inclusive, but the only acceptable business motive to expend a lot of time and money to change the culture is to enable the enterprise to become better at what it does. Culture change is not free, but it ought to be more than self-financing. As you change your culture, you need to routinely demonstrate that your culture change is paying for itself and producing additional enhanced performance.

> **Key Idea:** If you merely accept the belief that culture change is inherently good, and if you are therefore satisfied with achieving culture change independent of clear improvement in the business results, then you have confused the means of improvement with the goal of improvement—and that is usually a serious error.

Every business's objective is to improve strategic performance. One of the methods that you have chosen toward that end is to create and sustain a culture of engagement and inclusion. As you develop a measurement system, you will want some measures to demonstrate that you are deploying a new culture as intended. More important, you need measures that demonstrate the new culture is producing enhanced performance.

The measurements that you select will have a great influence on the actions of most people. This effect is well represented by the adage: "Be careful what you measure, because that is what people will do." As you undertake rapid improvement achieved through autonomous actions taken by many people, you need to be very careful to create measures of progress that cause people to take the right actions in the right way. If your improvement process does not cause a lot of change, then you have not been successful. And if your measurement process causes the wrong change, then you will have failed still more significantly.

For normal business activities, including big-event improvement, most businesses already deploy a well-known measurement practice that closely records and reports the events and results in great detail. For small-event autonomous improvement, use of such a detailed measurement practice would overwhelm the improvement results in many instances. In addition to creating new measures that track the results of culture change, you need to create a new "small-event" measurement practice to record the outcome of your autonomous improvements, without diminishing the results by the cost of measurement.

Principles of Measuring Small-Event and Autonomous Improvement

As you change your culture, you need a reliable measurement to affirm that your culture change is occurring as intended. And you need to measure the business performance that results from your culture change. Much of what is new at this time is small-event activity, which needs to be measured in a different way from the traditional measures used for big-event improvement.

Key Idea: Measurement has both objective and subjective components: your measurement system will both assess progress and communicate your intentions. In the case of small-event, autonomous improvement, your measurement system will assess a new type of activity and you will largely be communicating with a new group of people.

Following are a few characteristics of a small-event measurement practice that will enable you to meet these needs:

- The best indicator of successful culture change is the extent to which people join with you to improve your business.
- Bulk measures of strategic performance are the best indicator of small-event progress.
- Visible and intuitive measures of performance help communicate the specific intent of the changes to people at the front line.
- All measures need to be consistent and credible to the people whose work is being measured.

Each of these characteristics will be reviewed in detail in this chapter. In addition to reviewing the details of developing a small-event measurement system, I have a few other ideas on the topic of measurement that I have successfully used to achieve some remarkable results in an environment of rapid improvement. These are reviewed in detail later in this chapter, but here is a quick overview:

- Subjective performance can often be measured in a nearly objective way by utilizing a subject matter expert to provide credibility and consistency.
- It is possible to measure some performance criteria using bulk data even if there are no individual data.
- There are often meaningful trends in an aggregation of data, even when the individual elements of that data have no clear meaning.
- It is necessary to defend your measurement system against changes or abuse that will disrupt its credibility.

Before beginning the discussion of small-event measurement, though, it is important to be clear on a starting point. The information in this chapter assumes that you already have a fully satisfactory system of standard measures for regulatory reporting, shareholder reporting, and other financial accounting, and that you also have a good system for measuring and managing the traditional big-event portion of your improvement portfolio. Similar to other parts of this book, this chapter looks primarily at creating, managing, and sustaining the practice of large-volume, small-event improvement as a supplement to the practices and measures that are already in place in your organization.

Measuring How Engaged Your People Are in Improving Your Business

As you move toward a culture of engagement and inclusion, the best indicator of successful culture change is the extent to which people join with you to improve your business. There are many aspects of culture change that can be measured, but autonomous participation in improvement is the exact reason that you have undertaken culture change, so by measuring that effect as directly as possible, you will know with some certainty that you are achieving your objective. The accepted measurement of participation is the number of implemented improvements per person each year. Thinking of this in a traditional way, this measurement would be the product of the average number of suggestions from each person each year multiplied by the average rate at which those suggestions are adopted.

In North America, where autonomous improvement is still rare, this "suggestion" format is the way in which these data are most commonly displayed. In most places where the practice of autonomous improvement is mature, the number of improvements per person per year is reported directly. In recent data, the average company in North American industry yielded seven suggestions for each 100 people during a year. Those suggestions were implemented at an average rate of 20%, producing an average annual rate of 0.014 improvements per person. This is widely reported through several organizations, such as the American Productivity and Quality Center in Houston, Texas. There are also a great deal of existing benchmark data published for highly successful companies and individuals, such as

- Canon: 100 improvements per person per year.
- Toyota: 40 improvements per person per year.
- My personal performance: 40 improvements per person per year, which has been reported in *Business Week*, *Industry Week*, and *Maintenance Technology* magazines as well as in several books and in Europe's *L'Usine Nouvelle*.

> **Key Idea:** The power of culture is apparent in these numbers. The best companies and the best practitioners are receiving small-event improvement at a rate approximately 3,000 times as fast as the North American average. When those improvements are also strategically focused, you can begin to understand the performance advantage of a world-class business.

That being said, the measurement of improvements per person is not a rigorous or objective measure in the way that a ton of bricks is measurable. Fortunately no one uses this result as an objective measure of business performance. Rather, it is used only as an indicator of the extent to which people are joining or participating in the improvement process. (I will discuss the measures of performance next.) Although external references from the best businesses are available, I do not know of anyone who perceives this as a competitive measure. It is generally used internally within a business to track changes in participation from period to period as the culture change progresses or is sustained. As a subjective indicator of the evolving state of participation within a single company, it is quite a reliable measure, and more important, it is a measure that is very useful.

I have never asked for an auditable number for this measurement in the way that I would for other measures, such as cost, quality, or customer service. I normally accept the count that is produced by the leader of each quality station team as a fair representation of the number of separate contributions made by that team. There is some objectivity brought to the counting at the several different quality stations because I normally use a single individual to gather the data from all the teams. Use of a subject matter expert (SME) for data gathering makes the data fairly consistent even if it is not objectively precise. This practice of using a SME for data gathering and analysis is discussed further later in this chapter. For the purpose of assessing the trend in participation over time in a single organization, consistency of the data and analysis is largely all that is required. My belief is that team leaders have a record of team activities to know what has occurred in their group, and they know that they ought to have documentation of a physical change to correspond with each improvement claimed.

Key Idea: Most of the uncertainty in accumulating a good count of separate improvements occurs in situations such as the exhaust fan improvement described in Chapter 4 (where we dramatically changed the way the rooftop fan was repaired and saved significant maintenance time and costs by doing so). In that case, the original idea of improving the safety guarding evolved into a much better project through a continuing series of related ideas before any physical work was undertaken.

That sort of project development is clearly a good thing and is one of the attributes that makes improvement proposals at a quality station so much more valuable than suggestions submitted to others for a one-off review. I encourage teams to adopt that practice of building better ideas from an original idea, and as a result, I encourage teams with similar experiences to count each evolutionary step that is finally implemented as a separate improvement.

In any event, although this measurement practice is imprecise and somewhat subjective, for the purpose of understanding trends in participation, I have always been satisfied with the use of these data. And I have always been satisfied that increased participation was a good measure of the culture change that I intended to create. Certainly when people begin to participate at a rate nearly 3,000 times the prior rate, something more has changed than the existence of goals and quality stations.

> **Key Idea:** Autonomous participation represents the potential for rapid business progress. Good strategic focus and continuous careful management is still required to turn the potential for improvement represented by this increase in action into real performance.

I have two more thoughts on this topic. First, I never allowed teams to publicize their individual performance against this criterion. In operations that I have managed directly, the data were only publicly reported in aggregates of at least a full division. Because the data were not part of the performance system that determined personal reward and recognition, and individual team performance was not publicized, no one had an incentive to bump the numbers.

Second, the teams that are truly not engaging with you to improve the business are normally failing to do so for an identifiable reason. In my experience, someone on these teams wants management to know that they are not participating. They either want management to know so that they can get help to resolve the problem, or they want management to know so that they can make a statement about the fact that they have chosen not to participate. Therefore, tracking participation reported by individual teams is useful to management even if you do not allow the teams to post their results for this measure as you do with other matters.

Using Bulk Measurements to Ensure You Are All Working toward the Same Goal

In simple terms, the bulk measurement of small-event improvement is much the same as the bulk measurement of other high-volume small commodities. For example, no one measures the weight of each grain in a truckload of rice and adds the results to determine the total weight of the load. The accepted practice is to measure the bulk weight of all the rice and to know that by doing so, the individual weight of each separate grain has been included. In addition to representing a great simplification, bulk measurement improves the measurement by eliminating many potential measurement errors. Using bulk measures to know the aggregate result of many small-event improvements achieves the same result in measuring improvement.

If you were to use the same measurement system that you currently use for measuring and reporting big-event improvement for determining the results of each small event, then the cost of the measurement system would often be on the same scale as the value of the individual improvements. That is, the act (cost) of measuring would materially diminish the value of the performance being measured. You want to learn as much as you can about the performance of small-event improvements without interfering with them or diminishing the resulting performance. More candidly, you want to learn as much as you can about small events without employing an army of data gatherers and accountants.

The practice of bulk measurement takes advantage of the goals translation process. If goals translation has been done well, then all your teams are pursuing the same improvement outcome for your enterprise. The differences among the teams are in the exact nature of the task at each place, not in the nature of the intended outcome. For example, if you intend as an enterprise to increase output, then each team will take its own best steps to increase output. The tasks will be different, but the outcome will be the same. You can see the bulk effect of many small efforts to increase output by measuring only the increase in the bulk output of the enterprise, or of the major operations within the enterprise. The use of bulk measures reinforces commonality of purpose across your organization. If you are all working together to increase output, then together, you will all measure output.

There is no need to capture each of the individual project results and add them together. This characteristic of the bulk measurement practice is a great simplification and improvement in the measurement practice for your project teams. A team might have completed a project to increase the reliability of its equipment, and now they are able to report with some certainty that the equipment is available for service an additional 10 hours each month. For a variety of reasons, including product mix or dependency on other operations, they might not know with the same certainty what that additional 10 hours of equipment availability means in terms of output. With a lot of effort, and a lot of uncertainty, the team could probably estimate the output effect of each separate project, but there is little value in doing that. Increased output, per se, is independently apparent at all organizational levels, including the team level, the enterprise level, and any level in between. If capacity has been usefully improved, then the aggregate of the improvements appears everywhere that you may choose to observe it.

There was an important phrase in the prior paragraph: "If capacity has been usefully improved." Business operations are complex, interconnected, and often cyclical. As a result, most manufacturers do not have the luxury to adopt a strategic goal that is as simple and single-minded as "increase capacity." Instead, they have a more complex goal for the future that includes several companion goal elements that reflect different potential contributions to manufacturing success. In the sample goal shown in Figure 2.3 (in Chapter 2), the strategic goal was to "increase capability and capacity." Capability in that example included such additional operational factors as quality, variety, cost, and productivity.

Over a five-year strategic horizon, there will be times when each of these different performance elements has more value to the enterprise than the others. This is especially true if your business operates in several different product or market segments, and even more true when considered in the intense detail available at the front-line team level. For the CEO, it may be straightforward to identify that for extended periods some products need growth and others need lower prices, as discussed in Chapter 2. At the team level, the cycle time for those prioritization decisions is much shorter. Bulk measures help the teams with this assessment. When a team completes a few capacity improvement projects, but is not able to report increased output, then they have an objective indication that their projects are not currently useful.

That result may occur for many reasons, including the existence of an unresolved rate-limiting step either within their own team or at the interface with another team, a downturn in the market, or something else. Whatever the cause may be, when a team is successfully completing projects to increase capacity, but they are not physically increasing output, then the bulk measure is telling them that they are possibly working on the wrong thing at this time. The team may want to refocus their efforts on finding the rate-limiting step, or on addressing another of the possible tactical improvements described by their translation of the strategic goals. When they meet next as a team to select a project to advance, they may want to select cost, quality, or product variety (flexibility) improvement rather than another capacity project. At a minimum, they will want to use this information in the next conversation with a manager who visits their quality station.

Measuring Visible Results Reinforces an Intuitive Understanding of Performance

Whenever it is possible to do so, I always prefer to construct a measurement system for small events that measures visible or physical results. This is strongly recommended. If you possibly can do so, measure something that people can see so that the measurement corresponds to their intuitive understanding of the business. In this way, the measurement assists you in communicating the exact outcome that you seek. You may be successful in communicating among managers using highly complex metrics, but people at the front line live in a very tangible world. To the extent that you measure physical results, you greatly increase the communications value of the measurement. For example,

- If you are interested in increasing volume, then measure physical output.
- If you are interested in labor efficiency, then measure physical output divided by the total number of people employed in the business.

Key Idea: As shown above, I believe that when you measure something, you ought to measure all of it at once (all the output or all the people). The issue is that when you have a fungible population and measure only a part of it or measure it in different pieces, you have created a big hole in your measurement system that someone is certain to exploit. The classic experience with this phenomenon is to observe how fast discretionary work is assigned to maintenance once management begins to measure the efficiency of production workers. Nothing at all has improved, but the measured efficiency goes up.

Tangible measurements such as these have two great advantages:

1. They are both objective and certain.
2. They confirm in numbers the subjective feel for the business that people carry with them each day.

It is possible to add as much detail to this sort of measurement as you need for analysis of performance. For example, if you are initially measuring the efficiency of a loading team's output by counting the number of rail cars they process (which might vary between 180,000 and 190,000 pounds each), it is possible to add a measure of loading effectiveness by also measuring tons or even pounds that they load into each rail car. When you are measuring tangible results, there is a physical manifestation of performance, and it can be measured as precisely as your instrumentation and budget allow.

In addition to reporting performance, a tangible measurement system also enables analysis of processes and reinforces communication of expectations. Measuring visible performance is perfect for both of those purposes. For management, using a physical indicator of success enables you to measure outcomes very precisely. It is then possible to conduct process analysis and improvement using powerful data tools such as statistical analysis or designed experiments. Process improvement can be very scientific with data of this sort. For people other than management, measurement of an outcome that can be personally observed communicates an unambiguous understanding of performance and expectations.

In contrast, alternate measurement systems based on performance to theoretical standards (as in an industrial engineering practice) or composite measurements comprised of several factors, such as the overall equipment effectiveness ratio (OEER), are much more difficult to understand, and they often have little value in either process analysis or in communication at the front line.

Make Sure Your Measures Are Consistent and Credible to the People Being Measured

Through the measurement system, management attempts to summarize into a few numbers the many interesting things that happen in operations. For many people, particularly those at headquarters who rarely observe operations, the numbers have to tell the whole story. One consideration of great importance is that the folks at headquarters who rarely see the operations often use the numbers to compare one operation with another. For that reason, you need to be very careful that your measurement system is consistent and credible and that the people being measured and compared believe that your system of measurement fairly represents actual performance. There are two fundamental components of credibility for a measurement system:

1. The measurement system must measure performance as directly as possible.
2. The measurement system must be managed on an ongoing basis to sustain fairness and accuracy.

These requirements are described in detail in the following subsections.

Make Your Measurements Direct and Exact

As you develop and deploy your goals, the business outcomes that you intend to achieve will be quite clear and very specific. In order to measure business outcomes directly, you need only to sustain the understanding of performance that you established as you were setting your goals.

Unfortunately the staff people who develop measures for use within the business often do not retain that direct linkage with the goals. Measurement systems often take on a life of their own for no good reason and with no good outcome. More important, the people who develop internal measures often do not consider the communication value of measurement. Many internal measures are too indirect to be certain that you are truly measuring the intended outcome and too complex for most people to comprehend as they make operating judgments.

> **Key Idea:** An even greater oddity is the recent practice of combining many different results into a single highly complex number. An example of a highly complex combined measurement is the OEER, which is the product of multiplying the rate of utilization of theoretical equipment availability by the rate of utilization of theoretical production speed, multiplied again by the percentage of good quality production. After making five calculations using three data points and two theoretical numbers, a single numerical result is presented to represent performance. This OEER is very popular, and as a consultant, I often use it myself. Because it is commonly used or readily calculated, it is a great tool for consultants. That being said, no one can look at this sort of number and obtain operationally useful information. Certainly a number such as this has no value in communicating at the front line of any business.

When you adopt indirect and complex measures, you often wind up measuring something other than what you intend. For example, mechanical uptime represents a potential for production, but not production itself, which is the true business intent. Also, by measuring success indirectly, many businesses invite people to do the wrong thing in pursuit of the measure rather than in pursuit of improvement. For example, when production success is measured as a percentage of theoretical capacity, many managers underreport capacity or delay reporting completion of capacity-improving projects.

When you have a practice of well-translated goals, then it is clear that many of the direct measures of business expectations and performance used as corporate goals apply directly at the front line. Use those measures. When you use simple measures, it is clear that you are measuring the right thing and doing the right thing. When people can see the direct linkage between their measured results and business performance, the communication value of the measurement will be very strong. This is not as easy as it sounds. Your business will certainly have some very theoretical and complex measures that management loves to use. Those may be fine for management reporting, but as you initiate serious participation at the front line, give those people measures that relate directly to their work and measures that link them to the business.

Keep Your System Fair and Accurate

By far, the most serious challenge to the credibility of your measurement practice will be any recognized version of unfairness or inaccuracy. This sort of concern often arises when there are differences among your operations that are outside the influence of management. For example, consider the following differences:

- In France, the standard work week is only 35 hours long, and there is almost zero use of overtime to increase work hours.
- In the United Kingdom, there is a 40-hour work week, and there is some, but very little, use of overtime.
- In the United States, the standard work week in a chemical plant is often 44 hours long, and there is common use of abundant overtime.

As a result of these national policies, if the measure of productivity is total output divided by total people, then the local differences become very important. To perform 1,000 hours of work in one week might need 29 people in France, 25 in the United Kingdom, and fewer than 20 in the United States. The same work necessarily requires more "people" in France, fewer in the United Kingdom, and still fewer in the United States. Therefore these differences in reported productivity are caused by structural inconsistency, not performance.

This example is easy to comprehend, but there will likely be several complex situations in your business where the measured outcome is determined by something other than performance. If you fail to accommodate those differences as you create your measurement system, then the conversations that should be about performance will in fact be about the differences. It is necessary to create a measure that people accept as fair before you can have meaningful conversations about performance.

Create a Subject Matter Expert for Measurement

A related reporting issue is normally associated with some major change in the business, such as a new product or a substantial change in product mix, or some major physical event such as a flood, snowstorm, or a strike at a customer site. The most common manifestation for this concern is that because a change (either permanent or temporary) has occurred, someone wants to change the system of measurement or perhaps just wants to adjust the reported result in order to accommodate the change. This will certainly happen, and when it does your measurement system will be facing a very serious challenge. The response that I favor is the designation of a single individual as the SME on the measurement system who will be the sole clearinghouse for that sort of request. The important consideration is that changes, exceptions, and accommodations (when and if they occur) must allow you to retain the credibility and consistency of your system. Credibility and consistency require that someone who is primarily responsible for the measurement system itself manage the changes.

Example: At Exxon Chemical, we once had a severe ice storm in Baton Rouge, Louisiana. Obviously this was unexpected and caused significant loss of production as well as cost to recover. The managers in Baton Rouge believed that they were fully justified in adjusting their performance to remove the effects of the storm. The problem is that the plants in Canada experience ice and snowstorms on a regular basis. If Baton Rouge can adjust performance to remove the costs of recovering from an unexpected freeze, then can the Canadians adjust to remove the costs of preparing for anticipated freezes? Our SME, in collaboration with several others, ultimately decided that weather-related costs in some form are common to all plants and something more (perhaps a hurricane?) would be required before local adjustments would be allowed. Because we employed the services of a SME for administering our measurement practice, the request for adjustment was received, considered from a general-interest perspective, and resolved in a way that everyone respected.

Without that clarity of central responsibility, managers who feel the need for a change in reporting will simply check with their boss or perhaps just make a change on their own initiative. As different people make different changes, your measurement system soon becomes arbitrary and local rather than objective and global.

Other Interesting Measurements

In addition to the general characteristics of creating a system of measurement for small events described so far, there are several short topics related to the practice of measuring within an environment of small-event or autonomous improvement that may be valuable to you.

Useful and Nearly Objective Assessment of Subjective Data

There is often great informational value in measuring attributes of a business that are not objective. Usually this sort of measurement is best used for providing forward guidance to an activity, rather than as part of the reward and recognition of past events. For example, Chapter 13 discusses personal competence. Assessment of personal competence (this is different from assessing personal performance) provides a great management tool for guiding training and development as well as personnel assignments. Unfortunately, assessing the competence of many people in many different assignments and many different places is far more subjective than the measures we normally use.

Objective performance can easily be measured broadly across an organization by providing specific definitions and rules of practice and allowing each manager to make their own measurement and report the results. This is the most common form of corporate reporting. That practice certainty is not equally appropriate for gathering subjective information. An alternate way to obtain useful albeit imprecise information from subjective data is to conduct all of the measurements using a single individual, or a very small group of individuals, who personally are known to be experts in their field as well as people of strong credibility and integrity. Limiting the assessment team to one person or a very small group often provides sufficient consistency to make subjective results credible and useful, including making them useful for some comparative purposes normally reserved for very objective data. The criteria for this measurement practice include

- Externally applying consistent standards of data gathering and assessment in all places.
- Applying lessons learned from the several unique experiences gained while assessing many places during the assessment of each different place.
- Revisiting prior assessments, at least by telephone, if not in person, when new information or experience becomes available in order to sustain the consistency of the data and assessment.

A SME (or a small team of SMEs) can do all that in a way that most people accept. I used competency assessment as an example of the practice of subjective assessment using a SME because the specific practice of competency assessment is discussed as a detailed example in Chapter 13. There are a great many situations in which such an assessment provides the best information available. Normally these situations involve human characteristics in some way, or they involve physical situations that are so highly varied that a fixed set of rules for objective measurement is too complex to write or sustain.

Use Bulk Measures When Individual Data Are Not Available

Bulk measurement was originally introduced to measure many small changes without overwhelming the benefit of the small improvements with the cost of a traditional measurement system. It is possible to measure and aggregate the individual results, but it is not practical to do so. It is also possible to use bulk measures to report results for which it is not possible to gather individual data.

Example: In the banking business, it is well known that the best customers—that is, the most loyal and most profitable—are the customers who use several services from the same institution. A customer who has several accounts (such as checking, savings, certificates of deposit, a credit card, and a car loan) will be much more loyal and profitable than a customer who has only a free checking account or a single deposit account.

I am currently chairman of a credit union, and we know that customers with more accounts are better customers, but the current state of our information system does not allow an automated assessment of that data. We would need to make a manual search of our records to determine the number of different accounts that each member has and then use many individual data sets for assessment. That process is so slow that the data would change before we could complete the exercise. We certainly could not do that frequently enough to sustain an ongoing measurement practice. Because we understand the value of creating customers with multiple accounts, we are training our customer service agents to cross-sell additional accounts whenever they talk to a customer, and we have both individual goals for each branch and an organizational goal for the entire credit union to increase the number of accounts that each member has.

The problem is how to measure the success of the effort. In this case, bulk measurement saves the day. For each branch, and for the organization as a whole, we know the total number of accounts of all types, and we know the total number of members. It is difficult to obtain individual account data, but it is easy to know the average number of accounts held by all individuals. With that data, we can track improvement of this interesting data at each of the seven branches and also for the entire credit union.

Key Idea: There are many situations in addition to small-event improvement where gathering and analyzing individual data is impractical or even impossible, but with bulk data, the analysis is often both easy and useful.

Look for Useful Trends in Meaningless Data

The objective of culture change is business improvement. When considering improvement, I believe that the *trend* of the data is often more useful than the *absolute value*. For example, in 1970, the absolute data were clear that

General Motors was a much larger company than Toyota. However, the trend was equally clear: General Motors was shrinking, and Toyota was growing. Of great interest in this regard is that it is possible to usefully measure trends in data that otherwise have no significant meaning.

There are two situations where I have used trend analysis in this way. The first opportunity to do this occurs when the individual data are consistent, but the absolute value is uncertain. One example of this sort of data is the count of improvements per person as an indicator of the health of our efforts to increase participation. I have always allowed each team at each quality station to count for themselves how many separate improvements they created and implemented. Several people, including our SME, have checked the reported numbers, and it appears that the teams were painfully honest. The fact is, though, that we were measuring a trend in uncertain data. The counted number of improvements per person was not precise, and we all knew it. But we also believed that our practices ensured that the count was consistent with time. In this situation, a measured trend in the consistent data told us what we needed to know, even though the absolute number of improvements was somewhat uncertain.

The second situation in which we trended uncertain data was with data that truly had no individual value. Exxon was clearly on the very forefront of converting process industries to statistical quality methods. As a result, the preferred indicator of product quality was the statistical process capability index, or Ppk (this would be Cpk in discrete manufacturing, but that difference is not important here).

For those who are unfamiliar with Ppk, here is a brief description. Process capability is a statistical comparison between the range of the product specifications and the natural variation of a process. If the process operation is "centered" within the range of the product specification and the natural variation of the process operation around that centered value is fully contained within the allowable range of the product specification, then there is very little likelihood of producing bad product, absent a special cause of unnatural variation.

Normally the natural variation of a process is measured using standard deviation, which is indicated using the Greek notation of sigma (or σ). In round numbers, all of the natural variation of a process occurs within three standard deviations on either side of the center. When a process is so consistent that 3σ of natural variation on each side of the center (6σ total variation) is fully contained within the product specification, there is no expectation of producing a bad product, absent a special cause. This is the origin of the concept of 6σ production.

From that description, it is apparent that the process capability index is specific to individual products and processes. But for my purposes as manager of a very large business with many products, I had no value for 250 or more separate measures of product quality. Instead, I wanted to have a single number that represented the trend of improvement across the business. (I recognize that this is starting to sound like OEER, but remember that this is not a measure for the front-line teams, this is a measure for me. OEER is often useful, but not for front-line teams.) So I began to compute an average Ppk that represented the quality of all our production. Anyone with any statistical training recognizes immediately that the concept of an average Ppk has no meaning. I also believe that is true. The instantaneous or absolute value of the average Ppk for 250 separate products does not convey any useful information. At the front line, and for most purposes, the only acceptable report of product quality is the direct measure of statistically correct individual Ppk for each product.

That being said, the trend of the average Ppk for all the products that we produced provided interesting information that pretty well represented the progress of product quality improvement in a very large multiproduct operation. I used to tell statistical purists that they could think of this as a dimensionless number. It had no precise meaning, but as it got bigger, I knew that was good.

Key Idea: For the purpose of understanding the business or gaining useful information, it is possible to find interesting trends in data, even when the individual values of the data are without meaning.

Defend Your Measures

There are a lot of ways that intelligent managers can make improvement appear to happen as the result of actions taken at the analyst's desk without causing any change at all in the way that the business is conducted. Unfortunately, over the last 40 years, I have seen most of them.

> **Example:** In one interesting case, a process unit could equally produce either of two different products and normally produced a mix of the two. During a period when the market demand had changed to substantially favor one of these products, a new executive was assigned responsibility for that unit. He convinced his analyst that the product currently out of favor in the market was not a primary product, but only a by-product. By simply changing the definition, the analyst stopped considering about half of the prior manager's total production. As a result of analytically reducing previously reported output, and thereby changing historical performance, this manager was able to report that efficiency was now higher than it had been. In fact, the actual performance was worse, not better.

Managers who are measured by comparing output to capacity frequently find a way to justify underreporting capacity, or they delay reporting completion of capacity-improving projects. Both have the effect that output is being compared against less capacity than they truly have, so they are able to report that they are more successful at utilizing available capacity than they actually are. There are many ways to find a hole in an otherwise objective measurement system. When the measurement system becomes complex and unobvious, it enables even more of this practice. Every weakness in every measurement system that I have ever known about was exploited by some manager or analyst. And not one of these people believed that what they were doing was improper. They were simply doing their best to report good performance within the system created by senior management. If you create a system where it is easier to make improvement by sitting for a while with the analyst than it is by visiting the plant floor, then you will certainly get some managers who do just that.

The SME for your measurement system needs to monitor performance reports for evidence of this sort of behavior. When history changes, when capacity projects routinely are "closed out" months after the equipment begins production, or when it just seems that the reported results do not conform to your knowledge of the operation, your SME needs both access and authority to put the measurement practices back as they should be. This may be very difficult. Because the manager is apparently reporting according to the formal requirements of the system, it often takes a long time for the SME to identify the problem, and the reporting manager may have a well-rehearsed rationale for reporting as he or she has done. By the time that it is clear that a problem exists and requires resolution, issuing a correction may be an embarrassment. But you need a person who defends the credibility of your measurement system, and you must have management who supports that defense. Without that, your measurement practices will soon have no value.

Summary of Chapter 12

- *Measurement* is the strategic goal element with the greatest influence over what people will do.
- The best indicator of successful culture change is the *extent to which people join with you* to improve the business.
- *Bulk measures* of strategic business performance are the best indicator of small-event improvement.
- The most visible and intuitive measure of any outcome is the physical value of a *tangible* result.

- Whatever you chose to measure, the measurement will be more valuable *if you measure all of it at one time.*
- Measures must be *credible* and *consistent.*
- It is possible to measure subjective performance in a useful way by using a *subject matter expert (SME)* to provide credibility and consistency.
- It is possible to measure the *bulk effect* of performance for which there are no individual data.
- It is possible to measure *meaningful trends* in an aggregation of data that has no individual meaning.
- It is necessary to *defend your measurement system* against changes that will disrupt credibility.

Chapter 13

Managing the Competence of Your Employees, Especially in Business-Critical Roles

> **Key Idea:** There is a clear relationship between the competence of people in critical positions and the performance of their organizations. Understanding and managing that relationship can provide a very powerful tool for improvement.

A critical issue in business performance is the active engagement of all people working toward a common purpose: that is the essence of this book. However, as I have gained more and broader experience with the success derived from engaged people, it has become apparent to me that another factor is also important. That factor is the competence of a few people working in business-critical assignments. Achieving truly great performance, at the upper end of world-class results, requires that, in addition to an engaged workforce, a few people in business-critical roles must demonstrate high competence.

For the purpose of understanding the relationship between corporate performance and personal competence, the only relevant consideration is the current, real-time performance of highly competent people in critical assignments. General personal competence, future potential, and suitability for other roles are all important attributes, but they are irrelevant to this discussion because they have no direct impact on current corporate performance. A person may have broad general competence in many areas (i.e., a jack-of-all-trades), but unless that person is highly competent now in a specific critical position, that general competence does not have an impact on corporate performance. The same is true of a person who may have future potential to be president of the company but today is a modestly competent second-line supervisor. It is also true of a person who might sometime be a great sales representative but today is a poor engineer. In contrast, a person who has no general competence, no potential for career advancement, and no suitability for other roles may have a current positive impact on performance by being highly competent at just one critical task.

I began to understand this issue after I commenced a formal assessment of the relationship between the competence of individuals and the performance of their organizations. Since then, I have done this assessment many times in many places, with surprisingly similar results. In some cases, without conducting a formal assessment, it has been possible to use the general knowledge gained by several years of assessing competence to look for attributes of an organization that indicate a focused change in competence would be of immediate value. This chapter describes the genesis and process of competence assessment as well as some of the general knowledge and lessons for management that I have obtained from those assessments. Finally, the chapter includes a few practical recommendations for management action that I have distilled from the knowledge gained during this process.

Early Assessments of Individual Employee Competence

When I began to study the relationship between the competence of individuals and the performance of their organizations, the study was associated with my other work to continuously enhance the engagement of all the people in practicing improvement. At that time, I believed it would be appropriate to look at the competence of *all* people. To facilitate this assessment, I developed a simple standard definition of the states of competence that I believed would be effective across the complete spectrum of occupations that might be encountered within a manufacturing organization. That standard is shown in Figure 13.1.

During these first assessments, I looked at all the people in an organization and gathered a lot of demographic data on individuals, such as age, formal

Level I	Competence level I describes a person who is only able to conduct the basic elements of the task and who requires some supervision to achieve that performance. This is the level of competence normally associated with a poor performer or someone who is new to the job.
Level II	Competence level II describes a person who is able to conduct all the basic elements of the task with no supervision. Such a person may be able to do more advanced elements with some supervision and ought to be able to create and implement small event improvement associated with the basic elements of the work. This is the level of performance normal to most of the workforce.
Level III	Competence level III describes a person who is able to perform all of the task elements, both basic and advanced, with no supervision. Such a person ought to frequently initiate improvement to the basic elements of the task and regularly initiate improvements to the more advanced elements of the work. This person also provides task help (normally mentoring, not supervision) to enable others to achieve competence level II.
Level IV	Competence level IV describes a person who is a master of all the elements of the task and is competent enough to frequently improve the both basic and advanced elements of the task and to create valuable extensions to the work itself. This person provides task help (normally mentoring, not supervision) to enable others to achieve competence level II or III.

Figure 13.1   Competence matrix used in assessments.

education, length of employment, and other attributes that I thought might have some bearing on competence. This was intended to be a comprehensive assessment, and until I had some indication where the end point would be, I wanted to make certain that I had gathered adequate data to enable several possible analytical routes.

After 20 organizations had been assessed, I began to analyze the data. As you might expect, organizations with a more competent population generally performed better than organizations with a less competent population. However, the correlations between individual competence and organizational performance were weak, and the exceptions to the correlations were plentiful. It was clear from that first analysis of the data that the general competence of an organization's employees is important, but not much more important than many other factors. The small performance benefit of improved general competence could easily be overwhelmed by other small differences. Something more was needed before this work would have the value that I believed was available.

Recognizing the Importance of Critical Positions to the Overall Performance of the Organization

The something more that was needed was the concept of critical positions.

> **Key Idea:** A critical position is defined as one in which the incumbent has personal influence on the performance of an important aspect of the organization's business or has personal influence on the performance of several other people who collectively influence the performance of an important aspect of the organization's business.

It may sound as if I have just defined most, if not all, supervisory and managerial positions as critical, but you should wait before coming to that conclusion, because it is not accurate. Critical positions vary from place to place. Here are a few examples:

- A specialty chemical operation with many products and a product portfolio that changes rapidly to reflect new technical capabilities of the manufacturer as well as ongoing customer developments defined two analytical chemist positions in the manufacturing support laboratory as critical.
- Another operation with a stable but very wide variety of products defined the production planner/scheduler position as critical.
- A pump manufacturer decided that it was critical to have a true subject matter expert in each of the maintenance craft areas.
- Several operations defined nonsupervisory "group leaders" as critical, while defining many of the front-line supervisors as noncritical.
- Several plants defined a nonsupervisory engineering specialist position that served as a technical resource to the organization as critical.

Surprisingly often, critical positions turn out to be individual contributors, and not supervisors or managers. These are positions where someone personally does an important task that must be done very well for the business to succeed. As an alternative, these are positions where a credible individual with great personal expertise can help others to become better at a more general task. There are certainly critical positions that are supervisory or managerial positions, but I have found those to be less than half of the total of critical positions in most places.

Having assessed nearly 200 organizations in different companies, different nations, and different industries so far, I have found that critical positions are normally between 8% and 12% of the total positions in the business. Especially in multishift operations, some of these critical positions are occupied by more than a single individual. However, recognizing that many of these critical positions are individual contributor positions, the people who occupy critical positions are generally between 10% and 15% of the total population of a business. Notice that there are two distinct concepts here: first, there are the critical positions themselves, and then there are the people who occupy critical positions.

As I began to understand the relationship between critical positions and organizational performance, the collection and analysis of data focused only on critical positions, and the result began to become very valuable. In fact, everything of useful management value that I have learned about the relationship between individual competence and the performance of organizations was learned with respect to people who occupy critical positions. The material in the rest of this chapter reports those findings.

The Basis of Data Gathering to Assess Employee Competence

To assess competence, I look at two measures of a business, described in the following subsections.

Measure the Percentage of Critical Positions Occupied by Highly Competent People

The first measure of importance to this assessment is the extent to which the critical positions of the business are currently occupied by individuals considered to have competence at level III or level IV, as described in Figure 13.1. For simplicity, I routinely describe people at competence levels III and IV as "highly competent people." The measure used was the simple percentage of critical positions occupied by highly competent people. The range of possible results for this measure was from 0% (representing a business with no highly competent people in critical positions) to greater than 100% (representing a business with all or most critical positions occupied by highly competent people and also at least some "excess" highly competent replacements trained and available to ensure a continuation of high competence at all times).

There is a possibility that an organization could have a very high result for this measure because it has several highly competent people staged for a few critical positions, while other critical positions are without any highly competent person. That being said, when organizations were careful enough with formal training programs to have many highly competent people aligned with critical positions, those people were normally fairly distributed. Even when there was a small gap in their training program due to an unrecognized critical position, the analysis of their performance was consistent with other data in the comparative assessment that will be described later in this chapter.

> **Key Idea:** It is important to note that highly competent people who did not occupy critical positions did not demonstrate an impact on the business performance. These highly competent people, and also other natural leaders or naturally influential people, certainly make a contribution, but that contribution alone does not appear to significantly change the competitive performance of their organizations.

Measure the Overall Performance of the Organization

The second business factor for this analysis was a measure of the performance of the organization. Since I have looked exclusively at manufacturing organizations while conducting the competence assessments, the measure of performance that I selected was the overall equipment effectiveness ratio (OEER). The OEER is a popular combination measure of manufacturing success comprised of three factors:

1. The reliability or availability of the means of production (normally equipment).
2. The productivity or the rate at which available capacity for production was actually utilized.
3. Product quality, or the rate at which utilized capacity produced good products.

As discussed in Chapter 12, the OEER is not my favorite measure for many purposes associated with small-event improvement because it is too complex to be intuitively comprehended, therefore it has little communication value. The OEER is also fairly easily manipulated by a manager who underreports available capacity. But OEER has two good attributes that make it very valuable for the purpose of this assessment:

1. It is in common use among people practicing lean manufacturing.
2. The data to create reasonably good information for computing the OEER is readily available, even in those plants that do not currently use the measure for their own reporting.

The Process of Data Gathering to Assess Employee Competence

The assessment that I am about to describe probably does not seem very sophisticated, and it is not. For a business with 100 or fewer total people and a good manager who has been in place for several years, a similar assessment and use of data like this is almost intuitive. The importance of this more formal and structured approach to competence assessment is that it allows larger organizations or managers with short tenure to routinely achieve the same knowledge through a disciplined process.

> **Key Idea:** As with many of the ideas in this book, in small groups, there often are successful individuals who can easily and naturally manage all the aspects of the human side of the business. The reason for developing formal practices is to enable most people in large organizations to do the same.

Step 1: Identify the Critical Positions in Your Organization

The first step in gathering the data at a particular plant or business is to identify your critical positions. Remember that the test for a critical position is that the person in that position does one of two things:

- Individually performs a business-critical function, or
- Influences the performance of several other individuals who collectively perform a business-critical function.

Identification of critical positions is not a scientific undertaking. Do not overwork the process. A prompt good start followed by evolutionary improvement is the way to approach this sort of task. In organizations having up to 500 people, I have worked with local managers to get this task completed in less than half a day. You may recall that Chapter 12 discussed the use of a subject matter expert (SME) to bring some objectivity, or at least some consistency, to subjective analysis. Competence assessment is a perfect example of a good use of that technique to facilitate the process and to give results from diverse operations greater consistency than they might otherwise enjoy.

Step 2: Assess the Individuals Working in Your Critical Positions

The next step is to assess the individuals who currently occupy those critical positions. In most cases, you should also assess others who have previously occupied those positions, along with those individuals who might occupy critical positions in the future. The assessment is made against the competence criteria described earlier in Figure 13.1.

With the right people in the room, including the need to change the people in the room as the positions being assessed move through the organization, it should be possible to complete this assessment in about 5 minutes per person. For an organization of about 500 people, with a maximum of 15% of the people potentially occupying critical positions, this assessment should be complete in one day. It may be a long day, but get it done. And again, the use of a SME to facilitate the discussions results in both better and faster completion.

Correlating Personal Competence with Organizational Performance

As described earlier, the competence of the total population has some correlation to the performance of the organization, but the correlation is not strong, and many organizations present obvious exceptions to the rules of practice derived from the correlations that exist. That is not true of critical positions. Competence of the people in critical positions corresponds very closely to organizational performance, and there are very few exceptions to the rules of practice suggested by that correspondence.

As I analyzed a growing number of businesses, I created a "competence" ranking of organizations based on the percentage of critical positions occupied by highly competent people and another "performance" ranking of the same organizations based on the corresponding OEER results. As a result, I had produced a rank-ordered list of the critical competence of each business (from the most competent to the least competent) and also a rank-ordered list of the performance of each business (from the highest OEER to the lowest). The result was almost amazing.

With a modest allowance for measurement error (currently with data on about 200 assessed operations, I allow plus or minus five positions on the competence list), almost every business that has been assessed occupies a comparable position on both lists. Even more important for the purpose of using these data for management action, there are very few operations that appear to be clear exceptions to developing a rule of practice that highly competent people in critical positions are an important factor in the success of the enterprise. For these purposes, a "clear exception" is considered to be a business that is "out of position" by more than plus or minus 15 positions on the competence rank, when comparing the business's position on the competence ranking with the predicted position on the performance ranking.

> **Key Idea:** The theory of industrial competence provided by this result is straightforward. Highly competent people in critical positions are a significant factor in determining the extent of business success that can be achieved.

With the confidence derived from a lot of data, that statement is the basis for a general rule of management practice with strong correlation and few exceptions. The next issue is to apply that knowledge to benefit individual businesses.

Management Lessons from Competence Assessment

Having identified the general rule that, with some confidence, more highly competent people in critical positions corresponds to more business success, I began to torture the data to see if it would confess other things as well. Indeed, there are several other very interesting lessons of general applicability. I have often used these lessons to great benefit even without conducting a formal assessment. Here are several that may be of value to you and your business.

Focus Your First Personnel Development Actions on Critical Positions

In the early assessments, data were gathered on all people. Those data did confirm a general correlation between overall competence and performance, but the correlation was weak. Because there were also many exceptions, it was uncertain if an investment to raise the competence of all the people would actually provide improved performance. With a large training cost and an uncertain business return, the prospect of mass competence improvement was not a management strategy that I could recommend.

In contrast, the problem of low efficiency for the training effort and uncertain expectations for the business outcome of providing training does not exist when considering critical positions. The correlation between highly competent people in critical positions and business success is very strong, and there are very few clear exceptions. As described before, critical positions are normally around 10% of total positions, and less than 15% of the total population occupies critical positions. Therefore it is possible to recommend a management practice that you formally manage the competence of the people who will occupy your critical positions. The training or development effort is reasonable, and there is high confidence in the outcome.

In fact, I have found that most businesses that have existed for some time already have about 10% of their total population who are highly competent as incumbents in critical positions or who would be highly competent in one of the critical positions if they were reassigned. Further, normally a minimum of about half of the critical positions are currently occupied by a highly competent person. The practical task of obtaining the business benefit from managing the relationship between personal competence and performance is quite achievable. Most businesses need to train or reassign only about 5% of their people to greatly improve performance.

Begin Promptly

With the assessments of people (one day) and positions (half a day) completed, even in a large organization of 500 people or so, you can begin actively managing competence by noon on the second day after you initiate the assessment. There is no reason or value to delay realizing the benefit of this assessment process. You should begin the assessment with the intent of getting immediate results.

You begin by specifically identifying the critical positions that currently do not have a highly competent incumbent. With that information you can do two things.

First, you can attempt to find someone in your existing organization who would be highly competent if he or she were in that position. If that additional data were one of the considerations in your initial assessment, as recommended, then you already have that information. To the extent that you have highly competent people who can fill critical positions through reassignment, you can have that improvement as fast as you can make the change. At several plants, the first reassignment to benefit from this work had occurred before I left the plant.

Second, if no highly competent person is immediately available, then you want to find someone in or out of your organization (including the incumbent) who can become highly competent with the addition of some focused personal development. This route takes longer, but it is one of the few training efforts that you will ever undertake with real confidence that there will be a direct correlation with future improvements in business performance.

The important thing is this. Referring to the existing competence normally found in organizations as described above, even in a large organization of 500 people, you are only looking at training or reassigning about 25 people (i.e., 5%). You can do that. In fact, most businesses already have a better situation than the worst-case scenario of maximum need and minimum availability. And most organizations are already planning to do more training than this, but they do not anticipate such a great result. It takes a very long time and a lot of money to change the competence of an entire organization, but it is both affordable and relatively fast to change the competence of a few people to staff your critical positions. The demonstrated benefit of doing that is both large and relatively certain. The issue for management is to identify the correct few people for reassignment or focused development, and this process helps you do that.

> **Example:** During one consulting assignment, I encountered an operation with truly severe mechanical reliability problems. After some discussion, I learned that they had an agreement with the local union that caused every job in the plant to be assigned purely on the basis of seniority. Because nearly all jobs except the maintenance crafts were rotating shift positions, the maintenance crafts were entirely populated with older workers who had entered the craft world with no experience and little training.
>
> New management who had inherited this unusual situation believed that they were faced with a nearly insurmountable training burden before they could get out from under their reliability problems. In fact, although they had a few people eager to become excellent craft workers, they were concerned that many of these older workers were not willing to make the effort to become expert at their crafts. Based on the insight gained from my experience with the competency assessment process, I was able to teach them that what they really needed for an immediate improvement was only a single person of high competence in each craft. With some very intense, highly focused training, they were able to rather quickly develop some real expertise in their five best craft people.

Most of the existing craft people were competent (at level II in Figure 13.1), and now they also had some highly competent people (at levels III and IV in Figure 13.1) available for special situations and for mentoring the others. These managers never undertook a formal competency assessment, but they benefited from the general understanding of the results.

Spread the Word about Competence Management

Although I generally limited the discussion with the senior managers with whom I worked to analysis of critical positions for the business as an entirety, some of the most successful businesses promptly spread the word about managing competence broadly throughout their organizations, with real benefit. It is common in a manufacturing environment to have very well-known differences in performance among small teams doing the same or similar work. The performance of one team is known to be good, and the performance of another team is recognized to be bad. This sort of disparity is very apparent in multishift operations, where several teams operate the same equipment, producing the same products, but with very different performance. In most cases, the differences are not addressed because they are assumed to be personal to the team leader, or just a coincidence of good or bad people accumulating on the same team.

The fact is that accumulation of good and bad people in one place is exactly what has happened. Good people enjoy working together, working for a good team leader, and producing a superior outcome. Similarly, poor performers enjoy working for a weak supervisor. That result of differing performance among several teams is very quickly manageable. Although it does not fit the definition of managing business-critical positions for the entire business, this sort of situation may very well be business critical to the performance of a second-line supervisor. When senior management communicates the simple concepts of competency management broadly, I have often seen middle managers decide that certain positions were critical to their part of the business and take their own prompt action to manage competence locally.

The most common response of middle management is the immediate reassignment of a few high-performing individuals to spread the wealth by breaking up the teams that have accumulated all the good people. Some focused training to enhance local competence is also possible at levels below the enterprise level. And, honestly, in some situations, the people on the poor teams with the weak supervisor usually are already more competent than they are demonstrating. They do not need further training to improve. Breaking up the bad teams often produces an improvement, with nothing more required. Again, competence awareness and management is just another tool for organizational analysis and improvement that you can easily deliver to your organization with great effect.

Recognize That Not All Managers Need to Be Highly Competent

One finding that was of real interest to me is that no organization that I have encountered has believed that it was necessary for all of its top managers to be highly competent. On average, the result was that most organizations believe it is necessary that only about three out of five top managers be highly competent. The most interesting thing about this finding is that, unless you have a truly incompetent member of senior management or a dictatorial and modestly competent most senior leader, it does not seem to matter which three of the five senior leaders are highly competent. I think that this is good news, not bad. Leadership is definitely important. But there appears to be plenty of space to accommodate management development and other assignments that take leaders out of their comfort (and competence) zones for a while.

There is also space to accommodate leaders who have reached their limits. The Peter Principle suggests that highly competent people are promoted until they become incompetent. That probably is an exaggeration. Based on my experience, highly competent people are probably promoted until they become merely competent. And this study suggests that there is room at or near the top for some of those people to make good contributions, with no adverse impact on the business success.

Many Critical Positions Are Underappreciated

A longer-term management issue is that during the assessments, it was relatively easy to identify critical positions using the simple definition provided. When we sat managers down and systematically sorted through the organization looking for jobs that had a critical impact on the performance of the business, they quickly identified them, and normally there was little disagreement among the several managers present. Many of those critical positions were individual contributor positions.

The management opportunity is that, prior to exercising a formal discipline of identifying these nonmanagement positions as critical to business success, most managers had not spent much time thinking about either the position or the incumbent. Except in the very best organizations, it was extremely unusual to find a formal development or succession plan in place to ensure competence in these positions. Managers appear to be strongly biased toward managing development and succession in management and supervisory positions. In contrast, the critical individual contributor positions often had received no prior thought at all in that regard.

In several cases, it was clear that I was brought in as a consultant because the business was not as good as it once had been. During the assessment, the older members of the management team frequently recalled that when the business had been more successful, the critical individual contributor positions had been occupied by highly competent persons. However, no one was specifically managing the competence of nonmanagerial positions. When the previous highly competent person retired, quit, transferred, or died, a new person of only modest competence took that critical job. There was no plan to create a new highly competent person. As a result, business performance declined, and few members of senior management recognized the reason why that had happened. This situation is very common when businesses merge or sell. A great many people of lengthy experience and high competence disappear at the time of the event, and because this is just one of many changes in progress, no one notices until the effect of the lost competence appears on the bottom line some time later.

This experience of institutional memory of prior competence corroborates the concept. It also is a useful management tool. Often the person who once was highly competent is still around, but in another job, or has retired but is available to return as an advisor to the organization. That person can either be quickly reassigned or at least promptly return for a while to provide a focused development program for the current incumbent. The lesson derived from this exercise is to develop the discipline of succession planning for critical individual contributor positions exactly the same as you practice for management positions.

Key Idea: Remember that the correlation between business performance and the extent to which critical positions are occupied by highly competent people extended past the 100% mark on the occupancy scale. Organizations with highly competent people in all the critical positions as well as highly competent backfills for those critical positions performed even better than the organizations with only highly competent incumbents. A formal development and succession plan to provide a continuous presence of highly competent people in critical individual contributor roles, including even temporary replacement to cover for absence, is a good investment for most businesses and a good discipline for management.

Lessons to be Learned from the Exceptions

As discussed earlier in this chapter, one of the problems with the early assessments that attempted to consider the competence of all the people was that there were quite a few clear exceptions to the rule that higher competence produced better performance. The existence of those exceptions made it uncertain that we could predict success even for an organization that was willing to undertake a massive program to improve competence of the general population.

There were also a few clear exceptions in the assessments that considered only the competence of people in the critical positions. In that case, because the relationship between performance and competence was clear and the exceptions were few, it was possible to establish a beneficial rule for management practice. It was further possible to look closely at the relatively few exceptions to see if there was anything to learn. If the correlation between competence in critical positions and performance is really strong, why would some organizations not follow it? It was a real revelation to me that in several situations, when we studied the exceptions closely, what we found actually reinforced the general rule that competence in critical positions corresponds to performance. Once we understood the mechanism or the special cause that resulted in the exceptions to the rule, we found that the rule applied even where it did not appear to do so.

> **Example 1:** In the first exception that I studied closely, the measured performance (OEER) was much greater than would have been predicted by the competence of the people in the critical positions. Upon detailed examination, it was determined that this particular plant had quite a few more people than similar plants. Nothing in the OEER measurement of performance considers the efficiency of the workforce. The managers of this plant were achieving operating performance that exceeded what was predicted by their competence because they had deployed a larger workforce to accommodate the lack of skills. Plant management and business management was aware that their workforce was out of line with peers, but they did not know what to do about it. They believed (correctly) that they needed all the people they had in order to perform well in production and quality. Because they were fielding superior performance at the customer interface in a highly profitable business, they did not receive a lot of adverse attention for the problem of an excess workforce. Competence assessment set them on the path to sustaining their good performance with an appropriate workforce and even better profitability.

Example 2: The other interesting exception was a plant where the actual performance was far less than would have been predicted based on the assessed competence of the people. As we studied that plant in detail, we came upon a truly odd result. As I have described it, the competence assessment process is largely based on a SME interviewing local management and drawing on their knowledge of the business and the people. That is recognized to be somewhat subjective, but the use of a SME for consistency provided generally good results across a wide variety of operations, nations, and businesses. Unfortunately, in this case, that practice let us down.

When we found that this plant was reporting very high competence for people in critical positions but delivering very low overall performance, we undertook a serious examination in even more detail than normal and with more external resources than normal. What we learned was that the plant manager and the entire senior staff of that plant had very little knowledge of either the business or the people. Because they did not have good knowledge of the business, they failed to understand that they were by far the worst plant of their type. Because they did not have good knowledge of the people, they reported to us that all their folks were highly competent.

We had somehow encountered a plant where the entire senior management team did not know what they were about and in fact knew so little that they did not realize that they even had a problem! They were nice people, and at least one of them was considered to have good potential for the future. But in that plant, at that time, we did not have three out of five senior managers who were highly competent in their current assignments. Once again, the discipline of competence assessment proved that the rule of competence corresponding to performance is correct and the apparent exception led to a significant opportunity for immediate improvement.

Summary of Chapter 13

- A critical factor of business success is an engaged workforce. With an engaged workforce, truly great performance correlates strongly with a few highly competent people in business-critical roles.
- This assessment is a real-time determination of an individual's ability to contribute to the success of the enterprise.

- There is only a modest correspondence between the competence of all the people in a business and the performance of that business, and there are many clear exceptions to suggest that the influence of general competence cannot be distinguished from many other factors that modestly influence performance.
- Critical positions are positions where the incumbent has personal influence over some aspect of business performance or personal influence over other people who collectively influence business performance.
- Critical positions are often nonsupervisory or individual contributor positions.
- The correspondence between the competence of people in critical positions and the performance of their organization is strong, and there are few clear exceptions.
- Competence data gathering should utilize input from several knowledgeable managers and preferably also a SME to produce a result that is as consistent and credible as possible.
- Management action to fill critical positions with highly competent people can begin immediately after completing the assessment either through reassignment or focused personal development.
- Use of competence assessment as a senior management tool for the business often results in greater awareness and valuable general management action throughout the enterprise.
- Not all managers need to be highly competent. Generally, only three out of five senior managers at the highest competence levels is sufficient.
- Individual contributor positions are often unrecognized and unappreciated despite being critical to business success. Competency management and succession planning for those positions often produces surprisingly strong benefits.
- If you find organizations that are reporting competence that does not correspond to their reported performance (both good and bad), it is often possible to learn valuable lessons from those exceptions.

GETTING STARTED IN YOUR ORGANIZATION

In the Preface, I suggested that by the end of two years, you ought to enjoy substantially improved performance and have all the elements of a culture of rapid improvement in place. When I encounter businesses where the improvement efforts have been "in progress" for longer than two years without achieving a step change in the pace of improvement or without achieving autonomous participation, there is always an identifiable problem.

There are several possible causes for the problem of a business that has a case of the chronic slows, but four failures of leadership are the most common:

- Reason 1: Management has attempted to jump directly to autonomous action, but did not establish the required foundation. This is common when management hopes that everyone else will change, but that management will not have to.
- Reason 2: Management has focused its improvement efforts toward implementing a tool of improvement (such as 6σ) rather than toward strategic business goals. The people of the business often become excellent practitioners of the tool, but they rarely make the business more successful.
- Reason 3: Management believed that a great deal of training and other preparation was required before improvement could begin. The business therefore devoted a lot of time and money to preparation, but never got to the stage of actually practicing improvement.

■ Reason 4: Management has attempted to reproduce the specific practices (such as quality stations) observed at a successful business rather than learning why those practices work and adapting that theory to the special needs of its own business and people. The theories of improvement and culture travel well, but most successful practices are local.

The Path Forward

One of several possible ways to avoid getting a case of the slows in your improvement process and get a good start toward establishing your new culture is to manage your activities and measure your progress in six-month segments. Tracking progress in six-month increments ensures prompt action, but avoids the confusion of shorter periods when early systemic improvement can be overshadowed by natural variation in the conduct of the business. A two-year plan with four well-defined six-month increments allows management to focus on conducting the business, including the business of improvement, with some clarity and assurance of success. During each of these four phases of implementation, you will need to address the five critical elements of culture change:

1. Provide clear *goals* that people can achieve.
2. Provide new *tools* or capabilities for people to make changes.
3. Change the *culture* or the social interactions that define teamwork and inclusion in your workplace.
4. Conduct formally organized *pilot projects* that demonstrate your goals, tools, and culture and provide immediate improvement to the business.
5. *Sustain* or prepare to sustain the improvements that you are making.

The material that follows in Chapters 14 through 17 is more detailed than the rest of this book. It will describe clear guidelines and milestones for specific activities to be achieved in each of the four six-month improvement cycles during the first two years of your implementation. However, there is no suggestion here that improvement can be reduced to a cookbook or formula that you can follow without the creative input of your own team. In fact, many of the activities during this period call specifically for the creation of strategies and practices that are special to your business. But I think it will be useful for your planning if I describe a specific path that I have followed with some success as a reference.

If you want to vary from this path or add and subtract from the details according to the character of your own business and people, that is fine. But as you proceed with planning and implementing your new culture, this model can be a good reference for the sort of things that you ought to be doing or the pace that you ought to be achieving in order to make the best possible progress.

Chapter 14

Phase I: The First Six Months

During the first six-month period, you will set the foundation for the rest of your work. This does not imply in any way that this is a period when there will be no improvement. Instead, real, measured progress in performance, not just in implementation, needs to occur in each six-month period. As described in the Section V introduction, the activities will be in five areas. For Phase I, these key initiatives are

1. Create strategic goals for the business.
2. Give your people new capabilities or tools to practice improvement.
3. Begin the discussion of new social interactions and a new culture for the business that is more inclusive for individuals and more autonomous.
4. Conduct at least one pilot project that will put real examples in place of how the tools and strategies for improvement work within your business.
5. Establish the basis for sustaining the improvements.

This chapter describes each of these five initiatives in more detail.

Task 1: Create Strategic Goals for Your Business

The work of creating strategic goals was the subject of Chapter 2. It will probably take senior management the full six months of Phase I to formulate the initial set of strategic goals. This is because you will need serious internal and external research to fully understand the future demands of your external environment as well as the current internal capabilities of your enterprise. From that assessment of strategic strengths and needs, the team of senior leaders will need to agree on the few changes of real importance that are both necessary and sufficient to close the gaps between what you can do now and what you will need to do during the next five years. Although I do not often believe that true consensus is required, because the goals established during this phase will be the basis for focused action throughout the organization for several years, this is one case where I do believe that the management team must reach actual consensus before you begin to disseminate the goals to others.

This is a six-month task because you will not be working all day, every day on the development of strategic goals. There are necessary breaks in the action while you wait for information or analysis or as you experience delays in scheduling meetings with external stakeholders, such as customers. The leaders of your business also need time during these six months to manage the existing demands of conducting your ongoing business. Six months allows time for a thorough analysis and also for obtaining consensus among the senior management team before going forward.

Do make sure, however, that you have finished establishing and writing your goals within this first six months. Your business will be better if you proceed with goals that are directionally correct (even though they may be imperfect) than if you delay for additional months in what is sure to be a futile attempt to achieve a perfect statement of your goals.

Task 2: Give Your People New Capabilities or Tools to Practice Improvement

The second task of Phase I is to provide new capabilities for improvement. Chronic operating problems generally exist today because your people do not have the capability to fix them. In addition to problem resolution, the same concept is generally true for improvement opportunities that have gone unrealized. Even without a new culture, there are honest hardworking people throughout your business who would be glad to fix the chronic problems they have to live with and equally happy to capture the new opportunities you present to them. But they need the capability to do that.

For example, a key element in lean manufacturing is greatly increasing the flexibility for product-to-product transitions along with greatly improving the reliability of your plant and equipment and supply chain to enable you to produce good products on demand. Together, these physical improvements enable the logical improvement of lean manufacturing. The important breakthrough that has brought about the recent progress in lean manufacturing is not the knowledge that large inventories and the associated problems are caused by inflexibility and unreliability: everyone in manufacturing has known that for decades. For example, the practice of calculating economic order quantities originally developed by F. W. Harris in 1913 was an attempt to optimize the inflexibility that could not be avoided with traditional tools for product-to-product transitions. The critical breakthrough is that now we have the technology to enable rapid and inexpensive product transitions as well as several new capabilities in equipment design, maintenance, and reliability. We are fixing well-known problems because we now have the capability to fix them, not because we just discovered them.

During Phase I, as senior management develops your goals, you also need to select some new tools for improvement that are appropriate to your goals as you understand those developing goals. Clearly, if you know of new technical capabilities that will resolve long-standing problems, you will want to include those. This first set of new tools will not likely be the complete set that will exclusively serve your business needs in the future. However, it does need to represent a set of new capabilities that will quickly enable you and your people to demonstrate improvements that are aligned with your goals. Management will gain tremendous credibility for your initiative if you simply enable people to fix a problem that is well known and has high value.

Fortunately, introduction of a new capability for improvement is often more practical than it sounds. You may have identified or even initiated the use of some new tools already as a result of a current improvement effort. (Even if the initial results with a new tool have not been as successful as you wish, try again, but organize the effort differently, as in the pilot project described below.) Most manufacturing plants have one or more chronic reliability problems and several well-known problems with flexibility that can be solved with the enabling tools of lean manufacturing. Whatever direction is developing for your strategic goals, for most manufacturing businesses, fixing one of these well-known problems will be consistent with your goals as they progress.

There are several great new technologies of this sort for operating improvement that can be deployed with prompt results. A few of these will often get you off to a good start—for example, within this short list of technologies I have always found that one or more of them will produce a prompt improvement that will make a statement to your team about the new pace and success of improvement:

- Single minutes exchange of dies (SMED).
- Total productive maintenance (TPM).
- Reliability engineering.
- Value-stream mapping (VSM) or applying work management practices in administrative areas.

Although there are many good books that completely describe each of these new capabilities, for completeness here, I will introduce each one briefly in the following subsections.

Single Minutes Exchange of Dies

Single minutes exchange of dies is the technology for rapid transition of equipment from one configuration to another. It is useful for product-to-product changes that require mechanical reconfiguration of equipment as well as for a great many routine repetitive maintenance activities.

Here is a simple example that illustrates how it works: if you or I were to go out to our car and find a flat tire, it might take a half hour or more to change the one tire. Yet on television, we routinely watch racing professionals change four tires in 15 seconds. The difference is that they have made some modest modifications to the equipment (certainly modest relative to the total cost of the equipment and the value of what is at stake), and they have prepared in advance to do the task well and fast. Manufacturers can use the same logic and technology whenever you have a mechanical task that routinely needs to be done well and fast. Note that while you and I would have changed the tire alone, the professionals use several people. In industry, it is often very cost effective to use extra resources to make a transition that gets the equipment back in service quickly.

Total Productive Maintenance

Total productive maintenance devotees will hate me for saying this, but the essence of TPM is that the people who operate equipment learn the basic practices of caring for their equipment in much the same way that most conscientious car owners care for their cars. A conscientious car owner keeps his or her car clean, cool, and lubricated, and ensures regular performance of routine maintenance such as changing the oil and changing the filters. Conscientious owners also generally pay attention to the car, staying alert for anomalies in operation, sound, or performance. Sometimes the car owner does the work, and sometimes the owner arranges for the work to be done. When work is performed by others, the owner will "represent" the car to the mechanic.

In much the same way, TPM gives the owner-operator of industrial equipment the primary capability and responsibility for the routine repetitive basic care and monitoring of the equipment he or she operates. This generally results in improved basic care, conducted when most appropriate to the operation. And it allows the craft workers to move up the ladder from routine work to work that truly requires craft skills.

Reliability Engineering

Reliability engineering is the application of statistical analysis to equipment maintenance. There is great value in the sort of routine maintenance described in the previous section that owner-operators do. Those things generally constitute about one-quarter of all time-based maintenance (i.e., maintenance that occurs primarily because either calendar time or equipment run time has elapsed, and for no other reason). Beyond the work that is appropriate for owner-operators, most time-based preventive maintenance has little value. In fact, in round numbers, half of time-based preventive maintenance is useless: it has no impact at all on equipment performance.

Even more surprising, the final quarter of time-based maintenance actually causes harm. This generally occurs when a perfectly good part is replaced with a new part that immediately suffers infant mortality. Reliability engineering is the tool to move away from time-based maintenance to condition-based maintenance, which is less expensive and produces a better result. In fact, abandoning the three-quarters of time-based maintenance that is either useless or harmful (i.e., the time-based maintenance that is not included in the owner-operator routines of TPM) is often a good way to fund the initial work of reliability engineering.

Value-Stream Mapping

Value-stream mapping is the science of assessing work flow in search of activities that add little or no value. For light manufacturing and for administrative activities, value-stream mapping is the principle tool for identifying the accumulation of resources and associated non–value-adding work in order to resolve the cause of those accumulations. That is, VSM is the light industry and administrative approach to adopting lean practices.

As mentioned, each of these technologies is described in much more detail in other books, but this quick overview should give you some insight into these and other related new capabilities that are available to help you initiate pilot projects that will meet your needs in Phase I.

Task 3: Establish the Basis for a New Social Culture That Is More Inclusive and More Autonomous

The third task for Phase I is to begin the human part of culture change. This starts with enhancing the awareness of individual differences and personal cultures at the management level. This should include a lot of conversation about the differences that exist within the workplace now that prevent teams from forming and performing as they will need to do in the future. These will be difficult conversations for you. Therefore, now would be a good time to engage someone who has experience and expertise in this area to help you through this effort of talking about individual differences and preparing for the coming work of changing the way you manage the human side of your business. This will be the same person who trains your cultural team leader, to be described next.

During my seminars and workshops on culture, I routinely receive feedback that people cannot tolerate the fact that I talk about race, religion, and gender. Yet the undisputable fact is that in virtually all workplaces today, differences of race, religion, gender, gender orientation, and other personal attributes exist unresolved in a way that will, and does, interfere with establishing and operating high-performing teams. If you cannot tolerate hearing me talk about these topics in a classroom setting focused on culture, how will you ever have those conversations yourself with the folks who work for you?

Admittedly these are not conversations that anyone does well the first time with just natural empathy to guide them. You need a lot of experience to have this conversation successfully. During Phase I, you and your management team should begin to practice having cultural conversations of inclusion and autonomy. The focus of these first conversations among managers will be the design of your practices for including individuals and for establishing the social standards that will enable autonomous actions in small teams.

For the rest of the organization, the immediate implication of culture change that you can begin to communicate to your people is that in the future, most work will be done in small teams and that people will become more autonomous within their teams. The best basis for small-event improvement is work-oriented teams that are often described as "natural work groups." These teams include the front-line workers who share an easily identifiable, credibly common work set, along with one or a few other people who support their efforts. This support person might be an engineer, a craft supervisor, or a lab technician. As you begin to establish these small teams near the end of Phase I, either senior management or middle management can decide what teams are most appropriate to the task at hand, but you should make the relationships within the team natural and credible to the team members. Use the first six months to organize your front-line teams that will be the basis for future work. These teams will be months away from autonomy, but they need to be created now so that they can begin to establish their own standards and practices of working as a team and also so that during the second phase of implementation, they can conduct the goal translation.

Also near the end of the first six months, you should begin to communicate about the social elements of culture by describing the three-part model that we have been using throughout this book. Provide team leaders and managers throughout your organization (managers first) with an introduction to the three-part model as a basis for the cultural conversations described in Chapter 8, which bring people together intelligently and inoffensively. It would be premature to encourage a lot of inexperienced people to try cultural conversation yet. Managers need to get their own experience (as described above) before they can help others. But by describing the model of culture and the practice of using the model as a basis for future conversations that resolve interpersonal differences, you can achieve two things:

1. You will get managers and team leaders thinking about the personal behaviors that they practice and that they see around them as a derivation of larger values and beliefs. This often has real value and little risk, as it is an essentially private or personal introduction to the team conversations that will occur later.
2. As you begin to demonstrate some management-led examples of valuing individuals and some management-led examples of talking about culture in the new way, your people will recognize what you are doing as examples of what they will be doing soon.

Example: Try not to expect that people will naturally understand that your actions are intended to be exemplary. Always explain what you are doing. Because large chemical plants are huge expanses of concrete and equipment, we adopted the practice of having flower gardens near our shops, control houses, and other places where people gather. In what I believed to be an exemplary manner, I always picked a few weeds from the gardens whenever I entered one of those places. I hoped that others would see that example and adopt the practice. In my mind, the flower gardens would soon become self-maintaining.

One of our superintendents picked a few weeds one day and called me afterward. Although he was laughing nearly too hard to get the message out, he reported that he had been asked to stop. He was told: "Don't do that. Ray likes to do that himself."

During Phase I, you should select one person who can serve as the leader of your cultural design team and as an advisor to management on social issues, including the emotional health of the organization. This should be an internal person if you have someone who has the capability to do this work. This person will work with the consultant and also with management.

Key Idea: Senior management will need both the consultant and the internal resource until you are more comfortable with the activity. If you have a traditional organization and your only resource for cultural change is internal, you are not likely to truly address the tough issues that exist. A credible consultant can help ensure that you address issues with which you are truly uncomfortable.

Give the internal person you select specific training to develop formal skills in organizational culture. By the end of Phase I, you should be well along in developing your own internal subject matter expert (SME) in cultural matters. This assignment can be full time or part time, depending on the size and needs of your business, but it should be clear to you and to your organization that you have a new capability in human interactions.

Late in Phase I, as your cultural resource begins to be comfortable and competent in the assignment, you can begin to make those capabilities available to help team leaders as your teams begin to organize. Let your developing SME begin to practice and demonstrate the conversations of awareness and inclusion as soon as that capability has been developed. This is a great resource to keep your teams healthy and happy as they form. Forming work teams and keeping them healthy is not a new task, but now you can use your SME to demonstrate a new method of communications and new support for team leaders. Every time you demonstrate to people that you are working in a new and valuable way, you gain credibility.

Key Idea: You may already have work teams. Probably those teams are quite informal; you will benefit from exercising the team development described in this book to make your existing teams into the teams that you will need for the future.

As you begin talking openly about inclusion, awareness, and culture and obviously deploying a new resource, people begin to get accustomed to the idea and begin to expect cultural change. This may not sound like much, but cultural change is such an emotional topic that there is real value in getting people thinking about it before you begin to make more formal changes.

Task 4: Conduct Your First Pilot Project

The fourth management task for the first six months is to create a highly visible pilot project to demonstrate that your organization is now better able to fix some of its known chronic problems. Chronic problems suck the life out of a manufacturing organization, and visibly fixing an important one will go a long way to establish the credibility of your efforts. Even if you have tried the same tools before, try again. The tools and technologies of improvement are just like other technologies. They do work, and they will work for you. The most common cause for disappointing results is the support (or, more specifically, the extent of support) that you give projects in the early days of using a new tool. The tools of improvement are tremendously capable, but early efforts often need quite a bit of support to ensure success because the team is both learning the new tool as well as solving a problem. Think of solving this problem as a trial run for the sort of things that many people will be doing later. You truly need for this project to be successful, and therefore you need to support it in a way that will ensure success. Make it happen!

The way to initiate this pilot project to ensure success is to select a well-known, long-standing problem and then organize a team of your best people to use your new tools to fix it. Be sure that you put enough power on the team to ensure that the problem is successfully resolved. Establishing a basis for new activity is not a time to be stingy with resources. Doing a new thing for the first time is hard, and far too many new initiatives fail because of a simple lack of the resources and support needed. In chemical engineering, we refer to the excess capability needed at startup as "activation energy." Once you pass through the activation energy threshold, continuing the new activity requires more normal resources, but you need to be certain that the pilot project is well staffed and successful before you can get to the point of normal practice. In the first instances, you need people who have the excess capability to do three different things:

1. Learn the tool for themselves.
2. Use it on this project.
3. Teach it to others.

You should select team members who are capable of becoming either a team leader or a SME for other pilot projects that will be started in the future.

This first project might be a known reliability problem or a problem with inflexibility. I like to start with reliability or flexibility issues because I know that critical equipment that is unreliable or inflexible is often the most visible routine problem for people and because there are great tools to address these issues. However, if you decide that some other area is most important, then you certainly should start with correcting your own version of critical problems.

For communication purposes, pick a problem that demonstrates improvement that is consistent with your developing strategy and for which you have an appropriate new tool. For credibility, pick a problem that is well known as a chronic thorn in the side of your performance. It is never a good idea to demonstrate that your new tool for improvement can fix a trivial problem: instead, fix something that people recognize is valuable. More practically, if management-led pilot projects with strong project teams cannot address and correct meaningful problems, you will never convince other people that they ought to be able to address them either. Normally, if you have a large business, you will want to select a project implementation team that includes members from throughout the several different parts of the company so that they can return to their home organizations and become part of distributing the new capabilities.

With great visibility and with some fanfare appropriate to your existing culture, publicly identify the problem to be solved and its strategic implications for the success of your business. Identify the new capability that you will use to resolve the problem. Remember that your pilot project is not a good example unless people know what you are doing and watch as you do it. Then set your team of good people in motion to fix it. They have six months. While management is setting the strategic goals for the business, this pilot team will demonstrate to everyone that new progress is about to occur using new capabilities for improvement. The message that you want to send is this: the strategic focus is effective, the new improvement tools work, and we know how to use both in our business.

Project selection is important for another reason: performance. Never allow your improvement teams to waste six months practicing new methods on small problems that will not change your performance. The first project alone should provide a meaningful increment of the step change that you want to achieve in business performance. Selecting and completing the right pilot project with the right people on the team is critical. You need to be careful in launching the right project and team, and you need to be certain that you manage this event to be successful. The technologies of improvement actually work, and you need to make certain that they work for you.

You should also anticipate that when new methods of improvement make an appearance in your operation, there will be natural leaders throughout your business who immediately adopt them and, within their existing authority, conduct their own mini pilot projects. This is not yet autonomous activity, and you should be certain that even enthusiastic adopters follow existing authority and approval practices for this work. Autonomy is carefully managed; it comes later after you have created the framework for carefully managed autonomous work. However, these mini-pilot projects that pop up will also be immediately added to your base performance and will add to the credibility of your effort.

> **Example:** When I first introduced two of Shigeo Shingo's methods—single minutes exchange of dies (SMED) and Poka-Yoke (mistake avoidance)—into the chemical industry, we had two maintenance craftsmen, one a mechanic and one an electrician, who immediately

adopted both new methods as their own. These two men, together, were responsible for the maintenance of a group of balers that compressed synthetic rubber crumb into solid bales for packaging.

They hung a sign over their little office on the production floor and labeled it the "SMED-quarters." Thereafter, each time they had an opportunity, and in clear conformance with their existing authority, they made a series of changes to make the equipment more flexible and the quality more visible. In addition to the improvements that these men made, the obvious adoption of "management's new tool" by two very credible technicians had an amazing effect on the psychology of the effort.

Task 5: Sustain Your Gains

The final task for Phase I is to begin sustaining the gains. It probably sounds strange to begin the discussion of sustaining the gains during the first phase of implementation, but there are already aspects of your work that are both important and fragile. Sustaining them now is critical. The most obvious among these is the measurement system.

An important part of establishing and communicating your strategic goals is determining the measurements that will be used to track progress. Setting the measurements for the first time requires a collaborative effort between management and a SME who knows about measurement systems. (If you do not have such a person, you can create one now in the same way that you are creating the SME for culture change.) The SME will ensure that all the attributes of a successful measurement system as described in Chapter 12 are followed and that all the capabilities of the measurement techniques described there are available to management.

Of equal importance, as soon as you communicate your measurement system for the first time, the organization will respond. With nothing more than the measurement system as a basis for action, most managers throughout the business will begin to manage in a way that conforms to the measures. This will almost certainly begin to occur before the translation to tactical goals and the commencement of autonomous action is complete. During this period, the measurements will begin to apply to real-world situations. As a result, you will immediately begin experiencing all the possible problems, exceptions, and attempts to beat the system. Every flaw or weakness in your system will be exposed in some way. Having a measurement SME immediately available to address these issues as they arise is of real value in establishing a measurement system that you can use over an extended period.

Although a measurement SME is important, it is not a time-consuming role. Even in a global, multibillion dollar organization, the measurement SME function required less than 10% of one person's time. Find a credible, competent person who really loves details and designate that person as the clearinghouse for all comments, concerns, or changes to the measurement system, and it will serve you well.

Summary of Chapter 14

At the end of the first six months after initiating efforts to create a culture of rapid improvement, you should have at least the following activities completed:

- A formal, written business strategy that can communicate the goals of the enterprise throughout your organization.
- A new (probably incomplete) tool set for practicing improvement.
- A well-known pilot project that demonstrates the team process and the new tools.
- A step change in performance resulting from the pilot project and other less formal adaptations of the new tools.
- A cadre of future improvement team leaders and SMEs with experience gained while serving on the pilot team.
- A SME trained in cultural activities who has credibility among your team.
- A SME trained in measurement systems.
- An awareness among your people that culture change is coming.

Chapter 15

Phase II: The Second Six Months

During Phase II (the second six-month period) of your conversion to a culture of rapid improvement, you and your leadership team have another challenging set of tasks to complete in each of the five critical areas:

1. Leaders throughout the business need to complete the *goal deployment and translation process.*
2. Several *new pilot projects* will each resolve a visible and significant chronic problem. This will create a second round of prompt step changes in business performance.
3. The most senior leader of the business, in collaboration with your new subject matter expert (SME) on culture change, should form the *culture design team* (described as Diversity Pioneers in Chapter 9).
4. The list of *new tools and methods* that you will use to support your strategy will grow. More new tools may be selected for use in new pilot projects. More people should become experienced and expert in their use.
5. Management should establish and use a *formal practice of communicating and auditing communications* to enable you to sustain management information and management direction as the autonomous culture begins to grow. Also, an important step in sustaining progress is to develop and use a formal practice to ensure that tactical goals, as they evolve over time, always add to or exceed the performance required by the strategic goals. You can test this system as you deploy your goals for the first time.

This chapter describes these five areas in more detail.

Task 1: Complete the Process of Deploying and Translating Your Goals

The goal deployment and translation process was fully described in Chapter 3; during Phase II, the principle concern is that the strategic goals are leaving management and beginning to migrate through the rest of your organization. As a result of this migration, you will find that you are having frequent conversations about the strategic goals and developing tactics with many people. This is the famous "bulletin-board test," when management hangs their ideas about the future needs and current capabilities of the business on the wall for everyone to see. Be prepared to make the case for your view of things, and be somewhat flexible to accept input. Your strategic goals for the enterprise will become tactical goals for each team during this phase. This is the time during which strategic goals assume the additional characteristic as a tool of management communication. The goals, and the translation of the goals, will tell people in very specific terms how they can help improve the business.

It is critical that you very carefully follow the three-level view form of goal deployment as described. Recall (from Chapter 3) that this method of goal deployment considers, at each level, the input from higher levels and goals to be delegated to lower levels, as well as the goals and tactics adopted by peers. To use this process to strengthen your organization, you need to be certain that, at all levels, all people, including your middle managers, are thoroughly and personally engaged in the process of goal deployment. Through this, they will each define their personal role in leading and achieving your strategies. The three-level view also ensures that the tactical goals that result from the translation will produce actions that are additive and compatible throughout the business. To achieve the best rate of progress, you cannot accept any teams that make changes that are either counterproductive or strategically useless. Including managers at all levels of the organization in the activity of translation and ensuring that all tactical goals are additive and compatible requires the three-level view. Nothing else that I have encountered can achieve this effect.

The sum of all the performance targets established during goal translation at each level should be more than adequate to achieve the performance goals at the next higher level. If the aggregate of performance targets throughout the organization is not sufficient for the performance needs of the enterprise, then you need to rework the goal deployment. The performance needs of your business must be met: the goals were selected because you believed them to be business critical. You should establish and operate an accounting of the several performance targets, as they are set to ensure that this happens at each level during the initial deployment. This may well require some specific resolution or some balancing, as different parts of your organization offer you their best contributions to different goals in different ways (as described in Chapter 3). Later, as tactical goals evolve with time, you should run your accounting process at least once during every phase of implementation to ensure that the work of the several teams is always sufficient to meet the goals of the organization.

Remember that when the translation process is complete, each front-line team will have specific tactical actions to be taken. When you move into high-volume autonomous action during Phase IV (described in Chapter 17), the several teams throughout your business will largely have the authority to implement projects to advance those tactical goals, subject only to the rules of quality station practices. It must be clear to you, and to managers at all levels, that if each team advances their approved goals, using approved methods, the outcome will be successful. Now is the time to be certain that the translation is successful and accurate and that you have systems in place to ensure that the evolving tactical goals stay consistent.

Task 2: Initiate a Second Round of Pilot Projects

The second round of pilot improvement projects will be smaller and more local than the first pilot project (described in Chapter 14), but you should still expect that each pilot project will obviously resolve a visible and significant problem. Again, in this second round of projects, it will be necessary for management to provide each project with extra capabilities, both to ensure success and to ensure that the lessons of the new tool are well learned.

Each pilot project should make a real and immediate contribution to business success. At this stage, it is still intended that the pilot projects also demonstrate the use of the new tools. Each of the pilot projects should create new team leaders and SMEs for future teams. When all the pilot projects are completed at the end of the third six-month period (described in Chapter 16), and teams are routinely implementing autonomous change against their tactical goals, only the goals will define the project selection, not the tools. During each of the three pilot phases, though, tool demonstration and training of experienced team leaders and SMEs will also be important considerations in project selection.

Each part of the business that is separately managed by an individual member of the management committee that reports to the most senior manager should have contributed a SME, a team leader, or a team member to the business-wide pilot project of Phase I. During Phase II, each of those individuals will return to his or her home organization, and each of those organizational entities will conduct its own visible and significant pilot. Again, each project team has six months to complete its work. As with the first pilot, your intent is to make a significant step change in performance for the business and demonstrate the credibility of the effort. This demonstration will be occurring at the same time that most natural work groups are creating their own versions of the tactical goals in the goal-deployment process. The second phase of pilot projects will be a great communication tool during this goal-deployment activity.

Task 3: Take Formal Steps to Include Individuals in Your Culture Change

In Phase I (described in Chapter 14), you should have identified and trained a SME to help lead and implement your culture change. You should also have begun to communicate about the coming culture of inclusion and autonomy and started helping team leaders to organize new teams. You and your management team will have engaged with someone who knows about culture change and will have begun to discuss what a culture of inclusion and autonomy will mean to you and your business. During Phase II, you will take your first formal steps to address the social issues of culture change. The most senior leader of the business, in collaboration with your new SME, should form the culture design team that will help plan and implement culture change in a way that is appropriate and unique to your business and people. (This team and their work were described in Chapter 9.)

A good first assignment for this team of cultural designers, as they organize themselves for action, is to ask them to propose to management the social standards and expectations for small-team autonomous action that will apply throughout the organization. (These were described in Chapter 8.) Each small team will later have its own social standards, but those must be compatible with the enterprise-wide standards developed by the cultural design team and approved by management. Development of social standards for small teams throughout the enterprise early in Phase II will facilitate development of small teams as they begin to form. Most standards specific to individual small teams will be set late in Phase II of implementation.

Creating the cultural design team is a new and important task, so you will want to do it well. It is entirely appropriate to seek assistance from an external consultant, probably one of the people who provided the training for your SME. As in beginning the first cultural discussions described in Phase I (Chapter 14), management should recognize that this is work for which they have not been trained and for which no one is naturally prepared; therefore, use your external consultant and your internal SME hard and often. Practice among managers all the conversations that you expect to have with others. This is your version of using a new tool for a pilot project. Be sure to work it hard enough that you can be certain that you will be successful when the time arrives for conversations and actions on real situations that exist within your business.

You need to be clear that the work of culture change is being led and implemented from within your organization. The two most important attributes of the new culture are that it achieves your business goals and that it fits your people. You are building your own new culture, not copying a culture that has been successful for someone else. The consultant can provide training and experience to management and to the members of the design team, as well as advice to the senior manager and the SME. However, you should be very careful not to allow the consultant to become the leader (or even the facilitator) of your culture design team; also, your consultant may help management, but should never lead management, even though your lack of experience and comfort with the topic will likely make you wish for someone to help you lead. As management and the cultural design team creates a culture of inclusion for your business, it is important for everyone in the organization to be confident that senior management is setting the direction. People need confidence that the culture will last, and they know that consultants are going to leave.

If you have not already done so for other purposes, this is a good time to create and publish a formal statement from management on diversity or harassment or inclusion, whichever concept best fits your people and environment. This is an activity where senior leaders will benefit from the advice of corporate counsel. I personally prefer simple, direct statements, such as the following, but I have seen much larger manifesto-type documents. The key issue is to get a formal policy in place now that will provide a foundation for other work and other practices that will follow. A sample statement of inclusion that I like is this:

> We value all the individuals who are part of this business, and we want each individual to be included in the operation and success of the enterprise. We recognize that each individual has characteristics that form his or her personal identity. No employee of this company will be harassed or excluded by any other employee on the basis of any characteristic of his or her personal identity.

Although this statement is short and sweet, when you personalize it for your business and your people, it describes a corporate value for individuals, it includes all people, and it prohibits harassment. All those considerations will be appreciated by your people, and they all will serve you well as valuable foundation elements for your future actions toward an engaged and inclusive culture.

The members of the cultural design group should all be natural leaders. They may or may not have a position of authority in the formal organization, but they should all be well recognized as leaders among your general population. Fortunately it is easy to identify natural leaders, because natural leaders already have followers. Other people already seek their opinions and guidance. Other people already refer to them when talking about the business in order to add credibility to their own comments.

> **Key Idea:** You can identify the natural leaders in your organization by observing who has followers.

The natural leaders that you select should be ready and willing to represent others in the process of cultural design. And they should also be ready and willing to represent the cultural design team to their constituents. Team members should be selected so that the central design team has a fair representation from all the natural constituencies within the enterprise. If your business has several important subdivisions, then each of those should be represented. Your business will likely have several important differences in occupations, and those should be represented. For example, we had operating technicians, craft technicians, engineers, accountants, physicians, sales representatives, administrative support people, first-line supervisors, middle managers, and several other occupations represented when we commenced the Pioneers team described in Chapter 8.

We tried to have a fair selection of people with different aspects to their own personal cultures. Obvious in that consideration are the issues of race, religion, and gender, but we also tried to have a mix of younger and older people, as well as other attributes of personal culture.

The difficult part of the selection process is that if you want your design team to be an effective working group, then you will need to cover the waterfront of different personal, professional, and organizational attributes within a relatively small group. This generally results in team members who fill multiple roles. For example, we had a middle-aged black man who was also a maintenance technician in one of the operating divisions. We also had a young, white gay woman who was a first-line supervisor in another operating division. At the end of the day, to represent a population of several thousand people, we had a cultural design team of about 20 people.

Task 4: Implement New Tools and Methods in Your New Pilot Projects

As you progress through the second and all future rounds of pilot projects, you will be addressing new types of problems and new opportunities for improvement as you expand the scope of your work. So you will continuously need to use more of your new tool set, or even expand your tool set, to make it appropriate to the developing needs of your business. An important issue is to thoroughly demonstrate and communicate the capability and credibility of the new tools. Finally, your intent is to produce still more experienced people who can lead and advise others in the future use of the new tools. Obviously you should be certain that everyone involved understands that all pilot projects are expected to produce immediate benefit as part of creating a step change in performance. A project management discipline of establishing specific project goals and obtaining measured results will serve you well now and into the future.

As front-line teams practice autonomous improvement in Phase IV and beyond, the improvement effort will always be focused only on the goal of improving the business. When people begin to routinely practice autonomous improvement, the tool will just be a tool. During the pilot phases, however, you still want to consider demonstration of the new capability as a goal for project selection. In the future, you will want to carefully limit the amount of time that you devote to training so that the efforts of your teams are focused on improvement, not training. During the pilot projects, however, you are producing future team leaders and future SMEs, so a little extra training now is appropriate. Either through training or experience, you want to produce people during the pilot projects who thoroughly understand the applicability and practice of the new tools. As you begin to do new things, there is no substitute for someone who knows what to do. The pilot phases are your most immediate opportunity to produce those people.

Use Quality Stations

As described in Chapter 4, during Phase II, you will need to develop the corporate set of rules of practice and rituals for your quality station teams. This will ensure that all teams share some minimum formal expectations for such things as documentation and reporting of completed projects and results. You do not want an army of accountants, but you do need to have good information from each of the teams. You need rituals that ensure the teams will produce consistent and useful information. In Phase III, your teams will create their own local versions of detailed quality station rituals, but they will do that on the foundation of the general practices and rituals established during Phase II.

The general rules of practice will also ensure that you have clear limits on the available range of autonomous action. For example, as discussed in Chapter 4, within the chemical industry, we allowed autonomous action in many areas, but we never allowed any autonomous project that penetrated the "hydrocarbon envelope" that contained the potentially hazardous materials we processed.

Most industries have some equivalent activity that requires special consideration. Teams can conceive and recommend changes within those areas, but all of those changes must be designed and implemented under the supervision of a professional engineer.

There are other rules of practice that you may want to specify. For example, we liked to have a minimum time between the first appearance of a new idea on the quality station and the time that it could be advanced to action. This ensured that reasonably attentive engineers and managers would have a fair chance to review all of the small team projects for any potential consequences that were unforeseen by the team itself. This is the ongoing version of the three-level view of tactics that was discussed in Chapter 3.

Finally, you will want to identify and document the methods and limits for practice of each of the new tools of improvement as they will be practiced by autonomous teams. Some new tools (such as basic root cause analysis) will be available for practice by anyone who elects to do so. Other more complex or more rigorous tools (such as reliability engineering and statistical analysis) will be available for teams to use, but only with the assistance of someone who is a SME in that discipline. You need to decide and document these rules of practice during Phase II. When you launch your quality station teams during Phase III, you very rarely want to stop a team activity once it is in progress. The rituals and rules of practice need to be in place by the end of Phase II.

Task 5: Sustain Your Gains in Communication and Performance

The sustaining tasks for Phase II are in communication and performance. As described in Chapter 11, it is necessary to have a formal process for communicating and for auditing communications. This will become vitally important as you enter Phase III (described in Chapter 16), as late during that phase, autonomous activity may begin to occur throughout the organization. At that point, communications from management—especially instructions—will need to be very clear and very certain. Establishing your own version of the communication delivery and audit process described in Chapter 11 to achieve that goal during Phase II will serve you well as you go forward.

Similarly the tactical goals of teams will evolve continuously, much faster than the strategic goals that they support. That is nothing to worry about. It is a natural consequence of the relationship between tactics and strategies. However, as the tactical goals evolve, it will always be necessary for management to be certain that the current tactical goals, if achieved, will result in the performance required to meet the strategic goals, including the four subsets of strategic progress that you establish for the six-month periods of the first two years. During your original goal deployment process (described earlier in this chapter), you should have created a formal process to aggregate the team goals into an enterprise result. You should establish a sustaining practice of using that process at least once during each phase of initial implementation, and you should maintain that practice as you move into future years with fresh goals.

Finally, this is the time to create a specific discipline for managing small-event improvement projects. Use the experience from the pilot projects as the basis for this work. Similar to the discussion of measurements, you want a system to ensure that you are in control of autonomous projects, but in a way that also does not overwhelm the project with administration. The quality stations will answer much of the need for communication, but there will still be the need to provide the routine project discipline of managing time, cost, and results to even small-event project teams. Develop your standards for that practice now, and use it from here forward.

Summary of Chapter 15

At the end of the second six-month period, after initiating your efforts to create a culture of rapid improvement, you should have completed at least the following items:

- *Complete goals translation and deployment* to all parts of the organization, including all individual contributors and all front-line teams.
- *Complete a second round of significant and visible pilot projects* with at least one project within the organizational area of each person who reports directly to the most senior manager.
- Use your pilot projects to *create an expanded cadre of future team leaders and future SMEs* for deployment in the third phase of pilot projects.
- *Create a second step change in the business performance* resulting from Phase II pilot projects.
- Organize and *launch an in-house cultural design team*.
- *Increase the list of available tools and methods* of improvement available for the autonomous teams consistent with your strategies and needs.
- *Develop and publish enterprise-wide rituals and rules of practice* for your quality station teams.

- *Establish formal practices to communicate messages, including instructions,* from management to an autonomous workforce and a process to audit those communications to ensure that they are received in a timely and accurate manner.
- Establish and operate formal practices to ensure that the current *tactical goals always aggregate to the strategic needs* of the business.
- Establish and use a formal practice to ensure that a minimum of *project discipline*—especially for schedule, cost, and results—is in place for quality station projects.

Chapter 16

Phase III: The Third Six Months

During Phase III, the leaders again will address the core issues of goals, pilot projects, tools, inclusion of individuals to the new culture, and sustaining the gains. During this phase, you will be approaching and even, in some cases, commencing the autonomous activity that will take off in full measure during Phase IV (described in Chapter 17). This round of pilot projects will be at or near the front-line teams, although all projects done during this period will continue to be treated as pilot projects with team leaders and SMEs assigned by management ad hoc to the task. During this third six-month period, you should complete the following activities:

1. Establish quality stations as the last step in your goal deployment and commence formal small-team operations.
2. Initiate pilot projects deeper into the organization, reaching the organizational level just above the front-line teams in large businesses, or on the front line itself in smaller organizations.
3. Based on the completion of goal deployment, make your final selection of new tools to be approved for autonomous action.
4. Create affinity groups to support your people as they go through the culture change; also, the cultural design team should consider the first formal changes in your organization's human policies or practices to promote inclusion.
5. Sustain your gains by doing all of the following:

- Establish a formal practice to ensure that team leaders deliver the objective elements of employee engagement.
- Establish a formal practice of management engagement with the quality station teams to ensure that the teams recognize your ongoing commitment to their work.
- Establish the practice and discipline of routinely assessing the emotional state of your people and responding to it in an appropriate manner.

This chapter describes each of these activities in more detail.

Task 1: Create Quality Stations That Small Teams Will Use to Advance Your Goals

Your goal translation and deployment activity should have concluded during Phase II. As a result of that, each of your front-line teams and each of the individual contributors should have their own very specific tactical goals in support of your organization's strategic goals. These tactical goals at the team level should be formalized in the complete five-part goal format (as described in Chapter 2 and Chapter 3).

Therefore, during Phase III, your teams will need to create their quality stations (as described in Chapter 4), including each of the basic rituals of quality station practice. Assuming that the quality stations demonstrate the four required elements, then the quality stations themselves can look like anything that the teams want to create and maintain. I have generally found that the appearance of a quality station is more representative of the personality of the team than of any other attribute. Certainly the differences in appearance among quality stations have never been found to have any bearing on the productivity of the teams.

In addition to creating a physical quality station, each team needs to develop its local rules of practice and the rituals for its quality station. The corporate rules and rituals of quality station practice (which were created during Phase II) address common requirements and limits that are applicable to all teams. These local rituals and rules of practice at each quality station address team issues, including the time and schedule for regular weekly team meetings, and individual assignments for the team members who will fill the administrative roles in support of the quality station.

Some teams have rituals that require quite a bit of administration, with the expectation that the description of projects and the reporting of results and other elements will be computer generated with nice charts and graphs. Other teams have handwritten sheets of paper that are routinely scratched out and written over. Local rules include the responsibility for maintaining the quality station in whatever form is chosen by the team. An important rule of local practice is describing the process that the team will use for selecting projects to be promoted from idea to action.

The thing for team leaders to remember is that both the appearance and the rituals of the quality station are socially important to the function of the team. I have often found that after meeting the mandatory basic elements, it is best to let each team do what feels right for that team. With these quality station rules of team practice, as well as the social or interactive rules of practice that were developed during Phase II, most teams will be ready to operate.

By definition, Phase III takes place in the second budget year since you have commenced your work. By now, the team leader should be able to communicate in detail how management will provide the objective elements of engagement (as described in Chapter 5). It is very important, as the team establishes the quality station and prepares to commence formal autonomous improvement, that the team leader be able to communicate formally how management will provide the team with each of the requisite elements of engagement and autonomous action. Any team that is having trouble with this requirement will need help. Give it to them as soon as you recognize the problem.

Finally, at some time during Phase III, each of the front-line teams should begin to populate the "actions planned" section of their quality station. As they become ready to do so, and in accordance with the rules of practice that they and management have agreed on, each team may begin to advance some proposed improvements into work in progress. There are still pilot projects in progress throughout this phase, and those get priority. But if a team is well advanced and can complete its role in pilot projects as well as initiate some further work, let them do it.

At the front line, a lot of people with a lot of different issues and capabilities are involved during this time. Some teams will move forward very fast and be actively engaged in initial autonomous improvements as soon as they complete their Phase III pilot project. Other teams will move much more slowly. Some teams may experience one or more of the impediments described in Chapter 5 and Chapter 6 that can completely stop the teams from proceeding. As this activity ramps up, management should be very visible and interactive on the shop floor. You should be ready at any time during this period to support teams that are ready to proceed, and you should also be ready throughout this period to identify and help teams that are not proceeding.

The management-critical issue is that at the end of Phase III, all front-line teams should have

- A quality station.
- Good standards and expectations for the conduct of individuals as members of the team.
- Formal and well-known quality station practices and rituals.
- At least a few initial projects ready to propose for action.

Every front-line team must be immediately ready to start autonomous actions at the beginning of Phase IV, if not before. Any team that is not on a path to being fully active in autonomous improvement at the beginning of the fourth six-month period should receive help as soon as management recognizes the problem. You should be very accommodating to allow good teams to pull ahead. Once they are truly ready, there is nothing further to wait for. The big issue is that you cannot allow any teams to fall behind.

Task 2: Establish Pilot Projects on the Front Line

During Phase III, the pilot project phase of management-sponsored improvement projects is wrapping up with a big finish. The team leaders, team members, and SMEs from the pilot project teams should now be at an organizational level just above the front-line teams—except in small organizations, where there are no organizational levels remaining except for the front-line teams. Even if this phase of pilot projects is conducted at the front line, each project should continue to be conducted as a management-sponsored and management-led pilot project.

Communication, formal training, and experience with both the project format and the tools of improvement still need to be developed through the discipline of this pilot effort. There is also an ongoing need for management to have close association with each of the projects. Each project must be selected to be visible and significant, and each should be managed to ensure success. There is no value in teaching people that the new tools fix insignificant problems or that the tools are not successful. True autonomous initiation and execution of projects will generally begin during Phase IV.

Many of the project team members during this phase should be front-line team members or SMEs who, in the future, will work closely with (or as part of) front-line teams. Even in the largest organizations, every front-line team should have at least one person who is a member of a pilot team, either during this phase or in one of the prior pilot phases. If any team has not yet had a pilot team member, management should identify that situation and correct it before the pilot projects are completed. As before, the intent of the pilot projects is to fix a known problem that is both visible and significant. All pilot projects should make a real contribution to a step change in the business performance. This is especially true as the projects get closer to the front line. Use the pilot projects to clearly demonstrate the direction and nature of what will be expected from the autonomous improvement that is soon to come.

Task 3: Select New Tools That Support Autonomous Action

You will have started the initial pilot projects of Phase I with a limited selection of new capabilities to cause improvement. Those initial capabilities were selected somewhat theoretically to represent the tools most likely to cause immediate improvement as well as tools that were likely to be compatible with the strategic and tactical goals as they developed. As your pilot projects have progressed, and as your goals have been finalized and translated, you will have added more new tools that will have been selected to be appropriate to the detailed strategies and tactics that have been developed.

At this point, you should have a final list of the tools or methods of improvement that you will deploy for autonomous actions. You should formalize this list of tools that are available for use by autonomous teams and publish it so that the list is well known and readily available for reference. This list is not a limit on the tool set that is available to the business as a whole; your organization can utilize any tool that is appropriate for any project. The only limit that is set by your finalized list is a limit on the tools available to teams for autonomous action. Other tools will be available as needed, but those will require either management approval or ad hoc assistance from a special SME.

You might consider also maintaining and publishing a formal list of the improvement methods that you can support with appropriate expertise in support of teams that need additional capabilities. The use of an approved list of tools or methods for autonomous improvement is intended primarily as a limit on unexpected or inexpert team actions and also as a limit on training.

During the final phase of pilot projects, you will want to have at least one good example of each of the tools that you have selected as being appropriate to your work. This will be the last time that the tool itself has a role in selecting the project. For all future projects, the strategic business value alone will determine what needs to be done.

Task 4: Create Affinity Groups to Ensure Inclusion of All Individuals

There will be many improvement projects now, and although they are still pilot projects, you will begin to get a feel for the pace of change that you should experience when autonomous improvement begins. This is a good time to begin the conversations that allow you to make certain that both your people and your management are comfortable with how people, including managers, think and feel about the changes. (This practice of assessing the emotional state of your business was described in Chapter 10.) Senior management should spend plenty of time talking with people in the field, and management should have a reliable source of "confidential" information that people want you to know but do not want to tell you directly about their response to the changes that you are leading.

In Phase II, the cultural design team members were selected, trained, and organized. Therefore you and your design team will have already had some interesting discussions on the state of inclusion within your business. They probably will have developed and proposed some social standards for small-team autonomous action (as described in Chapter 8). As a first step toward formal action of the design team, early in Phase III, you can move the social standards and expectations for small teams that were developed during Phase II out to the work teams that you have launched at the front line. Most front-line teams are not yet ready to begin autonomous action, but they can begin to experience the rituals of small-team behavior that will be expected of them within the new culture as they take the steps to prepare for autonomy.

During Phase III, each of the several cultural design team members will begin active, although informal, discussions with the several constituencies that they represent. They will develop an ability to get information for the design team and also to represent the cultural team to others. Some team members may voluntarily drop out at this point because they do not like this sort of work. Others may need to be removed because they demonstrate that they are unsuited to the work. This turnover in team members at the initial startup of a cultural design team is not unexpected and is not a bad sign. Some people (including some who are otherwise considered to be natural leaders) are simply uncomfortable or inappropriate for work as a representative of others. You may also find some who are so communicative that they are unwilling or unable to maintain the confidence that this activity will require.

The critical issue related to this situation is that as early as possible, but certainly by the end of Phase III, you should make any personnel changes needed to the membership of the cultural design team. You need to go forward into Phase IV with a stable team that is good at the work and completely trustworthy.

During Phase III, the design team will actually begin to select one or more tangible human initiatives that the team will progress. A convenient task for this time period—which is always more difficult and controversial than it seems it should be—is the creation of the affinity groups (which were described in Chapter 9). The affinity groups will provide a basis for all the good things previously described as well as providing a very specific constituency for the appropriate design team member to talk with and represent. Do not take any formal steps toward policy or practice change now. Instead, save that for Phase IV. During Phase III, begin the discussion and planning internal to the design team that will lead to the first formal changes when the time is right.

Similar to the pilot projects for improvement of the operations, the initial formal steps toward inclusion should always be well founded on visible and significant issues of concern to your own people. In collaboration with your design team, your culture SME, and perhaps your external consultant, you should be certain that these first actions are thoroughly planned and widely discussed before you take action. You will want to be certain that these initiatives will be perceived throughout the organization as well conceived and well implemented. You also want each of them to be good examples of your strategic intent for culture change. And the changes, when you implement them, must succeed. Take your time. Changes to policies and practices are sure to be emotional. Thorough preparation during Phase III to ensure that you do these things very well during Phase IV is good insurance.

Briefly, the principle human task for management at all levels during Phase III is to get the teams at the front line, as well as the cultural design team and the several affinity groups, off to a good start. For most people, this will be the first time that they have had both an expectation that they will engage in making the business better as well as a true capability to achieve that outcome. Support the initial efforts of the front-line teams visibly and often. You will need to make very certain that no team fails to be ready for autonomous action at the start of Phase IV. Now is the time for management to convince people that autonomous improvement will actually succeed for the business and for the people who operate the business. You and your leadership team should have a well-developed and practiced discipline of communicating belief and support, as well as an auditable process for communicating instructions (both were described in Chapter 11).

Task 5: Sustain Your Gains by Establishing New Formal Practices

During Phase III, you should establish a formal practice of regularly ensuring that team leaders can demonstrate that each team is receiving the five objective elements of engagement (which were described in Chapter 5). You should also have a ritual of management review to ensure that teams are fully and effectively functional.

> **Example:** Even when I was managing the huge chemical complex at Baytown, Texas, I personally met with every second-line supervisor once a quarter and reviewed all the quality stations in that section of the plant. These meetings were formally scheduled and very important to me and to the local managers. We also formally adopted the practice of spending 1 hour of each management team meeting in the field with a quality station team that had created a significant success. Each of the members of my management committee were very careful to be certain that their division was represented among the teams with significant success to report.

This practice is truly important if you want to achieve and sustain real gains. From the time when quality station teams first come into existence, the teams need to see that management is interested in their work and personally engaged with them. Unfortunately management always has new demands arising. The only practical way to continuously demonstrate interest is to have a formal practice of routinely visiting each part of the operation with enough time allotted to do it well. Develop a formal practice for every member of management to engage in the communication of belief and support (as described in Chapter 11).

The final task for sustaining the gains in this phase is to establish the formalities and expectations for your assessment of how people think and feel about the changes. This is another activity that needs to be conducted routinely by management during any period when you have major change in progress. Hopefully that will be most of the time from now forward. Unfortunately this is also an activity that is not very comfortable to conduct and does not fit naturally with any other management activity. You will need to decide on the discipline that will enforce your practice of this assessment and then formalize that practice to ensure that you do it regularly.

Summary of Chapter 16

During the third six-month period following your initial efforts to create a new culture of rapid improvement, you should have achieved at least the following:

- ■ *Establish quality stations at every front-line team*, including local rules of practice and initial proposals for action to progress the goals.

- Complete a third phase of *management-led pilot projects.*
- Achieve a *further step change in business performance* derived from the new set of pilot projects.
- *Finalize the list of tools or methods* of improvement authorized for autonomous actions.
- *Finalize the membership of the cultural design team* and begin discussions of the state of inclusion and engagement of your business.
- *Establish the affinity groups* that will support your people throughout the cultural changes.
- *Plan more formal cultural actions* that will be implemented during Phase IV, the fourth six-month period.
- Commence a disciplined program of *communicating belief and support.*
- Develop a discipline for ensuring that team leaders continuously *provide the five objective elements of engagement.*
- Develop a *discipline for routine and ongoing management engagement* with the front-line teams.
- Develop a discipline of *routinely assessing the emotional state* of your business.

Chapter 17

Phase IV: The Fourth Six Months

Throughout the fourth six-month period, a transition is occurring in your business. The initial goal development and deployment is complete. Each team now has tactical goals and a quality station with an appropriate quality station process and rules of practice to manage autonomous work. They have tools, examples from the pilot projects, and a team member or two who has participated in the use of the new tools. They have time, resources, and all the other attributes of an engaged team. Early in Phase IV, each front-line team should actually begin practicing autonomous improvement in a serious way, and each front-line team should begin demonstrating significant performance improvement that conforms to the strategic goals and measures of the business. Autonomous improvement should accelerate continuously during this period. Near the end of Phase IV, your pace of strategic improvement should be approaching world-class rates. However, during this period of transition, you will still need activities in each of the five focused areas: goals, projects, tools, culture, and sustaining gains.

Task 1: Ensure That the Goals You Are Implementing Are the Goals You Deployed

Leading a goal-focused organization in Phase IV gets very interesting. Everything that you have done before is the basis for the activities of this period and beyond. Now you should expect that each of the individual teams throughout your business will actually commence autonomous activity in response to your goals. This is when you need to take some time to formally and carefully ensure that the goals implemented in practice are the same as the goals you originally deployed. You should also be certain that the teams are working successfully as teams and effectively practicing autonomous improvement.

Therefore management at all levels should be highly visible and highly engaged with the front-line teams. The management interactions at the front-line should provide

- Strategic and other guidance to keep teams aligned.
- Feedback on specific project selection and success.
- Sincere, specific recognition of good work.
- Proactive assistance to teams that request or need help.
- Ongoing communication of belief and support.

Task 2: Select Only Projects That Improve Performance

The rapid business improvement that occurs during this period will be largely the result of autonomous team action. This is the time that you should begin to experience the synergy derived from combining the unique contribution of engineers and managers with a separate unique contribution from the front-line teams. In the pilot projects of prior phases, you probably had some engineers and managers personally engaged in each project to ensure that the projects were successful. As a result, some of the improvement work normally done by managers and engineers has not progressed as normal. As the teams become more autonomous, the engineers and managers will return to their regular activities and the beneficial interaction between small-event improvements and big events will begin to occur.

The pilot project phases are over. However, that should not imply that teams abandon the practice of formally initiating and conducting improvement efforts in the form of projects. The discipline of project formation and execution that the team members, team leaders, and subject matter experts (SMEs) practiced during the 18 months of pilot projects should serve them well going forward. Be careful that they do not lose this discipline as they shift to autonomous action. Remember that autonomous action is not unmanaged, it is simply not closely supervised outside of the front-line teams.

Also, this is a good time for management to ensure that teams develop the discipline of selecting and implementing only projects that lead to significant improvement. No team should select a project that is either cosmetic or trivial, and no team should select a project either to experience or to demonstrate a new tool. There has been a year and a half of preparation in the use of the new tools. Now is the time when only performance matters in project selection.

Task 3: Train People to Use the Specific Tools That Will Meet Your Goals

The new tool list will have been finalized during Phase III, and there will be a cadre of folks with both experience and skill in using the new tools. But there will still need to be more training during this period. You will need to train more people in the specific tools that exactly fit the improvement goals of their teams. You will need to train some additional people who will have real expertise in the new tools, including the new tools that are not available for autonomous action. These people will serve your organization broadly as SMEs, and they will become excellent individual practitioners of the new tools. You need to expect this further training, and you need to be prepared to support it.

However, this is also a good time to be certain that you are exercising the discipline of training for a purpose. It would be very unusual if there is any training that every person in your organization needs at the same time. Training should be personal and focused on the work that each person does or will do. Training should be delivered at the time it is needed and not before. The easiest way to ensure that you have the time and budget to provide people with all the training that they will need is to exercise the discipline to ensure that you do not deliver training that is inappropriate or untimely. There is a careful balance that will need some management judgment and intervention. For example, many team leaders will want to train more people than truly need training, and other team leaders will hope to get by without diverting anyone to training. Management should see that everyone who needs training gets trained, and management should equally ensure that people who do not need training do not receive it.

Task 4: Make Sure All Individuals Are Included in Your Culture Change

During Phase IV, you will actually begin to formally change the policies and practices of managing people in a way that will further your goal of including everyone and valuing individuals. During Phase III, you and your advisors and design team set the foundation in place by preparing a few proposals for specific actions that you will take in Phase IV. Now you should use that foundation and implement one or more changes that really demonstrate the path to a better culture.

> **Key Idea:** Generally it is best to start with something that is meaningful, but also something that will be well received by most people. You should not challenge the emotional health of your organization too hard or too fast with changes that are likely to be controversial. I was lucky to discover the issue of managing the process by which people become qualified for promotion (as described in Chapter 9). Everyone recognized that it was an important change, yet almost no one was distressed by the change.

During Phase III, you also selected and organized the affinity groups that enable people to discuss common issues for review with management. Now you need to make certain that you are available for those reviews. The principle path for this information to come to the attention of management or of the culture design team should be through the culture SME or through an individual member of your cultural design team who is also a member of the affinity group. But there are likely to be times when an affinity group wants management, most often a senior manager, to come to one of their meetings. When that request comes, remember that people are doing you a favor by discussing with you their personal thoughts, feelings, and experiences. This insight will be of great value to your understanding. This interaction will also provide you with a great opportunity to demonstrate that you are personally committed to real cultural change. This is where you deliver your message of belief and support. So do not treat the request for management interaction as a favor from you to them; it is just the opposite.

That being said, the normal communications path is through the SME and the design team contact. Exceptions to that practice need to be meaningful and appropriate or you begin to damage your normal path in the same way that you disenfranchise middle management if you communicate with the frontline operations too directly and too often. Always be certain that when you meet directly with an affinity group, the SME and the appropriate design team member are briefed in advance and by your side.

Phase IV is the time when you want to be certain that you use the capability you developed earlier (including your culture expert, your cultural design team, and any other resource that you can find) to begin a formal discipline of routinely and actively monitoring the way that people think and feel about the changes that they are experiencing in the workplace. (This practice was described in

Chapter 10.) You established the practices and began to do this somewhat informally during Phase III, but now it should be a very serious consideration as you go forward. In a time of significant change, including changes in the way that you manage people to increase inclusion, emotions will be strong and prevalent. Maintaining emotional balance will be critical to sustaining progress.

This is also the time when you need to be prepared to enforce your culture change in the same way as you would enforce any other operating policy or practice of your business. As you roll out real changes, the likelihood of a serious challenge to the changes increases, and you want to detect that and stop it as quickly as possible.

Communicate Your Belief and Support of Your Culture Change

There will be a lot of action during Phase IV. You will need to get messages to people. Many of these messages will be statements of belief and support to keep them enthusiastic about the changes and to ensure that everyone understands that management is consistent in their support of the new practices. You previously established a formal discipline to ensure that management at all levels participates in this. Making statements of belief and support is not natural behavior for many people, but your teams need to hear the message, and hear it often, from everyone they respect. Make certain that the practices you established are routinely followed and intervene promptly as soon as you detect places within your organization where communications are not occurring as planned.

You will also find that you have a need to communicate instructions. Never allow yourself to bypass the organization by communicating instructions directly to people who are more than two organizational levels removed from your personal position. You previously established, and now you must use, a formal practice of communicating instructions that are translated through the organization in an auditable way. The temptation will be great for management to communicate directly throughout the organization. Remember that this never works. Instead, use your organization and your regular processes for communicating instructions.

Task 5: Sustain Your Gains into Year Three and Beyond

If you have followed the advice and recommendations of this and the preceding 16 chapters, you will have developed many new disciplines and practices. Some of those will be difficult for management, but they are nonetheless vitally important. You simply cannot sustain anything as comprehensive as a new culture without some strong discipline of ritual and formal practice that requires both management and others to routinely do things in a new way.

That being said, as you prepare to enter the third year of your culture change, you and your people will have quite a bit of experience with the entire culture change process. At the end of Phase IV, it is time to reassess the practices that you have created. Some are important and valuable; others, in your context, or in the way that you have implemented them, will cause more confusion and added work than they are worth. You probably will have received a great deal of input from your teams and from your middle managers related to the practices that have less value and more cost. During the first two years, it was probably good general practice to implement your new practices as they were conceived without change. You will never succeed in establishing consistency and commonality if everything that you do is subject to prompt change. Just plow ahead for a while to get some real experience and to get the big picture established before commencing what could be a constant series of changes to the new practices.

Having established new practices and gained some experience in the use of those new practices, now is the time to change some as an improvement and also as a demonstration that management receives and values input. Use the input that you have, and get some more. A truly valuable part of sustaining change is demonstrating that you are willing and able to make the new culture appropriate to your business and your people. Certainly that was your intent all along. Take some time now to give your people the chance to use their new experience to shape the result. They will reward you for your effort!

Looking toward the Future

An important element of the business transition during Phase IV will occur as senior management looks further into the future. As described in Chapter 3, now is the time to refresh your goals to reflect both changes in the business environment and changes to the internal performance and capability of your organization. The balance for management to achieve during Phase IV is to look ahead during the very time when the front-line teams need the most current management attention—and, of course, you will still need to operate the business each day. But it is very important to refresh your strategies now so that you know your future strategies and the performance expectations for the coming years before you complete your current plans. Clearly this will be a very busy time for managers.

During Phase IV, the most-senior management will begin the process of refreshing the strategic goals. (This activity was fully described in Chapter 3.) At the end of the fourth six-month period, your original goals will be two years old. Therefore there will likely be a real need to formally review your external environment to be certain that you are still on a strategic path that will cause business success if your actions are sustained. There will also have been a big internal change in both your business's performance and in the capabilities of your organization. Together, changes in the environment and changes in the capabilities of your organization will create a fresh set of strategic gaps that will need to be reflected in fresh strategies. By refreshing your goals during Phase IV, you can commence your second two-year strategic period with a new set of four six-month cycles of improvement and culture that will be entirely your own. By refreshing a five-year strategic horizon and establishing four new phases of interim goals and targets every two years, you will constantly provide your organization with both the big picture as well as more specific direction.

When goals are refreshed, you should create new goals and translate those new goals as thoroughly and formally as you did the first time. However, this time, the process and infrastructure for goal setting and goal deployment already exist. People, including management, know how this is done. Also important is that unless there is some unexpected problem or development that disrupts what you have been doing (either in the environment or inside the organization), the new goals do not represent a complete new start, but rather a logical extension of work in progress into the future. As a result, both the refreshment of strategic goals and the deployment of the fresh tactical goals and actions should be completed by the end of Phase IV.

Beginning the Third Year

As you begin the third year of your cultural transformation, there will be a remarkable change in the business and people that you lead. Your business will have experienced four six-month increments of step change improvement, each larger and more valuable than the preceding increment. You will have new capability for improvement ubiquitously deployed in every front-line team throughout your business. Those teams will all have experience making their own improvements, and nearly all your people will be actively engaged in continuously making more improvements.

While people have gained experience making improvements, management will have gained experience setting strategies for the business and translating those strategies into tactical actions that others can execute. Managers will have experienced creating and delivering the elements of employee engagement and be actively practicing those elements and continuously improving the state of engagement.

You will have the infrastructure for changing the human side of your business for greater inclusion. You will have taken some early steps to make those changes a formal part of managing how your business is conducted. Your culture will continue to grow and mature with time, but all the elements for that journey will be in place.

Your business will already have better performance. Your teams will have fresh goals, expanded capability for improvement, and a fully engaged workforce. You will have an excellent foundation for a future that will be all that you want it to be.

Key Idea: The second two years of culture change are always exciting and enjoyable. You have developed a wonderful new capability and now you can focus that capability on making your business the best in your industry. I wish you and your team great success.

Summary of Chapter 17

During Phase IV, you should have achieved at least the following actions:

- *Each front-line team should be actively engaged in autonomous improvement* and demonstrating a real contribution to the strategic goals of the business.
- *Management should be actively engaged with the front-line teams* and provide strong support to ensure that early autonomous efforts are successful.
- *Complete training of teams and SMEs*, as needed, to ensure that each team has the skills needed to apply the new tools of improvement to their work.
- Begin to *implement the social or interpersonal cultural changes* that were planned by your cultural leadership team during Phase III.
- Begin *formally monitoring and responding to the emotional state* of the organization.
- Refresh the *strategic goals* of your business to reflect changes in the external environment as well as the new internal capabilities of your organization.
- Give your people a chance to shape the effort as it goes forward.

Index

W